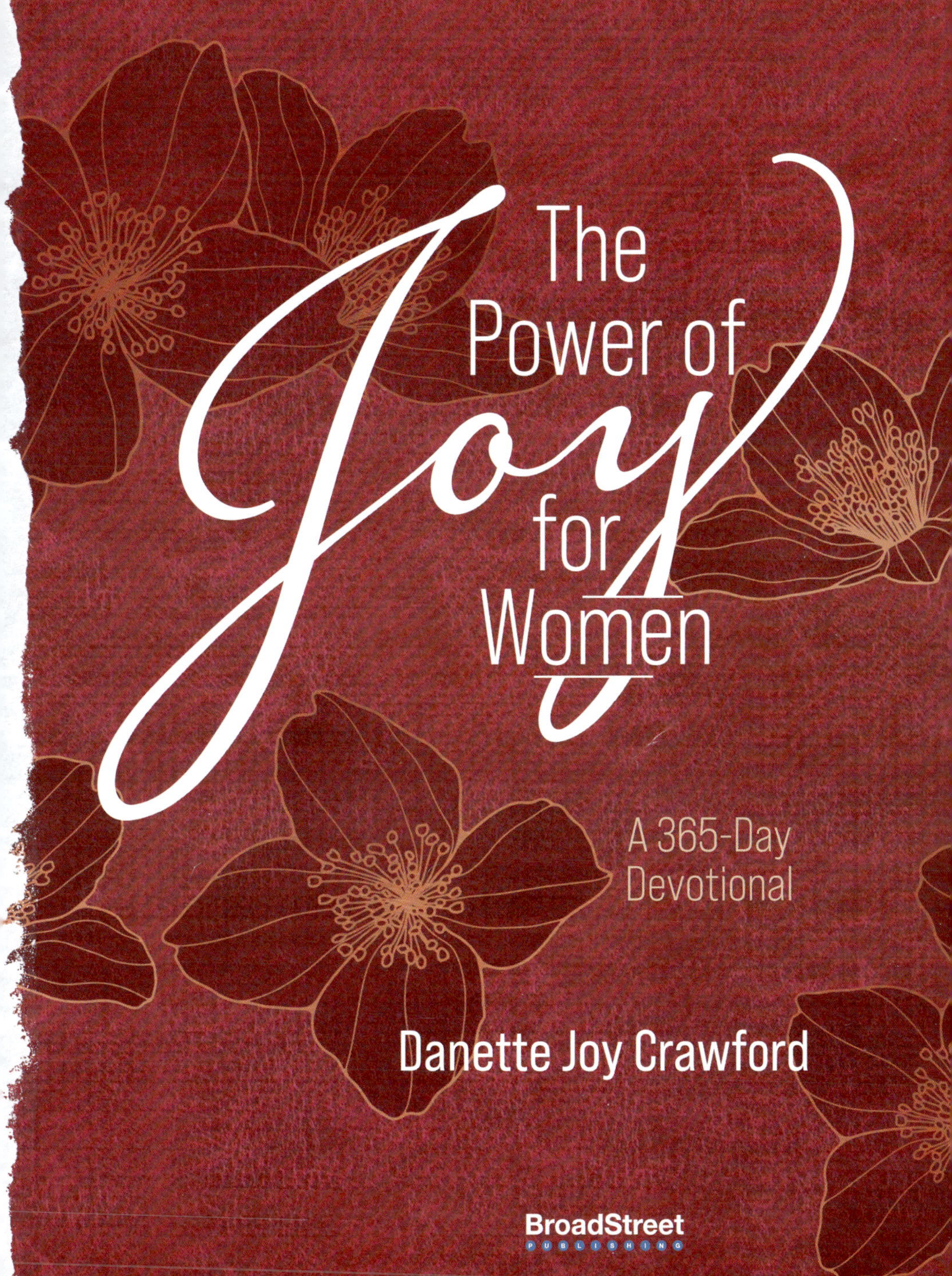
The
Power of
Joy
for
Women
A 365-Day
Devotional
Danette Joy Crawford
BroadStreet
PUBLISHING

BroadStreet Publishing® Group, LLC
Savage, Minnesota, USA
BroadStreetPublishing.com

The Power of Joy for Women: A 365-Day Devotional

9781424569267 (faux leather)
9781424569274 (ebook)

Please be aware that this devotional contains material regarding suicidal ideation. If at any time you find yourself experiencing suicidal thoughts, contact the 988 Suicide and Crisis Lifeline at 988.

Italics in Scripture quotations have been added by the author to indicate emphasis.

Cover and interior by Garborg Design Works | garborgdesign.com

Printed in China

25 26 27 28 29 5 4 3 2 1

Author's Note

Sister in Christ, have you grown weary? Are you starting to lose heart? As a new year begins, are you teeming with anticipation or trembling with dread? I've been in both places—on cloud nine and at ground zero. I've danced on mountaintops and despaired in deep valleys. I've tasted triumphs and tears, sweetness and sweat. From the precious moments of mothering to the pain and betrayal of divorce, from the sweetness of a close-knit family to the soul-crushing loss of loved ones, I have battled emotional and physical pain that I thought would end me. And I can tell you that there is one who will stay by your side through it all.

When I chose to keep going—with my eyes fixed on Jesus and my faith firmly founded on his Word—I found my burdens lifted and my way made straight (or at least straighter and more bearable than it otherwise would have been). I've proven what countless people in the Bible did long before me: God is near to the brokenhearted and a friend of sinners, a loving Father who never leaves us alone but who runs alongside us and even carries us when we need him to. Won't you take his hand today and let him do the same for you?

The Bible says in Nehemiah 8:10 that "the joy of the Lord is your strength." My heart in writing this book is to take you on a journey of proving the truth of this verse in your own life—to help you discover the only joy that will sustain you through every painful circumstance and strengthen you for every battle.

Each daily entry begins with a Scripture passage pertaining to the topic, followed by a brief meditation to encourage you. It closes with verses to deepen your joy—two additional Scripture passages for you to look up on your own, encouraging further familiarity with God's Word and the wonderful wisdom it contains—and an exhortation to go share the joy today. As the joy of the Lord unfolds to you, don't keep it to yourself. I encourage you to think of new and creative ways to reach out and share his joy with those around you.

Unspeakable joy and all-transcending peace are possible when we choose to pursue them and their source, when we have God as our anchor and his hope as our foundation. Join me today on a yearlong journey to proving God's faithfulness to you, his beloved daughter!

Go in grace,

Danette

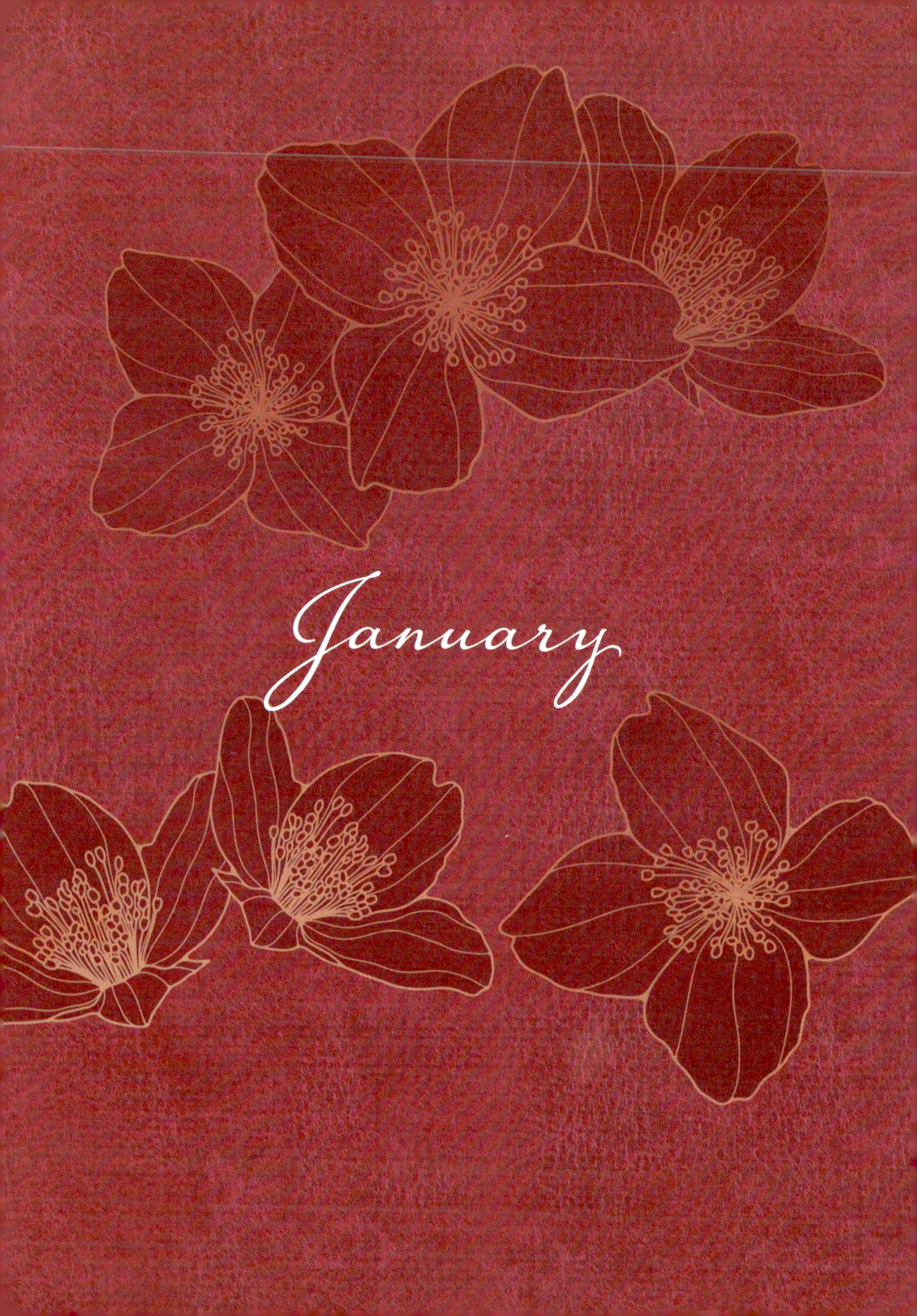

January

Running the Race of Life

I have fought the good fight,
I have finished the race,
I have kept the faith.
2 Timothy 4:7

If this life is a race, how will yours conclude? Only God knows, of course. But if you were to cross the finish line today, how would that look? What kind of declaration might you make? Could you say, like the apostle Paul in this verse from 2 Timothy, that you have "fought the good fight"? Would you be able to say that you'd "kept the faith"? These are tough questions, but they're important ones to ask if we want to live our lives in light of eternity.

However your race has been going—whether you've been running full tilt, overflowing with energy, or plodding along in search of your purpose—I want to encourage you: the race isn't over until God says it is. As long as you have life in your body and breath in your lungs, you have not yet fulfilled your ultimate purpose for living. And it is never too late to discover and pursue God's wonderful plans for you—"plans to prosper you and not to harm you, plans to give you hope and a future" (Jeremiah 29:11).

Wherever you are, whatever your pace, however swift or slagging your progress, God has great plans for your future! Find joy in this truth and trust that you will one day say, with the apostle Paul, that you have fought the good fight and finished the race to the best of your God-given abilities.

VERSES TO DEEPEN YOUR JOY

Jeremiah 29:11–13; Philippians 3:13–14

Go share the joy today!

Reassurance for the Weary

Let us not grow weary or become discouraged in doing good, for at the proper time we will reap, if we do not give in.

GALATIANS 6:9 AMP

Galatians 6:9 encourages us not to "grow weary." Have you ever seen a tree that has grown crooked? My neighborhood has several such trees, and if there's a strong wind when I'm out walking, I hurry my pace to get past them. You never know when one might topple over!

Maybe today you feel that your life's path has grown crooked. Maybe your heart has grown cold toward the Lord or toward other people. Or perhaps you find yourself growing weary for any number of reasons. This life can be downright discouraging, dealing gut punches and heartbreaking losses that threaten every day to rob us of our joy.

Yet a weary existence of despair and defeat was never what God intended for his children. He doesn't want us to grow weary but to summon his supernatural strength to persevere and overcome every obstacle that stands in our way. Don't succumb to discouragement but keep on "doing good"—pursuing the path God has put you on—and trust that he will reward your efforts fully.

When you remember the reward that awaits you for persevering rather than becoming so discouraged that you give up, you will find the motivation to keep moving forward and "doing good," as Galatians 6:9 urges you to do.

VERSES TO DEEPEN YOUR JOY

MATTHEW 11:28; JOHN 10:10

Go share the joy today!

Unshakable Joy

"Don't be dejected and sad,
for the joy of the LORD *is your strength!"*
NEHEMIAH 8:10 NLT

It's easy enough to want to press past our weariness. It's simple to decide in our hearts, *Today I won't grieve but will be joyful!* But if we're honest, our best efforts and our most earnest intentions can't produce feelings of happiness capable of overshadowing our doubts, pains, and fears. The good thing is that true joy doesn't depend on a mindset of our own making.

Today's verse from Nehemiah is both a statement of fact and a strong command. The fact is that our true source of joy is our almighty God, our heavenly Father, who never varies his character through the ever-changing seasons that we experience. We can count on him to carry us through all of life's circumstances. His joy is available to us anytime, anywhere.

As a command, Nehemiah 8:10 is just as relevant to us today as it was to the Israelites who heard it several millennia ago, when Ezra and the Levites were instructing them to take heart and quit crying. It's a call to rise above our circumstances and rejoice, not because of our sufferings but despite them. Even in the deepest pit and the darkest valley, God won't leave us or forsake us. That's why the apostle Paul could insist with such adamance, "Rejoice in the Lord always. I will say it again: Rejoice!" (Philippians 4:4).

We can rejoice in the Lord always because the Lord himself *is* our joy. And if our joy is unshakable, there's no stopping us.

VERSES TO DEEPEN YOUR JOY

DEUTERONOMY 31:6, 8; HEBREWS 13:5

Go share the joy today!

Worship and Walk with Him

Blessed are those who have learned to acclaim you,
who walk in the light of your presence, Lord.
Psalm 89:15

I can't emphasize it enough: the key to transcendent peace and all-surpassing joy is a life lived in the presence of God. It's only there that we find all that we need to thrive, including wisdom, strength, courage, conviction, and contentment. And, those benefits aside, in his presence, we have the best thing—God himself!

Funnily enough, it's our toughest trials that really prove this to be true. When our worldly comforts are stripped away, we discover just how sufficient Christ is and just how transcendent his joy can be. What had the apostle Paul endured before he reached the point of being able to say, "For Christ's sake, I delight in weaknesses, in insults, in hardships, in persecutions, in difficulties" (2 Corinthians 12:10)? Imprisonment. Floggings. Beatings to within an inch of his life. A stoning. Shipwrecks. Sleep deprivation. Extreme hunger and thirst. Exposure to the elements (11:23–29).

Yet, after all that, he proclaimed, "When I am weak, then I am strong" (12:10). Talk about someone who proved the all-sufficiency of God's presence! Clearly, the joy of the Lord was his strength, and we can draw from the same source when we cultivate a relationship of intimacy with our Lord and Savior.

VERSES TO DEEPEN YOUR JOY

Psalm 16; 2 Corinthians 12:9

Go share the joy today!

Abide in His Presence

In Your presence is fullness of joy;
at Your right hand are pleasures forevermore.

Psalm 16:11 NKJV

How can we abide in the presence of God and be confident that he is with us? The good news is that it doesn't depend on us. God promises never to leave or forsake us, and the psalmist acknowledged the omnipresence of God and his Holy Spirit when he wrote,

> Where can I go from Your Spirit?
> Or where can I flee from Your presence?
> If I ascend to heaven, You are there;
> if I make my bed in Sheol, behold, You are there.
> (Psalm 139:7–8 NASB)

The key is to live with a sense of God's presence. We must remind ourselves continually of his promises to guide, protect, uphold, and shelter us. When we dwell on who he is and how much he loves us, his kids, we can't help but worship in a way that draws us close to the Father's heart.

We can cultivate a consciousness of God's presence by setting aside time to study the Bible, meditate on Scripture, pray, and simply soak in his Spirit. The more diligently we do this, the more we want to do it. Our delight in the Lord will intensify as we deepen our faith and broaden our understanding of him and his ways. Nothing exceeds the power, awe, and peace of God's presence.

VERSES TO DEEPEN YOUR JOY

Psalm 84; Psalm 139:1–18

Go share the joy today!

Daughter of the King

See what an incredible quality of love the Father has shown to us, that we would [be permitted to] be named and called and counted the children of God! And so we are!

1 JOHN 3:1 AMP

The same promise God made to the Israelites—"'I will be a Father to you, and you will be My sons and daughters,' says the Lord Almighty" (2 Corinthians 6:18 AMP)—is the pledge he makes to his children today. The King of kings is a faithful Father who "keeps his covenant for a thousand generations and lavishes his unfailing love on those who love him and obey his commands" (Deuteronomy 7:9 NLT). That means you're royalty, girl!

And as a beloved daughter of the King, you have a host of covenant benefits just waiting for you to redeem. It's way better than cash and never expires. Belonging to God means, best of all, that his Holy Spirit dwells in you as your constant companion, comforter, and guide. Jesus described the Spirit's role like this: "He will teach you all things, and bring to your remembrance all things that I said to you" (John 14:26 NKJV).

Isn't that amazing? When God is your Father, his Spirit lives in your heart, and you can count on him to teach you, guide you, bring Jesus' words to your mind, and even pray on your behalf when you don't have the words (Romans 8:26). That's the best royal treatment I've ever heard of!

VERSES TO DEEPEN YOUR JOY

EZEKIEL 37:26–28; JOHN 14:16–17

Go share the joy today!

Divine Protection

Whoever dwells in the shelter of the Most High
will rest in the shadow of the Almighty.
I will say of the LORD*,*
"He is my refuge and my fortress,
my God, in whom I trust."

PSALM 91:1–2

When we dwell in the presence of God and his Spirit dwells in us, not only do we receive divine counsel and comfort, but we also have a royal guard protecting us. Living in the presence of the Lord positions us in the shelter of the Most High—a shelter like no other. And that place of shelter belongs to all those who call God their Father and friend. *Merriam-Webster* defines *shelter* as "something that covers or affords protection." When we are walking with the Most High God, he has us covered. He protects us and defends us.

The second part of Psalm 91:1 says that we will "rest in the shadow of the Almighty." What reassurance! I take such comfort in knowing that we can rest while God covers, protects, and defends us. When our opponents—even the devil himself—try to forge weapons against us, their efforts will be fruitless, for our Father promises us, "A thousand may fall at your side and ten thousand at your right hand, but it shall not approach you" (v. 7 NASB). Rejoice, for God is our sure defense.

VERSES TO DEEPEN YOUR JOY

PSALM 91:9–16; ISAIAH 54:17

Go share the joy today!

Holy Wisdom

If any of you lacks wisdom, you should ask God,
who gives generously to all without finding fault,
and it will be given to you.

James 1:5

Abiding in God's presence enables us to access his holy wisdom and divine guidance. God is so generous in giving us wisdom. We just have to ask. How many times have we missed out on receiving divine insight just because we forgot to consult our heavenly Father in the first place?

I love that God grants us his wisdom without rubbing our faults and flaws in our faces. He doesn't roll his eyes and say, *Great, here comes Danette again, bugging me for more wisdom.* No, he loves to give his children wisdom and discernment when they ask him for it. That's because asking him for wisdom shows that we understand just how limited our wisdom is. It indicates that we realize how much we need his supernatural insight to get through each day.

As we dwell in God's presence and keep our hearts open to his leading, we will receive his wisdom. And when we receive it, we have to believe rather than doubt what the Lord has said to us. One way that we can test the wisdom we receive is to hold it up to God's Word. What he says will always align with his Word—the Holy Scriptures. The two will never contradict each other.

VERSES TO DEEPEN YOUR JOY

1 Kings 4:29; Psalm 111:10

Go share the joy today!

Single-Minded Assurance

*When you ask, you must believe and not doubt,
because the one who doubts is like a wave of the sea,
blown and tossed by the wind.*

James 1:6

The very first time I received a word of knowledge from the Lord, I was in church, praying up front near the altar. By the time I got back to my seat, I had already begun to doubt, asking myself, *Did the Lord really say what I think I heard him say?* The Lord spoke to me through that incident and showed me how the Enemy comes immediately to steal God's words, as Jesus illustrated in his parable of the sower. We can't afford to loosen our grip on God's messages, or Satan will sweep in and steal them away.

If we begin to doubt, we become double-minded, and this attitude can spread quickly to all the other areas of our life, resulting in instability and ineffectiveness. But when we dwell in the presence of the Lord, we can remain stable and fixed under the shadow of the Almighty. And when the Enemy realizes we are not movable, he'll move on to mess with somebody else. Hallelujah! By the power of the Holy Spirit, we can maintain single-minded trust in the Lord and his perfect, failproof guidance.

VERSES TO DEEPEN YOUR JOY

Luke 8:4–15; James 1:7–8

Go share the joy today!

Permanent Peace

The peace of God, which surpasses all understanding, will guard your hearts and minds through Christ Jesus.

PHILIPPIANS 4:7 NKJV

Dwelling in God's presence also gives us permanent peace that we can count on regardless of our situations. We can find peace even in our most challenging circumstances, face challenges calmly, and fill our cups with refreshment during drought—be it literal, emotional, or mental.

Psalm 23 paints a well-known picture of the peace that is ours in Christ Jesus. The psalm says, "Even though I walk through the darkest valley, I will fear no evil, for you are with me; your rod and your staff, they comfort me" (v. 4). We can be at peace even when we're walking (or staggering or even crawling, as the case may be) through life's deepest valleys and darkest circumstances because the Lord has us covered. We can be refreshed and fulfilled in situations that would cause panic for those who don't know God. There's no limit to the peace and refreshment we find as we dwell in God's presence.

We need to keep in mind that the world's definition of *peace*—and how to find it—contrasts starkly with true peace, which comes from God alone. Jesus said to his disciples, "I am leaving you with a gift—peace of mind and heart. And the peace I give is a gift the world cannot give" (John 14:27 NLT). Many times, what the world prescribes for our peace results only in pain and confusion. But only in Jesus can we find true peace, which has the power to put all our worries and fears to rest.

VERSES TO DEEPEN YOUR JOY

PSALM 23; JOHN 14:1–4

Go share the joy today!

Unconditional Contentment

I have learned to be content whatever the circumstances.

PHILIPPIANS 4:11

When I read Psalm 91 and other verses that describe the benefits of abiding in God's presence, I feel unspeakable *joy*—yet another blessing that comes from dwelling in the presence of the Almighty. This is not circumstantial happiness we feel but rather a deep, abiding joy that can endure any heartbreak and sustain us through every challenge. When we can say, along with the apostle Paul, that we have "learned to be content whatever the circumstances," we show that our joy is founded on God's presence rather than on our present circumstances.

It sounds almost unbelievable: joy that persists through seemingly unbearable pain and gut-wrenching heartbreak, joy that carries us through unspeakable tragedies, joy that picks us out of the pit of despair and places us on a mountaintop of peace and contentment. But this joy has been proven possible by the apostle Paul and by countless other martyrs of the faith, for starters.

True joy does not depend on our circumstances; it depends on our relationship with the Lord. Our source of joy must be the very presence of God, for his joy fuels us to forge ahead through every hardship and helps us conquer every hurdle. Other sources of joy may fail us, but the Lord's joy cannot be cut down or destroyed. The schemes of Satan can't snuff it out. The joy of the Lord is a reliable source of strength.

VERSES TO DEEPEN YOUR JOY

NEHEMIAH 8:10; PHILIPPIANS 4:11–13

Go share the joy today!

Run with Perseverance

Let us run with perseverance the race marked out for us, fixing our eyes on Jesus, the pioneer and perfecter of faith.

HEBREWS 12:1–2

When we know that our peace and joy originate in the only source that won't run dry—Jesus Christ—we can take courage for life's race and run it with perseverance. When it comes to the race of life, we need perseverance if we're going to perform well and finish strong.

According to *Merriam-Webster*, to *persevere* means "to persist in a state, enterprise, or undertaking in spite of counterinfluences, opposition, or discouragement." When we persevere, we move forward *despite* hindrances and hardships. It can be tempting to think that our happiness and satisfaction depend on the absence of opposition and adversity in our lives. Yet the paradoxical truth is that our greatest joys usually come on the heels of our hardest trials and heaviest griefs. I've found this to be true in my own life, and I'm sure you've experienced this reality as well.

The strongest relationships, the longest-lasting marriages, and the closest bonds are between those who have persevered through the hard times and reached the other side of their pain together despite disappointments and heartaches. Overcoming difficulties together can reinforce and even deepen the bonds of loyalty and love. We're stronger together when we work out our differences in the face of conflict and come through on the other side closer and more committed to each other.

VERSES TO DEEPEN YOUR JOY

ISAIAH 40:31; HEBREWS 10:36

Go share the joy today!

Perfect Your Perseverance

We also celebrate in our tribulations,
knowing that tribulation brings about perseverance.

ROMANS 5:3 NASB

How do you develop and strengthen your perseverance? How do you hone this important trait that can propel you to run well and finish strong? You do it by greeting life's challenges with an attitude of maturity. You do it by cultivating a willingness to say, *Okay, God, how are you going to grow me through this experience?*

When you welcome opportunities to strengthen your character and reinforce your integrity, you set yourself up for a joy that surpasses understanding and stands through all circumstances. You prepare yourself to discover joy even amid the struggle—a joy that gives you the power to persevere.

The next time you find yourself at the end of your rope, remember to turn to God and ask him what he has in mind for your next step. Don't despair or throw your hands in the air unless it's in a posture of praise to the one who will get you through your storm. Perseverance that hasn't been tested and proven effective isn't perseverance at all. Whenever opposition and hardship come your way, invite God into the mess. It's a great way to train yourself in this all-important area of perseverance.

VERSES TO DEEPEN YOUR JOY

ROMANS 5:4; JAMES 1:2–3

Go share the joy today!

Throw Off Hindrances

Let us throw off everything that hinders…
And let us run with perseverance the race marked out for us.

HEBREWS 12:1

Any professional runner will tell you that when it comes to a race, anything that isn't helping your speed is hindering it. Training for a marathon or other sporting event may involve bearing extra weight to build endurance, but when you're vying for the fastest pace, you wear only as many clothes as you need and forgo any extras that would weigh you down and slow your speed. In the same way, we need to throw off certain hindrances to our personal race if we are to persevere effectively.

When it comes to our spiritual race, our life's journey, the extra weight of offense and unforgiveness is never helpful. Ezekiel 33:10 says, "Our offenses and sins weigh us down, and we are wasting away because of them. How then can we live?" Trying to run with the added weight of bitterness in our hearts is counterproductive and even destructive. That's because this burden drags us down and compromises our spiritual, mental, emotional, and even physical health.

We can't run with perseverance if we're dragging along a bunch of extra baggage. What baggage is burdening you today? What extra weight is dragging you down? Pray to God for wisdom as you seek to throw off burdens and run unencumbered.

VERSES TO DEEPEN YOUR JOY

HEBREWS 12:1–3; 1 JOHN 1:5–10

Go share the joy today!

Cast Off Comparison

A heart at peace gives life to the body,
but envy rots the bones.

PROVERBS 14:30

Nothing kills your joy like comparison. Some days, you may feel that the "racecourse" assigned to you isn't fair. Your friends and neighbors may seem to have the easy road while your path is riddled with potholes. But comparison is a major temptation you need to persevere through and move past, especially if you expect to run with joy.

That's part of what the author of Hebrews meant when he exhorted us to "throw off everything that hinders and the sin that so easily entangles" (12:1). It's no wonder that we lose our footing and trip when we're fixated on our neighbor's race; we're looking aside or over our shoulder rather than focusing on what lies ahead on our own path.

Don't be tripped up by envy or sidetracked by the comparison time waster. Don't get caught up in contrasting your assigned racecourse with those of your family members or friends. Stay focused on your own God-given course and rejoice that he has seen fit to run alongside you, steering and cheering you forward. Only he knows what hidden sins and struggles are affecting the pace of your peers. Keep your eyes on the track ahead of you and trust God to deal justly with everyone.

VERSES TO DEEPEN YOUR JOY

PROVERBS 23:17; ECCLESIASTES 4:4

Go share the joy today!

Avoid the Devil's Traps

Forgive...to keep Satan from taking advantage of us; for we are not ignorant of his schemes.

2 CORINTHIANS 2:10–11 AMP

Wherever we find ourselves along the racecourse of life, all of us have a common adversary: the devil, also called Satan, who is determined to do all he can to get God's kids to fail. Scripture says that the devil "prowls around like a roaring lion, seeking someone to devour" (1 Peter 5:8 NASB). Notice that it doesn't say he roars. That would be too obvious! No, the devil's schemes are subtle, and we need to be on the lookout for them lest we fall into the traps and snares that he so cunningly lays for us.

You can't run well if you're tangled up in a net or caught in a briar bush. That's why the Enemy delights in laying traps for God's children. He knows that if he can trip us up and cause us to stumble enough times, we're likely to become too discouraged or distracted to focus on God, and we won't finish strong—or maybe at all. But when we ask the Holy Spirit to reveal to us our areas of weakness and vulnerability, we can avoid the Enemy's entanglements and keep trekking ahead.

Again, the devil's traps aren't usually easy to identify. Satan is skilled at disguising his schemes and blindsiding us with his wiles. Ask God to open your eyes and help you discern the traps the Enemy has laid for you.

VERSES TO DEEPEN YOUR JOY

JAMES 4:7; 1 PETER 5:7–9

Go share the joy today!

Shed What Interferes

You were running [the race] well;
who has interfered and prevented you from obeying the truth?
GALATIANS 5:7 AMP

The Lord invites us to think and live without limits, seizing and possessing all the wonderful blessings he has in store for us. But only those who separate themselves from the things of the world and who consecrate themselves to the Lord will have the power and ability to finish the race and possess the "land" God has promised them.

Maybe today you need to throw off an offense you've harbored in your heart. Maybe there's a sinful habit you need to cut out of your daily routine. Perhaps you've been nursing a poor attitude that's kept you from tackling a problem or reconciling with an estranged friend or family member. The time has come to cast off whatever is hindering you today so you can press ahead with perseverance. Don't get dragged down by all the baggage that the devil would have you shoulder. Cast it off and prepare to speed ahead with a newfound lightness of foot.

Determine to throw off your entanglements and keep on running. Look to the Lord for strength and wisdom as you shed your sinful habits and strive toward godly living. Remember that because the Lord is by your side, "weeping may endure for a night, but joy comes in the morning" (Psalm 30:5 NKJV).

VERSES TO DEEPEN YOUR JOY

1 CORINTHIANS 9:24–27; PHILIPPIANS 2:16

Go share the joy today!

Separated and Consecrated

"'Consecrate yourselves and be holy,
because I am the Lord your God.'"
Leviticus 20:7

The power of God is released in and through us as we consecrate ourselves to him. Many people are trying to run life's race and possess God's promises but fall short because they are neither separated nor consecrated. They look like the world, think like the world, talk like the world, act like the world, and sometimes even smell like the world.

Separation from the world is the first step toward consecration to God. Without holiness, we forfeit the limitless lifestyle God desires for his children. It may seem as if things are working for a little while, but then, when we least expect it, everything will come tumbling down around us. We can only fake it for so long. But true holiness and pure consecration will keep us abiding in God's presence and advancing his kingdom on earth.

We must build our foundation to last through every storm, and the only foundation that promises such stability is a holy lifestyle. We cannot live a holy life if we aren't separated from the things of the world and consecrated to the things of God. Prayerfully consider today if you need to modify or eliminate any aspects of your lifestyle to separate yourself from the world and consecrate yourself to the Lord.

VERSES TO DEEPEN YOUR JOY

Joshua 3:5; Jeremiah 1:5

Go share the joy today!

Visibly Set Apart

"Let your light shine before men in such a way that they may see your good deeds and moral excellence, and [recognize and honor and] glorify your Father who is in heaven."

MATTHEW 5:16 AMP

My favorite definition of the verb *separate* comes from *Webster's New World College Dictionary*: "to single out or set apart from others for a special purpose." As we persevere in life's race, we must separate ourselves from the things of the world so we can consecrate ourselves to the things of God.

Once again, separation must precede consecration. Ask yourself the following questions: *Is it easy to distinguish my life from the lives of others around me? Can people tell that my life is different because of my commitment to God, or do I blend in with the crowd?* When we are separated from the world, people take notice. And when God has singled us out and set us apart from others, it's because of his special purpose for our lives.

It should be no secret that we're set apart. We don't need to flaunt our beliefs or put on airs because of our holy lifestyle, but it should be evident to others that we're running life's race with the goal of earning the only crown that lasts. We aren't in it to win it but to reach eternity with the ultimate Victor, our heavenly Father, who has already won the race in the first place.

VERSES TO DEEPEN YOUR JOY

MATTHEW 5:14–15; 2 CORINTHIANS 6:17

Go share the joy today!

The Prize Is Worth the Price

"'You are to be holy to me because I, the LORD, am holy, and I have set you apart from the nations to be my own.'"
LEVITICUS 20:26

I haven't attempted to live like everyone else since I was saved at the age of seventeen. The Lord made it very clear to me that I was to consecrate myself to him and to endeavor to lead a lifestyle of holiness based on his leading.

Many other faithful believers feel free to participate in certain worldly behaviors and practices, yet the Holy Spirit has constrained me from those habits. I don't judge such people; I never whine or complain about the narrow path God has shown me. I only know what the Lord has said to me year after year, time after time, based on Luke 12:48: "From everyone to whom much has been given, much will be required" (AMP).

The Lord has greatly blessed me with faith and anointing, and I am consequently required, in many cases, to pay a higher price than others for separation from the world and consecration to the Lord. But the price is always worth the prize.

Maybe today you are counting the cost. Let me assure you that the price you pay for living a holy, separated life is always worth it. When you are separated, you can be consecrated. And when you are consecrated, you experience God's power, presence, and glory in such a way that is beyond compare.

VERSES TO DEEPEN YOUR JOY

DEUTERONOMY 26:19; EZEKIEL 37:28

Go share the joy today!

Pure, Not Mixed

Know that the Lord has set apart the godly person for Himself; the Lord hears when I call to Him.

Psalm 4:3 NASB

When she was little, my daughter, Destiny, loved to combine random ingredients, whether in our kitchen or at restaurants, into a "secret mixture" of items that had no business being together: ketchup and applesauce, cottage cheese and Catalina dressing…you get the idea. This game usually activated my gag reflex.

And spiritual mixture in our lives has the same effect on God, who reproved a particular group of believers with the following words: "I know your deeds, that you are neither cold nor hot. I wish you were either one or the other! So, because you are lukewarm—neither hot nor cold—I am about to *spit you out of my mouth*" (Revelation 3:15–16).

Some Christians concoct their own secret mixtures of habits and practices, compromising in certain areas rather than holding fast to the righteous path Christ has purchased for them. But we are to be "hot"—on fire for the Lord—not lukewarm, wishy-washy believers who combine carnal desires with Christian disciplines, pious behavior with seemingly minor sins.

Sin separates us from the presence of the Lord and drags us down in our pursuit of the things of God. We can't live a lifestyle of compromise and expect the glorious presence of the Lord to surround us. But if we repent and turn to God, he cleanses and refreshes us with his pure, perfectly satisfying presence.

VERSES TO DEEPEN YOUR JOY

Psalm 51:1–2; Acts 3:19

Go share the joy today!

A Personal Process

"'I am the LORD your God;
so consecrate yourselves and be holy,
for I am holy.'"

LEVITICUS 11:44 AMP

Consecrating ourselves to the Lord involves making right choices and righteous decisions. And the process of consecrating ourselves is one we must do for ourselves as the Holy Spirit empowers us. No one else can do it for us. There's no such thing as "consecration by proxy."

Webster's New World College Dictionary defines *consecrate* as "to set apart as holy; make or declare sacred…; to devote entirely; dedicate." God has appointed us and called us to be set apart as his own. And how do we live out this calling? We do it by refraining from joining ourselves with people, places, activities, and organizations that are opposed to the holy lifestyle God has ordained for our lives. We must consecrate ourselves daily to his wisdom and ways.

Every day people make impulsive and foolish decisions that cost them their anointing. Let's not be among those people. There's too much at stake. God has planned a long list of contributions for you to make to his kingdom. Pay the price for holiness by living separated and consecrated. You won't regret it. I promise.

Ask God to show you any areas of your life that you have not yet consecrated to him. He will make the way clear for you to become set apart and sanctified for his plans and purposes.

VERSES TO DEEPEN YOUR JOY

NUMBERS 11:18; HEBREWS 12:14

Go share the joy today!

The Root of Bitterness

See to it that no one comes short of the grace of God; that no root of bitterness springing up causes trouble, and by it many become defiled.

HEBREWS 12:15 NASB

Have you ever tripped on a tree root? Those tripping hazards have been responsible for many a sprained ankle and twisted knee. In the same way, we want to avoid tripping in our spiritual lives. Living a consecrated life prevents us from getting tripped up by the sins and snares of this world. And the "root of bitterness," in particular, cripples us when we fail to notice it sprouting in our hearts. The Enemy loves to sow seeds of offense and unforgiveness in our minds, hoping we will nurture them with grudges and grow angrier as time goes on.

Because we live on a fallen planet in the presence of other fallen people, it's inevitable that we will be offended at some point. Jesus himself confirmed, "It is impossible that no offenses should come" (Luke 17:1 NKJV). But if we aren't careful to forgive and forget, we'll get caught in a relentless cycle of rehearsing and rehashing our hurts—a process that slows us down and produces only spiritual decay.

For many people, offense is a classic compulsion to sin. Offenses that we do not deal with quickly and effectively can sprout roots and spread. When a bitter root unleashes its tentacles in someone's heart, all relationships will suffer, not just the relationship with the person who hurt them in the first place.

Thankfully, God has provided a way for us to deal with this stumbling block, and it's called forgiveness.

VERSES TO DEEPEN YOUR JOY

MICAH 7:18; EPHESIANS 4:26–27

Go share the joy today!

Uprooting Unforgiveness

Make every effort to live in peace with everyone and to be holy; without holiness no one will see the Lord.

HEBREWS 12:14

Unforgiveness easily entangles many of us. This sinful attitude takes root too quickly in the human heart, spreading a spirit of bitterness and offense that is hard to eliminate. Praise God that we have a way of escape. Because of the cross, where Christ died for sin (including your sins and mine), we can extend forgiveness to other people, promoting healing for ourselves as well as for them.

Rather than watering and nourishing the root of unforgiveness, we need to yank it out before it gets too deep, giving it over to God and letting him handle our hurt. Through daily communion with God, we can tend the gardens of our hearts so that bitterness doesn't grow there. Believe me, you can't have true joy if you're holding on to unforgiveness.

Jesus emphasized the necessity of forgiving others when he said, "If you forgive other people when they sin against you, your heavenly Father will also forgive you. But if you do not forgive others their sins, your Father will not forgive your sins" (Matthew 6:14–15). We can't expect God to forgive and forget the wrongs we've done if we aren't willing to extend that same grace to those who have wronged us.

VERSES TO DEEPEN YOUR JOY

MATTHEW 18:21–35; 1 PETER 3:8–12

Go share the joy today!

The Ultimate Act of Forgiveness

"This is My blood of the covenant,
which is being poured out for many for forgiveness of sins."
MATTHEW 26:28 NASB

Lest we think that Jesus is asking too much of us when he tells us to forgive others, let's remember that he forgave the most unforgivable act—his undeserved death on the Roman cross. Even as he hung there dying, he prayed, "Father, forgive them; for they do not know what they are doing" (Luke 23:34 NASB). That's right. He actually forgave his murderers, and he asked God to do the same, even as those people were putting him to death.

No offense we'll face could be harder to forgive than that. Praise God that he forgives us and enables us to forgive the seemingly unforgivable in others. Praise him for showing the way and setting an example for us.

When the seeds of offense have been sprinkled in your heart by the hurtful words or actions of someone else or by a situation that caused you pain, think of Jesus, the only perfect Man who ever lived, taking the sins of humanity on himself and dying for the most despicable of sinners. It puts everything in perspective.

Maybe you've been hurt so much that you consider the person's offense unforgivable. If it weren't for Jesus, it probably would be. But he has made a way for us to forgive: through his perfect, all-powerful blood. In your own power, you may not be able to extend forgiveness, but God will empower you to forgive as you rely on him and invoke the blood of Jesus.

VERSES TO DEEPEN YOUR JOY

EPHESIANS 1:7; HEBREWS 9:22

Go share the joy today!

The Myth of Righteous Resentment

Do not be overcome and conquered by evil,
but overcome evil with good.
ROMANS 12:21 AMP

Today's culture tells us that we have a right to be angry toward those who've hurt us and even to get back at them. Blockbuster movies and popular songs praise the underdogs who exact revenge on their adversaries. Passively accepting pain and extending forgiveness rather than lashing out are seen as signs of weakness; those who do so are labeled doormats and worse. Yet the call of Christ is to be meek and mild-mannered as we remember the one who, "like a lamb that is led to the slaughter, and like a sheep that is silent before her shearers,...did not open His mouth" (Isaiah 53:7 AMP).

None of us have the right to hold on to offenses and unforgiveness. No matter what anyone has or hasn't done to us, we need to forgive them. It doesn't matter if we don't feel like it. In fact, it's rare to feel like forgiving until after we've made the conscious choice to forgive whoever has wronged us.

The Enemy delights in deceiving people and keeping them from knowing the truth. Someone who has been offended may be deceived into feeling justified in harboring anger and resentment toward their offender. And the rest of the world affirms this "right" of theirs.

Don't let yourself be deceived into thinking you have the right to remain offended. Don't allow the deadly deception of unforgiveness to steal your joy, weaken your relationship with the Lord, and jeopardize your eternal destiny. It isn't worth it!

VERSES TO DEEPEN YOUR JOY

ISAIAH 53; ROMANS 12:19–21

Go share the joy today!

Overlooking Offenses

Good sense and discretion make a man slow to anger, and it is his honor and glory to overlook a transgression or an offense [without seeking revenge and harboring resentment].

PROVERBS 19:11 AMP

When it comes to the hurts and wrongdoings that others have committed against us, I like to say, "Don't nurse it; don't rehearse it—just curse it in the name of Jesus!" Instead of internalizing the hurt, thinking about it continually, and venting about it to those around us, we should curse the hurt and extend forgiveness. God's Word cautions us along the same lines when it says, "Whoever would foster love covers over an offense, but whoever repeats the matter separates close friends" (Proverbs 17:9).

We shouldn't *nurse* or *rehearse* our offenses by dwelling on them and repeating them over and over in our minds. This kind of behavior only worsens our pain and increases our anger and indignation. It sinks us deeper into the mucky mire of self-pity, which is never a spiritually or emotionally productive place to be. We need to *curse* the hurt and move on.

Is this process easy? Of course not! But when we ask the Holy Spirit to soften our hearts and lead us past our hurts, he is always faithful to respond. By his power, we can forgive and even forget. Again, God set this example for us, and we can follow in his footsteps.

VERSES TO DEEPEN YOUR JOY

PSALM 145:8; JAMES 1:19–20

Go share the joy today!

Slow to Anger

The Lord is gracious and compassionate;
slow to anger and great in mercy.

Psalm 145:8 NASB

As we practice holding our tempers and keeping healthy lines of communication open with others, we can learn to overlook offenses and let them slide right off us. Reacting in this way brings glory to our heavenly Father, not to mention that it protects our own reputations, although looking good in others' eyes shouldn't be our motivation.

Endeavoring to cast off offenses rather than cling to them also aligns our hearts with God's, for he is the best example of extending forgiveness where it isn't warranted and forgetting altogether about our sins. When we remember how merciful and long-suffering he is with us, it softens our hearts and makes it easier for us to extend mercy to those who have hurt us.

Once we've overlooked an offense, we need to leave it alone. It isn't enough to push it to the edge of our consciousness, where it is likely to lurk and threaten to rebound at the slightest provocation. No, we need to forgive and forget. We need to release the person who offended us and choose not to complain about the matter to anyone else. We can take our hurt to the feet of Jesus and leave it there for good. The more we practice these steps, the more forgiving and merciful we will become.

VERSES TO DEEPEN YOUR JOY

Proverbs 17:27–28; Hebrews 8:10–12

Go share the joy today!

Become Offense Proof

Be kind and compassionate to one another, forgiving each other, just as in Christ God forgave you.

EPHESIANS 4:32

One of my favorite breakfast dishes is eggs cooked sunny-side up. I store my frying pan on the stovetop so it's handy when I need it. The Teflon coating used to enable me to slide those eggs right out of the pan and onto my plate when they were ready, but a few years ago, the Teflon coating wore away. No worries because I just started spraying the pan with nonstick cooking spray. The oil serves the same purpose as the Teflon did, making for a mess-free serving of sunny-side up eggs.

My frying pan has become a daily reminder of how I should treat offense when it comes my way. I need to oil my spirit with the presence of God's Spirit so that any offenses simply slide right off me. Just as I spray my frying pan daily with oil, so do I reapply my "Holy Spirit" coating. I immerse myself in God's Word. I pray continually to him, keeping his ways in mind and remembering his presence and all its benefits. And I worship him for who he is and what he has done—a never-ending list of attributes and actions that far surpasses any list of hurts I've experienced.

It may sound oversimplified, but if you live conscious of the fact that you are coated with the Spirit and that, no matter what others may say or do, God has the final word, you become a tricky target for the devil's snares of offense and hurt. Just let them slide and revel in the joy that results.

VERSES TO DEEPEN YOUR JOY

PSALM 27:1; PSALM 118:5–6

Go share the joy today!

Acknowledge the Offense

Rescue me, LORD, from evildoers...They make their tongues as sharp as a serpent's; the poison of vipers is on their lips.

PSALM 140:1, 3

After reading yesterday's devotion, you may be thinking, *Really, Danette? I'm supposed to think of Teflon and just let that person's cruel words and spiteful backbiting slide right off. As if it's that easy!* Okay, you're right. It isn't enough to pretend we have a Teflon coating that repels any and all offenses. I was simply trying to paint a picture of how we can act and react when we're adequately filled with the Holy Spirit. But sometimes we need a practical strategy—concrete steps toward forgiving and forgetting.

The first step toward healing from hurt and freedom from unforgiveness is admitting you've been hurt. In many cases, our pride keeps us from acknowledging that we have suffered emotional injuries. We put up a wall and say, "Me, hurt? Never! I'm not hurt."

This prideful wall is hard to pull down. We need to be humble enough to say, "You know, I *do* feel hurt. Those words really stung—almost as much as the 'poison of vipers.' That mistreatment made me feel lousy. That person's betrayal cut me to the core." Only when we acknowledge our pain can we have hope of recovering from it. Only when we make ourselves vulnerable by owning our feelings can we release the person we hold responsible for causing those feelings.

Acknowledging our pain can be difficult, and the process may take a while. But with the Holy Spirit's help, we can be strengthened through the process and find freedom on the other side.

VERSES TO DEEPEN YOUR JOY

PSALM 140; MATTHEW 6:14–15

Go share the joy today!

Lay the Offense Down

"Do not judge, and you will not be judged. Do not condemn, and you will not be condemned. Forgive, and you will be forgiven."
LUKE 6:37

The second step of healing from offenses is to lay your hurt at the foot of the cross of Christ. Go to God and say, *Lord, I forgive so-and-so for hurting me. I release that person from everything they've done that has hurt me. I choose to release and forgive them. As you have forgiven me of my sins, Lord, I forgive them for their sins against me.* As you humble yourself (once again) by praying this prayer of forgiveness, you also release yourself from the bondage of unforgiveness.

Many people feel that they are punishing their offender by holding unforgiveness against that person. Yet the only victim of unforgiveness is the one who is dealing it out—the offended person who fails to forgive. An attitude of bitterness will keep you trapped in bondage and oppression and is emotionally and physically ruinous if you don't uproot it. But when you forgive those who have hurt you, you release yourself from the bondage of bitterness. You free yourself from the chains of unforgiveness, and you will find once again the freedom you need to live with peace, love, and joy.

You may need to pray a prayer of release daily—or even twice or three times a day! Remember, forgiveness is a process that begins with a decision. Your decision to forgive and forget, paired with a prayer of surrender that invokes the Lord's help, will produce powerful healing in your own life and in your relationships so that joy can prevail.

VERSES TO DEEPEN YOUR JOY

JEREMIAH 31:34; COLOSSIANS 3:13

Go share the joy today!

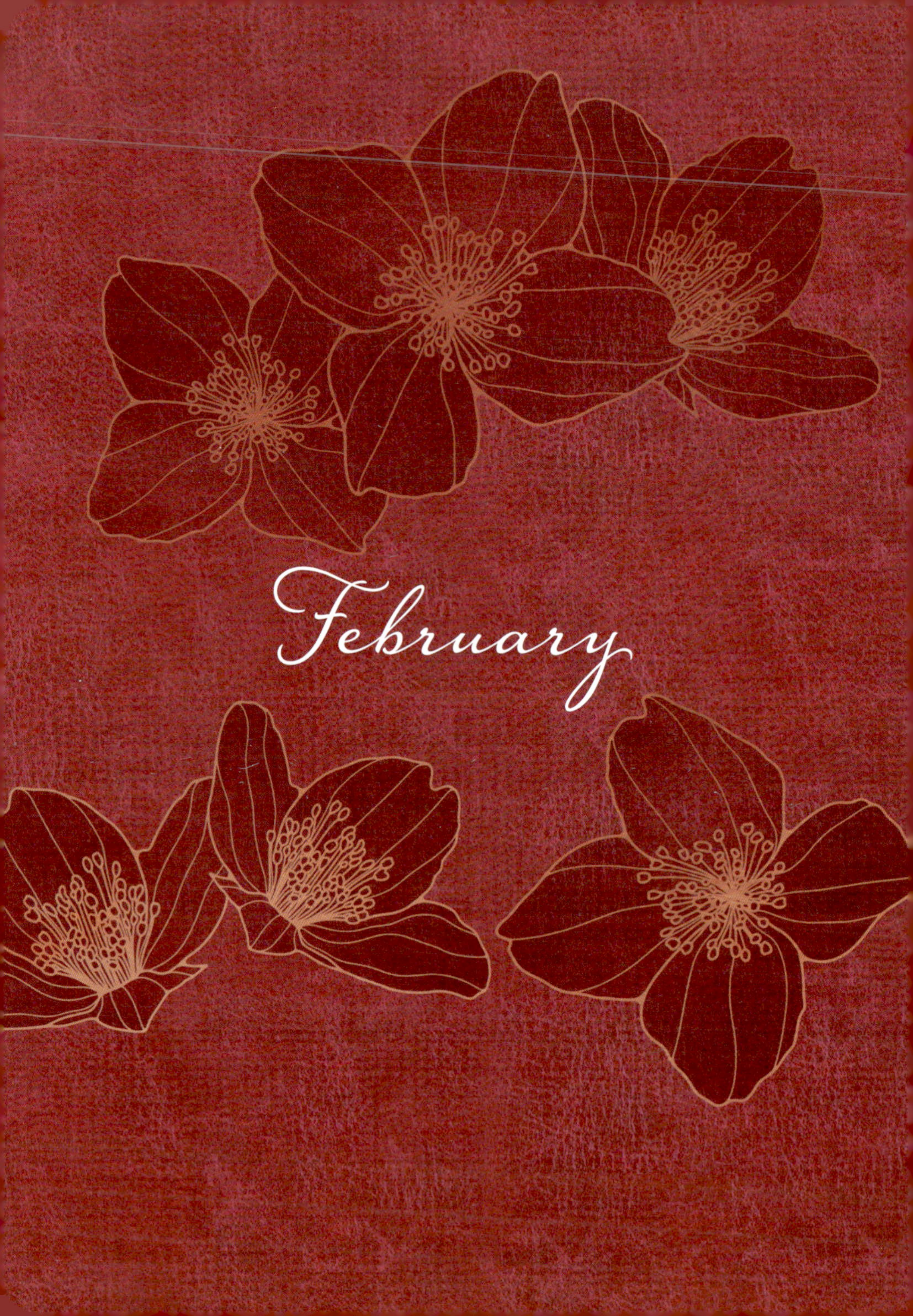
February

Replace Negative Thoughts

We are taking every thought and purpose captive to the obedience of Christ.

2 CORINTHIANS 10:5 AMP

When someone hurts us, it's tempting to wallow in self-pity as resentful thoughts of our wounds stew within our hearts. This behavior is hardly helpful for our healing. In fact, it drives us further down the path of unforgiveness, amplifying our anger and sometimes causing us to consider taking revenge. The best antidote to negative thoughts is just the opposite: replacing them with positive images and ideas, which is the third step toward freedom from offense.

There's just one problem. When we deliberately try not to think about something, that's just the thing that persists in our minds. Instead of focusing on *not* thinking about our hurts and offenses, we must replace those thoughts with wholesome, edifying, positive thoughts. We need to take our thoughts captive, as the apostle Paul says in 2 Corinthians 10:5.

When negative, sinful thoughts pop into your head, deliberately dwell on "whatever is true, whatever is honorable, whatever is right, whatever is pure, whatever is lovely, whatever is commendable, if there is any excellence and if anything worthy of praise" (Philippians 4:8 NASB). Focus your mind on what is good, pure, and holy. Then there won't be room in your heart and mind for negative thoughts. Since you have been raised with Christ, "set your mind and keep focused habitually on the things above [the heavenly things], not on things that are on the earth [which have only temporal value]" (Colossians 3:2 AMP).

VERSES TO DEEPEN YOUR JOY

2 CORINTHIANS 10:4–5; COLOSSIANS 3:1–4, 12–14

Go share the joy today!

Pray for Your Offender

"You have heard that it was said, 'You shall love your neighbor and hate your enemy.' But I say to you, love your enemies and pray for those who persecute you, so that you may prove yourselves to be sons of your Father who is in heaven."

MATTHEW 5:43–45 NASB

The fourth step in finding freedom from offense is to pray for your offender. (Please notice that I didn't call it the "final" step. Remember, these stages are cyclical, and we must follow them daily.) Praying for your offender is probably the hardest step, but it's mandatory if you're going to be free from offense and unforgiveness.

When you react out of your soul to the hurt you've experienced, your first inclination is to nurse and rehearse it. When you react out of your flesh, the temptation is to punch the person's lights out. But when you react out of your spirit—a spirit that's surrendered to the Holy Spirit—you overcome these tendencies by praying for your enemies because you know that's what Jesus tells you to do.

I realize that it goes against everything you *feel* like doing, but you must pray for your offender, asking God to bless them. Pray for favor for that person. Pray for them like you would pray for yourself. When you follow these steps, I'll bet you will soon find your bitterness melting and your heart softening for that person.

VERSES TO DEEPEN YOUR JOY

LUKE 6:37; EPHESIANS 4:31–32

Go share the joy today!

Loving the Unloving

Above all, have fervent and unfailing love for one another, because love covers a multitude of sins.

1 PETER 4:8 AMP

It's easy to love others when everything is going your way and everyone is getting along. Who doesn't respond positively to kindness and compliments? Who isn't eager to respond with love to those they find loving or lovely? But that's not the nature of unconditional love. God commands us to love even our enemies—those who have wounded us and caused us great pain.

It sometimes seems impossible, but that's why you need to exercise your heart by training yourself to walk in love and forgiveness. Such exercise is part of the process of maturing as a Christian. You can't do a whole lot of good for God if your heart is full of bitterness and offense.

Again, whenever we associate with other people, whether in our families, on the job, or in our church, we are bound to encounter offenses. How we handle those offenses determines our destiny. We must endeavor to love and forgive rather than to judge and hold grudges.

When all else fails, let's remember Jesus, the pioneer of our faith, who paved the way by forgiving the unforgivable. As he said, "Wide is the gate and broad is the road that leads to destruction, and many enter through it. But small is the gate and narrow the road that leads to life, and only a few find it" (Matthew 7:13–14). Loving those who love us back is the easy road. Let's walk in Jesus' footsteps and take the narrow road of loving our enemies and praying for those who persecute us.

VERSES TO DEEPEN YOUR JOY

MATTHEW 5:43–48; ROMANS 5:7–8

Go share the joy today!

Peace Flows from Forgiveness

There is a river whose streams make glad the city of God,
the holy place where the Most High dwells.

PSALM 46:4

One day, I was driving along a road that ran beside the banks of what appeared to be a beautiful river. From my vantage point, at first glance, the water looked clear and pure. But as I continued to travel, the road curved closer to the water, giving me a better look. Yuck! All kinds of junk and debris drifted in the river. Later, the Lord spoke to me about this experience and said, *That's how my children are when they have unforgiveness in their hearts. They have junk floating in their rivers.*

Not only does junk in the rivers of our hearts rob us of the beauty of God's presence in our lives, but it also keeps us from flowing in the power that comes from his presence. Only once we choose to let go of yesterday—the pain of the past, the memory of offenses—can we expect the river of God's presence to flow freely in our lives today, tomorrow, and into the future.

Don't stop up the river of peace with such junk as bitterness, unforgiveness, and vengefulness. Let go and let the river flow. Be a conduit of God's grace and mercy to those around you, and you will overflow with the all-surpassing peace of your heavenly Father.

VERSES TO DEEPEN YOUR JOY

PSALM 86:5; MARK 11:25

Go share the joy today!

Peace like a River

"If only you had paid attention to my commands,
your peace would have been like a river,
your well-being like the waves of the sea."
ISAIAH 48:18

What's the quality of your peace today? Does peace flow out of you like a river, or does it feel like your peace has simply dried up? Peace is an indication of righteousness, as the Bible says in Isaiah 48:18. Paying attention to Gods commands produces peace in our lives. Our obedience to the leading of the Holy Spirit and to the Word of God produces order in our lives. When we walk in disobedience to God's Word, we can open the door to stress, fear, and sometimes anxiety.

What has the Lord been leading you to do lately that perhaps you have been putting off? Don't delay your obedience another day. God will give you the strength today to follow through on what he has already told you to do. As you walk in obedience, even when it seems difficult to do so, you open the door for the peace of God to flow in your life. There is nothing in the world like knowing that you have obeyed what God has called you to do in a situation. When you do what God has called you to do, God will do what only he can do in your life.

VERSES TO DEEPEN YOUR JOY

PSALM 32:1; MARK 11:25

Go share the joy today!

When Offense Cuts Deep

The words of the reckless pierce like swords.

Proverbs 12:18

Sometimes forgiving does not mean forgetting. Sometimes the hurts we feel, the glares we see, and the words we hear will cut us to the heart, sprinkling seeds of insecurity, feelings of self-hate, and a sense of rejection. We may well have released the person who planted these seeds, but removing those seeds is often a different story.

I grew up in a tumultuous home, surrounded by volatile emotions and so desperately lacking affirmation that I developed unhealthy coping mechanisms and even struggled with depression to the point of feeling suicidal. God alone could redeem my rocky childhood and set me on a path of peace. And he did, but that path was not without significant, deep-seated issues I had to address along the way with the help of the Holy Spirit.

The negative words I repeatedly heard and the absence of any loving affirmations in my youth created within me a craving for acceptance, and for a while, I was desperate to earn it at any cost. Truly, Scripture is accurate when it says, "A gentle tongue [with its healing power] is a tree of life, but willful contrariness in it breaks down the spirit" (Proverbs 15:4 AMPC). My point is that I am not trying to minimize your pain. Whatever you've been through, God knows it, and he cares. He cries with you, but he wants you to find healing, and the only way to reach that step is to forgive.

VERSES TO DEEPEN YOUR JOY

Proverbs 12:18; Matthew 12:36

Go share the joy today!

Accepted in the Beloved

[God] hath made us accepted in the beloved.

Ephesians 1:6 KJV

As a result of the emotional tumult surrounding me as I grew up, my spirit was so broken that, for a while, nothing short of perfection would suffice. I masked my low self-esteem by earning many accolades and accomplishments during high school and college. I did all I could to get ahead, stand out, please others, and make it impossible for anyone to reject me. I did not know then what I have since learned: *perceived* rejection can be just as brutal as *actual* rejection.

Even when other people weren't intentionally treating me with unkindness or rejection, I would read into their words and actions malignant intentions that weren't actually there. Every look, every whisper, every sideways glance was a dart in my already deflating self-esteem. Yes, the rejection I perceived stung every bit as much as any real rejection. Our minds can create monsters where only murmurs exist. Self-deception can produce devastating results on our self-image and our relationships.

Praise God, for "he hath made us accepted in the beloved." Yet internalizing our status as accepted unconditionally by God and overcoming the sting of rejection, whether perceived or actual, are processes that take the Holy Spirit's help. Are you ready to begin? Don't delay but start defeating perceived rejection today.

VERSES TO DEEPEN YOUR JOY

Isaiah 41:9–10; Ephesians 1:3–10

Go share the joy today!

Guard against Rejection

The fear of man brings a snare,
but whoever trusts in the Lord shall be safe.
Proverbs 29:25 NKJV

A particularly effective scheme of the devil is to prey on our delicate self-image by making us susceptible to rejection. He loves to inflate our fear of ridicule and cause us to crave the acceptance and admiration of others. But God's approval is the only approval that counts, and he tells us throughout the pages of his Word just how valuable we are to him.

When you know who you are in Christ, receive God's unconditional love, and acknowledge that he has redeemed and accepted you, you'll become what I like to call rejection proof. You have to know God's approval of you in your heart and in your spirit, not just in your mind as mere head knowledge. And this knowledge comes only from regularly studying and meditating on God's Word and spending time in God's presence through prayer and worship.

Once God's Word makes us rejection proof, rejection, whether real or perceived, won't permanently affect or influence us. Once we become rejection proof, we are protected from and ultimately resistant to other people's negative words, opinions, and actions. God's Word assures us, "God has not given us a spirit of fear, but of power and of love and of a sound mind" (2 Timothy 1:7 NKJV). The fear of others' opinions can be paralyzing, but we don't need to give that fear a foothold. We can maintain a sound mind and confidence that God loves and accepts us.

VERSES TO DEEPEN YOUR JOY

Isaiah 41:9–10; 1 John 3:1

Go share the joy today!

Resist Perceived Rejection

"The devil...was a murderer from the beginning, not holding to the truth, for there is no truth in him. When he lies, he speaks his native language, for he is a liar and the father of lies."

John 8:44

As I've said earlier this month, rejection can be either real or perceived. Both types hurt if the truth of God's Word hasn't made us rejection proof. Perceived rejection is a device of the devil, whom the Bible calls "the father of lies." The devil loves it when God's children feel rejected, and if he can't send actual rejection our way, he's content to meddle with our perception so that we *think* we're being rejected.

If, for example, you walk into a room and nobody greets you, people seem to be ignoring you, or everyone suddenly stops talking, you might assume they've been talking about you. This is often a case of perceived rejection. Satan has a heyday trying to get you to feel rejected and left out, and he will wage wars in your mind, using thoughts that originate in the pit of hell.

The devil's goal is to get you to perceive rejection that doesn't exist. Don't fall for his deception! Don't be susceptible to fabricated feelings of exclusion. Instead, be rejection proof by intentionally giving others the benefit of the doubt and making no room for the devil's lies to take hold in your imagination. Refuse to entertain such thoughts. Renew your mind to the truth, and you will stay free from perceived deception.

VERSES TO DEEPEN YOUR JOY

Ephesians 6:11–12; James 4:7

Go share the joy today!

Deflect Real Rejection

"A good man brings good things out of the good stored up in his heart, and an evil man brings evil things out of the evil stored up in his heart. For the mouth speaks what the heart is full of."

LUKE 6:45

Although other people may genuinely reject us for various reasons, we can be sure that God never rejects us. He assures us of just the opposite. He has chosen us (Isaiah 41:9). He has called us by name and designated us as his own (43:1).

Keeping this truth in mind helps us maintain a clear perspective when we face actual rejection. If someone rejects us, we can be sure that their negative words or actions don't define us. In most cases, those who say negative things to you and about you are actually projecting the contents of their own heart. Maybe putting others down helps them feel a little better about their own insecurities. Maybe they're trying to mask feelings of envy. As the saying goes, "Hurt people hurt people." Whatever the case, their words and actions don't define your value or identity. God's Word alone defines who you are: his beloved child, fearfully and wonderfully made in his image (Psalm 139:14).

Whether someone else is deliberately employing the tactic of rejection to try to control you or whether they are ignorant of the harmful effects of their treatment, you can refuse to play their game. You can choose healthy ways of relating to people by refusing to be controlled by their rejection. Remind yourself of the truth—the Beloved has accepted you—and pray that those who reject you will work through their issues.

VERSES TO DEEPEN YOUR JOY

PSALM 139:1–18; LUKE 12:4

Go share the joy today!

Trust the Father Heart of God

A father of the fatherless, a defender of widows,
is God in His holy habitation.

PSALM 68:5 NKJV

Many people are nursing the wounds of rejection. In many cases, those wounds were inflicted by their own parents, whether in early childhood, during their growing-up years, or into adulthood. Some people wait years and years to hear their mother or father tell them they're proud of them. A lack of affirming words, paired with mostly critical comments, can plant seeds of rejection that may result in an eventual harvest of low self-esteem and poor coping mechanisms, not to mention broken relationships.

Broken relationships happen because people are broken. There's no getting around it. Broken people are bound to break ties and breach confidence. You can't live out something you've never received, so if one or both of your parents never had a strong example of loving, caring parents, chances are that they don't know how to be loving, caring parents themselves. They don't know how to break the cycle and start fresh with you.

But our heavenly Father never condemns or rejects his children. He loves us—his adopted daughters—so much that he sent his Son, Jesus, to die for our sins so that we could be confident of spending a blessed eternity with him. Praise God for being the perfect parent!

VERSES TO DEEPEN YOUR JOY

PSALM 27:10; JOHN 3:16–18

Go share the joy today!

A Father Who Never Forsakes

"The Lord your God goes with you;
he will never leave you nor forsake you."
Deuteronomy 31:6

The sooner we understand the Lord's heart for the poor, fatherless, and widows and the sooner we realize that he loves us with a constancy that no earthly father could ever exhibit, the better. You may not have known it until recently, but all your life, you've had a Father who loves you and desires to draw you to himself. He loves you with an everlasting love, and he longs for you to draw close to him. You can talk to him anytime in prayer. He longs for you to pour out your heart to him and receive his peace and wisdom in return.

Your heavenly Father will never leave you nor forsake you. He won't condemn you or rub your mistakes in your face. And once you know what his Word says about his faithfulness and loving acceptance, you can experience freedom from the bondage and brokenness that human relationships—or the lack thereof—may have brought into your life. You can find a love that never fails and an acceptance with no strings attached.

Won't you turn to the Father today and receive his love? Rest in the confidence that he is with you always and that his loving-kindness will never depart from you. He is the Father who never forsakes, and he can be trusted.

VERSES TO DEEPEN YOUR JOY

Jeremiah 31:3; Hebrews 13:5

Go share the joy today!

Perseverance in Weathering Rejection

"You will know the truth,
and the truth will set you free."
JOHN 8:32 NASB

The longer a stronghold has been present in our lives, the longer it usually takes to uproot it. I say *usually* because there have been certain instances when I've seen God deliver someone instantaneously. For me, however, overcoming the spirit of rejection was a gradual process, and I think this is most often the case.

As I grew in the knowledge of God's Word and developed a better understanding of who I am in Christ, I became increasingly free. The Lord allowed me to go through experiences that I now call Holy Spirit setups. These were encounters with rejection that took me to a new level of being rejection proof because I chose to trust in God rather than falling for the devil's deceptions. If someone rejected me and spoke negatively about me, I would stand on God's Word, speaking forth what God has said about me, which contradicted whatever my offender had said.

The Word of God always trumps the lies of Satan. Our heavenly Father has the final say no matter what! When we cling to what Scripture declares and internalize it in our hearts and minds, we can deflect the devil's deceptions and stand firm in our knowledge of who we are. Spend time in the Word, and you'll discover a sense of identity that can't be shaken.

VERSES TO DEEPEN YOUR JOY

1 CORINTHIANS 15:58; EPHESIANS 4:26

Go share the joy today!

Imperfect Fellowship

The God of all grace, who called you to his eternal glory in Christ, after you have suffered a little while, will himself restore you and make you strong, firm and steadfast.

1 Peter 5:10

Is it always easy to contradict the devil's lies with the Word of Truth? Is it a natural inclination of ours to rest in God's Word and reject what others may say? Definitely not. But for me, holding firm to God's truth has been key to my healing and gaining strength of identity, and it can be for you too. The thing is that I have probably suffered rejection from and been hurt by Christians more than from worldly unbelievers.

With God's help, we can overcome every hurt and pain that we experience in relationships. When we release offenses and focus on God's great love for us, we can become rejection proof. Although other people may reject us for various reasons throughout our lives, God never rejects us. He tells us, "I have chosen you and have not rejected you" (Isaiah 41:9). Remember, Jesus was perfect, and others still rejected him. It was that rejection that helped him to fulfill God's plan for his life.

God can and will use our trials and troubles for our ultimate good if we'll just trust him. He can even use rejection from others to fulfill his wonderful purpose for our lives. Isn't that a comfort?

VERSES TO DEEPEN YOUR JOY

Psalm 55:22; 1 Peter 5:8–9

Go share the joy today!

Blessings in Disguise

We know that in all things God works for the good of those who love him, who have been called according to his purpose.

ROMANS 8:28

It amazes me and brings remarkable comfort that God works all things together for our ultimate good. No matter how bad things may look or how hurt we may feel, there's nothing he can't turn into a tool for blessing and promoting us.

You might be in the middle of a major conflict or a financial struggle that has you thinking, *How could God possibly work anything good out of this mess?* Remember that he sees the big picture. He knows how the story ends. Our eyes see just the here and now, but his perspective is eternal, and nothing lies beyond the scope of his power.

Open your eyes and your heart to him. Allow him to work compassion in your heart for others who are experiencing the same or similar difficulties. Start reaching out to others and let God use you to bless them during their struggles. When we get our eyes off ourselves and start taking stock of the needs of those around us, our trials turn into an immediate blessing.

Don't make it your priority to skirt conflict and avoid difficulty. Face your challenges—maybe even embrace them—knowing God is by your side. Grow through them with a joyful spirit, and you will develop a heart of compassion that can't be broken by petty offenses or even deep emotional wounds.

VERSES TO DEEPEN YOUR JOY

LUKE 1:37; 2 CORINTHIANS 1:3–4

Go share the joy today!

Run with the Proper Perspective

Hope that is seen is not hope; for who hopes for what he already sees? But if we hope for what we do not see, through perseverance we wait eagerly for it.

ROMANS 8:24–25 NASB

Over the past few weeks, we've established the importance of ridding ourselves of offenses and unforgiveness and overcoming rejection so that we can persevere and run with joy the race that is this earthly life. Once again, while God desires for us to discover contentment, he never promised a journey free of trials and troubles. He does, however, guarantee us unlimited access to his abundant supply of wisdom and divine strength as we run the race marked out for us.

Heavenly wisdom is a key to unconditional joy because it gives us a proper perspective on everything that we face. God's wisdom is more valuable than any material possessions we could ever own. That's why the writer of Proverbs said, "How much better it is to get wisdom than gold! And to get understanding is to be chosen above silver" (16:16 NASB).

Wisdom teaches us to have patience in affliction because we know that by persevering through our problems, God is making us into the people he planned for us to be—powerful, principled, joy-filled kingdom builders. Running with the proper perspective means viewing obstacles as potential opportunities and staying open to whatever God might be trying to do through our trials.

VERSES TO DEEPEN YOUR JOY

GENESIS 39:2–6; ROMANS 8:5–11

Go share the joy today!

Faith from Prison to Palace

While Joseph was there in the prison, the LORD was with him; he showed him kindness and granted him favor.

GENESIS 39:20–21

During his years of imprisonment in the dungeon of Pharaoh's palace, Joseph easily could have given up hope. He could have gotten stuck in sadness and self-pity, assuming that his fate was sealed and there was no hope of leaving prison. After all, he had correctly interpreted the dreams of two of his fellow prisoners, yet the one who was promoted forgot about his promise to help exonerate Joseph. Joseph could have thrown in the towel, especially since he had been wrongly imprisoned in the first place due to the deception of Potiphar's wife. He could have thought, *Woe is me. Life's so unfair. God must have forgotten me. I guess I'm in this prison for good.* Yet Joseph knew that God was in charge, working all things together for his good. And God will do the same for us if we keep our hearts right.

Maybe God is working on your behalf, but you can't see it right now. Even if the Enemy is trying to steal, kill, and destroy in your life, God promises that he will work all things together for your good. And having wisdom will help you cling to the hope of that promise.

VERSES TO DEEPEN YOUR JOY

PSALM 100:5; ROMANS 8:35–39

Go share the joy today!

See the Big Picture

Consider it nothing but joy, my brothers and sisters, whenever you fall into various trials. Be assured that the testing of your faith [through experience] produces endurance [leading to spiritual maturity, and inner peace].

JAMES 1:2–3 AMP

Have you ever encountered a trial or tough situation that had you thinking, *How exciting! God must really be developing endurance within me*? Probably not. But that's the perspective we can have when we're filled with divine wisdom.

> Let endurance have its perfect result and do a thorough work, so that you may be perfect and completely developed [in your faith], lacking in nothing.
>
> If any of you lacks wisdom [to guide him through a decision or circumstance], he is to ask of [our benevolent] God, who gives to everyone generously and without rebuke or blame, and it will be given to him. (vv. 4–5 AMP)

According to James, wisdom is essential for spiritual maturity and completeness. The good news is that we can choose to live with joy even before perseverance has completed its work in our lives. This is because we know that whenever we go through trials, God will use them to grow us and develop our maturity if we'll turn to him and ask for his help.

We don't rejoice because of our sufferings, but we rejoice during them because we know what's really going on behind the scenes: God is working in us and through us to fulfill his purposes for us.

VERSES TO DEEPEN YOUR JOY

ISAIAH 55:9; PHILIPPIANS 1:6

Go share the joy today!

Purpose behind the Pain

"You meant evil against me, but God meant it for good in order to bring about this present result, to keep many people alive."

GENESIS 50:20 NASB

Keeping the proper perspective can carry us with joy over every obstacle. It helps us view roadblocks and other obstructions as opportunities for spiritual growth and for glorifying God. It helps us remember the big picture even if we can't see it.

Joseph is a great example of someone who saw the big picture and ultimately understood the greater purpose behind all the suffering he'd endured. When his brothers came to Egypt—where years before they'd sent him to be enslaved—to grovel for food during a predicted famine, Joseph revealed his identity to them. A major shocker! Even more shocking was Joseph's lack of bitterness and resentment over how his brothers had treated him all those years ago.

The brothers fully expected him to lash out in anger and to take revenge on them for what they had done. Instead, we have a beautiful picture of forgiveness from someone who perceived what God had been doing behind the scenes (Genesis 50:16–21).

Remarkable, isn't it? Joseph had the favor of God even when it didn't look that way in the natural realm, and he had the wisdom to see how favor had guided and graced his life all along.

VERSES TO DEEPEN YOUR JOY

ROMANS 8:18; 2 CORINTHIANS 4:17–18

Go share the joy today!

What Is Good?

Many are the plans in a person's heart,
but it is the LORD's purpose that prevails.
PROVERBS 19:21

It may be hard to believe in the middle of a desperate situation, but God truly can turn anything around for our ultimate good, as the Bible says in Romans 8:28. We must remind ourselves of this truth every day so that we build our faith for the tough times. But who determines what is good? Is it our decision? Or is it God's?

We have our answer in the Bible:

- "In their hearts humans plan their course, but the LORD establishes their steps" (Proverbs 16:9).
- "What I have said, that I will bring about; what I have planned, that I will do" (Isaiah 46:11).

We may think we know the best course for our lives. We may believe we know the difference between a good and a bad situation. We may despair when things seem to go wrong. Yet "there is a way which seems right to a person, but its end is the way of death" (Proverbs 14:12 NASB). Our human perspective is limited. God alone sees the big picture, the beginning to the end. And we can trust him to work out all the details for our good.

Whatever you're facing, God's got this! Nothing is beyond the scope of his sovereignty, and we can trust him in all things. In fact, that's what we must do if we are going to run with the right perspective.

VERSES TO DEEPEN YOUR JOY

PROVERBS 3:5–6; ISAIAH 55:8–13

Go share the joy today!

Obstacle? No, Opportunity!

Let me know Your ways, O LORD; teach me Your paths.
Guide me in Your truth and teach me, for You are the God of my salvation;
for You [and only You] I wait [expectantly] all the day long.

PSALM 25:4–5 AMP

Cultivating godly wisdom that gives us the proper perspective allows us to experience joy that doesn't depend on our circumstances. Whether the skies are cloudy or clear or whether the terrain we travel is rocky or smooth, we can experience joy when our hope is in God and when we keep the big picture in mind. We don't have to be puppets pulled along by the strings of situations and scenarios. When our hope is in the Lord, we believe he will use whatever happens to us for our ultimate good.

A person whose mind is governed by the flesh looks at hurdles ahead and turns immediately to thoughts of despair and defeat. But a person whose mind is governed by godly wisdom sees roadblocks and believes, *Here's a chance for God to show up on my behalf! Here's a challenge that will give me a chance to grow my faith and move to a higher level of spiritual maturity.*

For those who are guided by godly wisdom—for those who see everything from God's perspective—"wisdom is like honey…: if you find it, there is a future hope for you, and your hope will not be cut off" (Proverbs 24:14).

VERSES TO DEEPEN YOUR JOY

ISAIAH 40:31; 1 CORINTHIANS 1:20–30

Go share the joy today!

Upward and Onward

[God] said to me, "My grace is sufficient for you, for my power is made perfect in weakness." Therefore I will boast all the more gladly about my weaknesses, so that Christ's power may rest on me.

2 Corinthians 12:9

When we persevere with a godly perspective through our trials, we deepen our spiritual maturity. God takes us deeper into the things of him as we surrender our agenda and submit to his perfect plan. Remember, we already know the ultimate outcome. God is the victor! And he's right by our side, giving us full access to his wisdom and strength. It's like taking an open-book exam armed with the text and the teacher's answer key.

All we must do is ask, and God will grant us his wisdom. Let's pray to view every obstacle from his perspective, staying open to the opportunities he may have in store for us as we persevere. When the wisdom of God guides our perspective, we can view everything through the lens of his purposes and find hope in the confidence that he is in charge. We don't have to know what comes next. We can trust that God is with us and will guide us in his ways.

VERSES TO DEEPEN YOUR JOY

Romans 1:17; 1 Peter 1:3–5

Go share the joy today!

Zooming Out

Oh, the depth of the riches of the wisdom and knowledge of God! How unsearchable his judgments, and his paths beyond tracing out!

Romans 11:33

As we trust God, it's always good to ask for his help and to keep a prayerful ear open to his still, small voice. We never know just how he will guide us—whether by a word of knowledge, a vision in a dream, or a verse that the Holy Spirit brings to our minds. However he communicates with us, I find that it's often akin to zooming out from a photo to get an eagle-eye view of my situation.

Imagine you're standing in the lobby on the ground floor of a fancy hotel that you're staying at in the city. You might look out the window and see cars speeding by and tumbleweed-like trash blowing in the streets. But if you take the elevator and look out from the penthouse suite on the top floor, everything will appear totally different. You'll see the stunning city skyline. You'll revel in the glorious sunset.

Prayer gives us this type of panorama. Instead of seeing everything in the natural and interpreting life's events through a human perspective, we can filter our experiences through a heavenly perspective and maintain hope no matter the view. Regardless of how things may look, we can trust that God sees the big picture. He has seen it from the beginning, and he already sees the end. And from our prayer perspective, we will see more with his wisdom than we otherwise would. Let's make sure we run with the right perspective—a heavenly point of view.

VERSES TO DEEPEN YOUR JOY

Psalm 147:5; Colossians 2:2–3

Go share the joy today!

Faith When the Future Is Uncertain

"Declaring the end from the beginning, and from ancient times things which have not been done, saying, 'My plan will be established, and I will accomplish all My good pleasure.'"

ISAIAH 46:10 NASB

When we turn to God, he definitely grants us insights that we otherwise wouldn't have. But he doesn't always spell everything out from the get-go. Especially in situations when he reveals each next step as we move forward in faith, we need to place our trust in him and believe that his wisdom and ways will work for what is ultimately the best outcome for us.

This is how Esther had to operate when she became King Xerxes' new queen (Esther 2:15–18). When her husband approved an order to annihilate the Jews—which included Esther, though she had not disclosed her ethnicity—her cousin Mordecai begged Esther to do what she could to intervene on behalf of her people (4:13–14).

Esther's cousin had faith in the future deliverance of his people; he just wasn't sure whether he and his cousin would be spared. Esther shared his ambivalence but bravely decided, "I will go to the king, even though it is against the law. And if I perish, I perish" (v. 16). Trusting God to guide her, Esther laid out her request to the king in a way that reflected heavenly wisdom.

VERSES TO DEEPEN YOUR JOY

ESTHER 8:3–17; 2 CORINTHIANS 5:7

Go share the joy today!

Trust in God's Timing

"Still the vision awaits its appointed time;
it hastens to the end—it will not lie.
If it seems slow, wait for it;
it will surely come; it will not delay."

HABAKKUK 2:3 ESV

Thanks to Esther, a brave, young woman who trusted God no matter the outcome, the fate of an entire people was reversed. Thanks to the actions of someone who followed heavenly wisdom without knowing what would happen, the story of the Jewish people went from overwhelming despair to all-out exaltation. That's what happens when we determine to trust God and his good intentions for us.

I love the story of Esther. One day, she had an ordinary life; the next day, she found herself a resident of the palace, married to the king. When God's will and timing intersect, we are suddenly thrust into our purpose and place in his kingdom. The key is waiting for his appointed time, as Esther did.

If Esther hadn't arrived at the palace at the very time the Lord had ordained, she would have missed her appointment with destiny. Before the king decided to start interviewing for a new future queen, Esther had no place at the palace. The position wasn't even open. And if Esther had dragged her feet instead of answering her summons, she would have been too late. Somebody else would have gotten the position.

VERSES TO DEEPEN YOUR JOY

ECCLESIASTES 3:1–8; ROMANS 5:6

Go share the joy today!

The Speed of Suddenly

With the Lord one day is like a thousand years,
and a thousand years like one day.

2 PETER 3:8 NASB

Most of us would love to have our futures neatly mapped out on the calendar—a record of the dates and times of important events so that we can plan accordingly. But the only one with an eagle-eye agenda is God, and he moves at the speed of suddenly. Like we discussed yesterday, when God's timing and will intersect, his promises are suddenly fulfilled. You may have to wait thirty years for your "suddenly," but God's timing is perfect. He is always right on time. He proves this truth not only in the example of Esther but also in such biblical figures as Abraham and Sarah, Joseph, and Ruth, just to name a few.

Jesus himself was born at just the right time: "When the set time had *fully come*, God sent his Son, born of a woman, born under the law, to redeem those under the law, that we might receive adoption to sonship" (Galatians 4:4–5). Throughout his ministry and even to his death, everything happened according to a divinely orchestrated timetable. And we can trust God to orchestrate the events of our lives according to his perfect timing too.

Don't grow impatient but trust the one who sees the beginning from the end. He will be faithful to fulfill his promises—and it will happen *suddenly*, when you least expect it.

VERSES TO DEEPEN YOUR JOY

GENESIS 18:14; LAMENTATIONS 3:25–26

Go share the joy today!

Wait Patiently

Is anything too hard or too wonderful for the Lord? At the appointed time, when the season [for her delivery] comes around, I will return to you and Sarah shall have borne a son.

GENESIS 18:14 AMPC

We need to wait on God's timing, for he has an appointed time for each of his promises to manifest in its season. Seasons come and go automatically. We can't prevent a season from coming when God says it's time. Just as we can't force winter to end prematurely so that spring can begin, we can't rush the passage of seasons in God's kingdom. We can only embrace every transition and trust that God is in control of the schedule.

God fulfilled his promise of an heir to Abram and Sarai (later called Abraham and Sarah) at his perfectly appointed time, but it wasn't without a few hiccups on the part of the parents-to-be, who grew impatient and took matters into their own hands (Genesis 15–18, 21).

Waiting on God is far wiser than rushing him. If we fail to wait patiently for the proper season, we become stressed out and discouraged, all to no avail. We end up wasting time and expending unnecessary energy. We cannot do anything to prevent a promised season from starting, nor can we speed up its arrival. The schedule is entirely in God's hands. All we must do is stay attuned to the passage of God's seasons so we don't miss our time when it *suddenly* comes.

VERSES TO DEEPEN YOUR JOY

PROVERBS 27:1; 2 PETER 3:8–9

Go share the joy today!

Don't Rush the Ripening

There is an appointed time for everything.
And there is a time for every matter under heaven—
...a time to plant and a time to uproot what is planted.

ECCLESIASTES 3:1–2 NASB

Strawberries are one of my favorite fruits. Like most fruit, they taste best when they're in season. Where I live in Virginia, we have a strawberry festival every May in the middle of prime strawberry season. You can taste and buy just about anything made from strawberries at the festival, and it's all delicious.

If the festival were to be held in April, before the berries reached their peak ripeness, it would be a disaster. The fruit would be underripe, without the deep red color, luscious juice, and sweet flavor that make ripe strawberries irresistible to me. Strawberries aren't ready for picking or eating in February, but if I wait until they ripen on the vine and reach their height of flavor, I won't be disappointed.

Just as strawberries reach their peak ripeness in May (at least in Virginia), you will bear the highest-quality and most bountiful fruit for God's kingdom in the middle of the season God sets for your "ripeness." Stop trying to rush God. Stop straining toward the next season if God hasn't said it's time. Your fruit isn't ready yet. But when it reaches the proper ripeness, suddenly, you will be thrust into your proper position. For now, practice patience as you await the harvest.

VERSES TO DEEPEN YOUR JOY

PSALM 104:27–28; GALATIANS 6:9

Go share the joy today!

Don't Grow Weary in Waiting

Let us not become weary…
for at the proper time we will reap a harvest if we do not give up.
GALATIANS 6:9

I was nine months pregnant and about to give birth to my first baby—an event I had long awaited. And just when it was almost time to head to the hospital, my husband announced that he was leaving me. Still reeling from the blow of his decision, I gave birth to a beautiful, healthy baby I named Destiny Joy, and then I got busy praying, fasting, and standing in faith, expecting God to restore my marriage.

Despite all my pleas and prayers, our divorce was soon finalized. No reconciliation occurred. While I was still struggling to adapt to the challenges of single parenting, God said to me, *You will be married again. It will take longer than you thought it would, but it will be worth the wait!*

Two decades later, I was still waiting for the "longer than you thought it would take" blessing. I decided to remind the Lord about it, asking him again and again for a prophetic word concerning the situation. Oh, he gave me a word. Everywhere I went for the next seven days, he gave me a word, and it was the same one every time: *Wait!* I finally asked him, *Don't you have any other word for me?* He responded with silence.

I got the point. I needed to continue waiting until the appointed time that God had established for me from the beginning. Don't grow weary in the waiting today! God's best is always worth waiting for. And his best always comes "at the proper time."

VERSES TO DEEPEN YOUR JOY

PSALM 27:14; PSALM 40:1

Go share the joy today!

March

Why Wait?

Be still before the Lord;
wait patiently for Him.
Psalm 37:7 AMP

Why is waiting required of us? There are several reasons I can think of right now and probably dozens more we will never know on this side of heaven.

For one thing, I believe God requires us to wait so that the promise or blessing will not mean more to us than the One fulfilling that promise or granting that blessing. While we wait, we learn to value God and content ourselves with him rather than obsessing over the thing we're waiting for. While we wait, God will show us that he is always more than enough for all our needs.

Another thing that happens while we wait is that God builds our trust and strengthens our faith in him. God promises, "Those who hopefully wait for Me will not be put to shame" (Isaiah 49:23 NASB).

Finally, waiting gives us a chance to acknowledge and appreciate the blessings God has already granted and the promises he has already fulfilled. Focusing on these things nurtures our gratitude in a way that increases our joy and lifts our spirits. We can encourage ourselves—and others—by recalling and sharing the great works of God on our behalf. If he has done them before, he will do them again! Like the psalmist, we can say, "I have not concealed Your righteousness within my heart; I have proclaimed Your faithfulness and Your salvation. I have not concealed Your lovingkindness and Your truth from the great assembly" (Psalm 40:10 AMP).

VERSES TO DEEPEN YOUR JOY

Isaiah 55:9; Philippians 4:19

Go share the joy today!

Waiting with Hope

We wait in hope for the Lord;
he is our help and our shield.

Psalm 33:20

Waiting does not have to be a tedious, soul-draining process. When we trust in the Lord, we can wait in joyful expectation. Expecting and anticipating are vital steps to seeing God's promises fulfilled. Consider this hopeful statement of anticipation from the psalmist: "I remain confident of this: I will see the goodness of the Lord in the land of the living" (27:13). What an expression of confidence! Let your faith build as you wait for the Lord. Be assured that you will see God's promises to you fulfilled—every one of them!

The psalmist also said, "I wait for the Lord, my soul waits, and in His word I do hope" (130:5 NKJV). We hope in God's Word. When our soul is waiting on God, our mind, will, and emotions agree to patiently await God's perfect will and perfect timing. But waiting in our soul realm is probably the hardest. We may wait a week or two, or a month, before we get tired of waiting and decide that it's time to help God out—just like Abram and Sarai tried to do when Abram had a son with Hagar instead of waiting on God's promise (Genesis 16). The best thing to do while waiting is to practice what I like to call soul control, which means not being led by what we think, what we want, and what we feel.

VERSES TO DEEPEN YOUR JOY

Isaiah 26:8; Hebrews 6:18–19

Go share the joy today!

Keep Hope Alive

Everything that was written in the past was written to teach us, so that through the endurance taught in the Scriptures and the encouragement they provide we might have hope.

ROMANS 15:4

We are to put our hope in God's Word, especially while we wait on the Lord. And what better source of encouragement than the scriptural record of the saints of old who proved God's faithfulness time and again? That's what the apostle Paul was talking about in Romans 15:4.

When you're dealing with the sting of betrayal by a loved one, look no further than the story of Joseph. If you grow weary while waiting for the fulfillment of God's promise to you, the story of Abraham and Sarah offers ample encouragement. When your own personal Goliath is staring you down and you're quaking in your shoes, just consider the story of David and take courage. And if you feel as if you've sinned beyond remediation, look to the example of Zacchaeus, the thieving tax collector whose house Jesus deliberately graced with his presence to prove that none of us are beyond the scope of God's grace.

The Bible is full of examples of those who kept hope alive, even during seemingly impossible circumstances, and then rejoiced when God fulfilled his promises to them. As we wait to see him fulfill his promises to us, we can keep hope alive by clinging to these examples and standing on them in faith.

VERSES TO DEEPEN YOUR JOY

PROVERBS 13:12; JOHN 8:34–38

Go share the joy today!

Don't Lose Hope

Let us hold unswervingly to the hope we profess,
for he who promised is faithful.
HEBREWS 10:23

We can't afford to lose hope. The Enemy is out to steal our hope and cancel our encouragement in any way he can. He knows that if he can get us to lose hope, our faith will erode, and we will easily be drawn away from our God-given assignments. But if we hold fast to the truth—the Word of God—we can be free from Satan's strongholds. We can cling to the rope of hope that is the Bible and find strength to resist the devil and his schemes.

Jesus said, "If you hold to my teaching, you are really my disciples. Then you will know the truth, and the truth will set you free" (John 8:31–32). We can be free from fear, free from discouragement, free from frustration, and free from false thinking. The Enemy most often seeks to set up his strongholds in our minds, and the seed of each stronghold is usually a lie.

Don't let those devilish seeds germinate and bear fruit. Don't buy the lie but keep hope alive. Hope causes us to think, ask, and expect big things from our great big God. And he is an endless source of hope for each and every challenge we face.

VERSES TO DEEPEN YOUR JOY

JOB 11:17–19; PSALM 9:18

Go share the joy today!

The God of Hope

May the God of hope fill you with all joy and peace as you trust in him, so that you may overflow with hope by the power of the Holy Spirit.

ROMANS 15:13

As long as our hope is in the Lord, whether we are waiting, suffering, or celebrating, we will never be disappointed. As long as the "God of hope" is our God and our hope is in him, we can be filled with joy and peace no matter what comes our way.

If we are suffering while we wait, we can take courage, for God will use even our trials to fine-tune our character if we let him. Consider these inspiring words from the apostle Paul: "We also glory in our sufferings, because we know that *suffering* produces perseverance; perseverance, character; and character, hope. And hope does not put us to shame, because God's love has been poured out into our hearts through the Holy Spirit, who has been given to us" (Romans 5:3–5). We don't rejoice because of our sufferings, but we can rejoice in the midst of our sufferings.

Paul was not advocating a morbid view that celebrates evil and embraces pain. He was saying that we can and should live joyous, victorious lives even during challenges. Won't you trust God to enable you to do just that?

VERSES TO DEEPEN YOUR JOY

ROMANS 8:17; 1 PETER 4:13

Go share the joy today!

The Author of Only Good

Every good and perfect gift is from above, coming down from the Father of the heavenly lights, who does not change like shifting shadows.

JAMES 1:17

Many people lose hope when they mistakenly attribute their sufferings to the wrong source or base them on an ill-founded reason. They think that God must be punishing them for some sin or trying to teach them a lesson. But God is never the author of anything that isn't good. As the Bible says in James 1:17, God gives us "every good and perfect gift…[and] does not change like shifting shadows."

God does not put sickness on his children. He does not send suffering on purpose to punish us. He won't get fed up and frustrated with us to the point of planning hardships and trials for us to endure. But he can and does produce good outcomes from bad circumstances. Though he may allow us to experience suffering and pain, those problems are not the endgame. His purposes will prevail no matter what.

When he lets us go through challenging times, we can trust him to work all things together for our good, for he blesses us with all that is good. Matthew 7:11 says, "If you, despite being evil, know how to give good gifts to your children, how much more will your Father who is in heaven give good things to those who ask Him!" (NASB). We can trust that any growth we experience in faith, character, hope, and trust will prepare us for upcoming seasons of life and qualify us for greater responsibilities in God's kingdom.

VERSES TO DEEPEN YOUR JOY

MATTHEW 19:17; JAMES 1:12–14

Go share the joy today!

Bold Declarations Build Hope

"The mouth speaks from that which fills the heart."
MATTHEW 12:34 NASB

While you're waiting for the fulfillment of God's promises to you, one key to building your hope is to declare God's Word over your situation. Even if defeat seems inevitable, remember that God "gives life to the dead and calls into being things that do not exist" (Romans 4:17 NASB). There is such power in faith-filled declarations. As you speak God's Word over yourself and your situation, you are giving life to seemingly dead things. You are commanding your circumstances to align with God's unstoppable plans and purposes. You're affirming what he has decreed.

Of course, to declare God's Word, you need to be familiar with what the Word says. Maybe you weren't raised in the church. Maybe you didn't grow up reading the Bible. Now is a great time to start. I recommend you begin by reading a chapter or so a day. You might even follow a Scripture-reading guide or a study that highlights verses pertaining to a specific topic. Whatever your approach to studying Scripture may be, you will quickly discover that "the Word of God is living and active, and sharper than any two-edged sword, even penetrating as far as the division of soul and spirit, of both joints and marrow, and able to judge the thoughts and intentions of the heart" (Hebrews 4:12 NASB).

VERSES TO DEEPEN YOUR JOY

PSALM 40:10; ROMANS 10:9–10

Go share the joy today!

Powerful Professions

The tongue has the power of life and death.

PROVERBS 18:21

Whatever is in your heart will eventually come out of your mouth. What you're expecting is what you will declare. That's why it is so important to keep your heart full of faith. Your expectation becomes your declaration, and your declaration becomes your reality.

In a sense, you can prophesy your own future. Make sure you speak words of bold faith and transcendent peace, for your tongue has a lot of power—the power of life and death. Don't allow your mouth to spew forth negative announcements of despair and death. Keep complaining and self-criticism far from your speech. Avoid repeating negativity and naysaying, or negative outcomes and naysaying people will plague your existence.

Speak positive, faith-filled declarations while you wait for God's promises to manifest. Don't drag yourself down in doubt with expressions of despair and frustration. God fashioned the world using words, and we fashion our world with our words. Truly, what we profess has power. Be sure that you're using your words carefully, in a way that's calculated to bring life rather than death. Voice only that which edifies and uplifts, never that which demeans and drags down.

I challenge you to guard your mouth today and avoid giving voice to any criticism or complaining. At the end of the day, reflect on what has happened and the way that you feel. I'll bet you'll notice a big difference.

VERSES TO DEEPEN YOUR JOY

PROVERBS 15:4; EPHESIANS 4:29

Go share the joy today!

Words as Worship

"To obey is better than sacrifice,
and to heed is better than the fat of rams."
1 SAMUEL 15:22

The practice of speaking God's Word runs contrary to how most of the world talks. You've probably noticed that people in the world generally speak their mind without foresight, seeming not to care what comes out of their mouths and its potential effects, for good or for evil. Loud cursing, substantial criticism, and crude jokes are commonplace. People who speak carelessly prove the point James made when he said, "The tongue also is a fire, a world of evil…It corrupts the whole body" (James 3:6).

Our speech should be positive and edifying. When we obey the Lord with the words that we say, we are actually worshiping him. That's because obedience counts as worship. And God prefers the pure, true worship of obedience to any sacrifices we make to try to compensate for disobedience.

In Isaiah 55, the Lord declared that his Word never returns to him empty but always accomplishes that which he desires. That holds true when his Word is on our lips. Our job is to speak his Word, pray his Word, and proclaim his Word.

God's Word produces fruit. That's why the Enemy delights in distracting us from spending time in the Bible. Neglecting Bible reading keeps us from speaking words of truth and being effective. We need to keep God's Word as our foundation, reading it routinely, speaking it regularly, and praying it over our circumstances. That's the way we use our words as worship that God considers worthy.

VERSES TO DEEPEN YOUR JOY

ISAIAH 55:10–11; JAMES 3:3–12

Go share the joy today!

Rest While You Wait

Wait for and confidently expect the Lord;
be strong and let your heart take courage;
yes, wait for and confidently expect the Lord.

Psalm 27:14 AMP

All of us are waiting for something. It may not be that we're expecting something specific at the moment, but all believers are waiting for the resurrection of our bodies that will come when our earthly journey ends and our heavenly life begins. We can wait patiently when we know what we're hoping for. Keep hopeful expectation alive and rest in God's love for you as you await the fulfillment of his promises to you.

And while we are expecting and declaring the fulfillment of God's promises to us, we must be sure to rest. Resting does not mean doing nothing. On the contrary, resting implies having full faith and trust in the Lord while we are waiting on him as we continue doing all that he has appointed us to do.

Rest often seems to imply lazily lounging around, doing absolutely nothing. But that isn't what it means at all. We can rest in the knowledge that God is handling things once we have done our part. When the Israelites were waiting to inhabit the promised land, Joshua gave them this message from God: "The Lord your God is giving you rest and is giving you this land" (Joshua 1:13 NKJV). We must learn to rest while we wait. The land is already ours; we are simply waiting for the time God has appointed to release it to us.

VERSES TO DEEPEN YOUR JOY

Exodus 14:14; Hebrews 4:9–10

Go share the joy today!

No Naysaying

Sin is not ended by multiplying words,
but the prudent hold their tongues.

PROVERBS 10:19

I wonder how many of God's purposes for us have been temporarily postponed because of our own defeatist attitudes. How often have we thwarted the plans of God for a time by speaking against him and voicing only skepticism? When we fail to speak in faith and instead give voice to our fears and doubts, we often delay the fulfillment of God's blessings and prolong the waiting process. We must resist the temptation to engage in negative talk and naysaying.

This lesson is illustrated by the Israelites' journey to the promised land under Moses' leadership. Poor Moses had to deal with some serious doubters. The scouts he sent out to survey the land returned with a report that although the land was flowing "with milk and honey" (Numbers 13:27), its inhabitants were so big and so strong that the Israelites were "like grasshoppers" (v. 33) in comparison. Instead of talking with bold faith and encouraging the people to follow God's instructions, most of these men "spread among the Israelites a bad report" (v. 32).

Bad reports yield only bad results. But positive affirmations leave room for the power of God. When the Enemy makes you feel as weak as a grasshopper, go to God for a boost of confidence. Don't whine about your inadequacy and end up missing out on the wonderful plans God has for you.

VERSES TO DEEPEN YOUR JOY

PSALM 50:15; JAMES 1:6

Go share the joy today!

Silence Declarations of Defeat

Do not be overcome by evil,
but overcome evil with good.
ROMANS 12:21

Of the scouts whom Moses sent to scope out the promised land, only Caleb and Joshua refused to give in to defeatist thinking. Caleb exhorted the Israelites, "We should go up and take possession of the land, for we can *certainly* do it" (Numbers 13:30).

And Joshua said, "The land we passed through and explored is exceedingly good. If the LORD is pleased with us, he will lead us into that land, a land flowing with milk and honey, and will give it to us. Only do not…be afraid of the people of the land, because we will devour them. Their protection is gone, but *the Lord is with us*. Do not be afraid of them" (14:7–9).

That's the kind of pep talk that pleases God. Joshua voiced his confidence that however things looked, God was strong enough to protect the Israelites as they took possession of the land. Caleb and Joshua maintained their hope because it was built on the strength of their God, not on their own apparent strength in the face of their formidable-looking opponents.

We can overcome the evil of defeatism and despair when we proclaim the powerful Word of God and our confidence in the one who backs it up.

VERSES TO DEEPEN YOUR JOY

PSALM 34:19; 2 CORINTHIANS 4:8–10

Go share the joy today!

Winning, Not Whining

Do not let unwholesome [foul, profane, worthless, vulgar] words ever come out of your mouth, but only such speech as is good for building up others, according to the need and the occasion, so that it will be a blessing to those who hear [you speak].

EPHESIANS 4:29 AMP

During my first several years as a single mom, I faced the temptation to whine and complain like never before. From the hormonal changes that follow childbirth to the sleepless nights, dirty diapers, and everything else in between, I felt that nobody else had it as hard as I did. I truly felt like the only single parent in the world with the most demanding job description ever—even though my daughter really wasn't that difficult as far as babies go.

But as I turned to the Lord in my misery, he started showing me the differences between whiners and winners. He opened my eyes to a winning strategy that did not include whining. I had to choose daily to silence the whiner within and to let the Holy Spirit raise up the winner within me. There is a little whiner in all of us, and we win only when we focus on keeping that whiner as quiet as possible.

Pay attention to the words you speak and the conversations you have. Do you tend to whine, perhaps more than you thought you did? Are statements of self-pity common in the phrases you speak? Notice whether you have been talking like a whiner or a winner. In the coming days, we'll discover more about what traits distinguish these two personalities.

VERSES TO DEEPEN YOUR JOY

PROVERBS 16:24; ISAIAH 30:18

Go share the joy today!

Winning Thoughts and Words

I will say of the LORD,
"He is my refuge and my fortress, my God,
in whom I trust."

PSALM 91:2

A major difference between whiners and winners is that whiners tend to talk about whatever they're going through. They dwell on their present misery, wallowing in moans and groans, hardly quieting themselves long enough to listen to anyone who might speak words of hope and reason into their situation.

On the other hand, winners don't live in denial of their circumstances or gloss over their problems but talk mostly about where they are headed. They focus on the finish line. Turning their troubles to God, they trust him to be with them in their struggles and to guide them past their pain. They trust in God's perfect timing and live out their belief that he is sovereign over every part of their lives.

Whiners won't look past their immediate problems; they feel mired in defeat and doubt. But winners proclaim the powerful Word of God, which buoys their faith and keeps hope alive until its fulfillment.

Have you been living like a whiner or a winner? It's never too late to change your tune and proclaim the positive while silencing the negative. What you choose to declare makes a big difference in your outlook. Discover the joy that comes from focusing on the finish line.

VERSES TO DEEPEN YOUR JOY

PSALM 96:10; 1 CORINTHIANS 15:57

Go share the joy today!

Escape Your Comfort Zone

"Be strong and courageous, do not be afraid or tremble in dread before them, for it is the Lord your God who goes with you. He will not fail you or abandon you."

Deuteronomy 31:6 AMP

These days, there's a lot of emphasis on stretching ourselves and getting outside our comfort zones. In many cases, escaping our comfort zones can be an avenue to major personal growth. But we can acknowledge that the process is rarely comfortable; that's why we'd rather stay inside our comfort zones. Braving the unknown can be scary. But when God is leading the way, we can be confident that we're going onward and upward to higher places of spiritual maturity.

Whiners tend to do whatever they can to stay inside their comfort zones. They avoid any pressure to try something new or to inconvenience themselves at all costs. Winners, on the other hand, eagerly accept the challenge to push past the boundaries of their comfort zone. That's because they know that only outside their comfort zones can they discover their true potential.

We'll never know how far God can take us until we follow him where we never thought we could go. Trust him to guide you beyond your limits so you can do great things for his kingdom. Don't get stuck inside the cushiness of your comfort zone. Let God lead the way past former boundaries and into new territories for him.

VERSES TO DEEPEN YOUR JOY

Romans 5:3–5; 1 Corinthians 2:9

Go share the joy today!

Christ's Example

For the joy set before him [Jesus] endured the cross, scorning its shame, and sat down at the right hand of the throne of God.

HEBREWS 12:2

Even Jesus had to choose to press past his comfort zone to reach his full potential. In the garden of Gethsemane, just before his arrest and subsequent crucifixion, he prayed in desperation to his Father, "If it is possible, may this cup be taken from me" (Matthew 26:39). Staying in his comfort zone would have meant staying alive—and failing to secure the salvation of humankind. And so he added, "Yet not as I will, but as you will" (v. 39).

Dying on the cross—suffering a death he didn't deserve and even asking why his Father had forsaken him—took Jesus further than anyone else has traveled from their comfort zone. Yet he yielded to his Father's will and escaped his comfort zone because he knew what the outcome of his obedience would be. Because he knew the joy that awaited him once he had fulfilled his mission, Jesus moved outside his comfort zone, endured the agony of death on a cross, and rose again, returning to heaven to sit at his Father's right hand.

Praise God! We, too, can brave whatever lies beyond our comfort zone, knowing God will use it to take us to our full potential. Follow Christ's example and leave your comfort zone behind.

VERSES TO DEEPEN YOUR JOY

LUKE 9:22; HEBREWS 12:1–2

Go share the joy today!

Winners Ask, "Why Not?"

I can do all things through Christ who strengthens me.

PHILIPPIANS 4:13 NKJV

Whiners want to play it safe. They avoid risk at all costs, always asking what-if questions: *What if I fail? What if I'm rejected? What if I make a fool of myself?* Fear paralyzes whiners and keeps them from stepping into what God has for them. They trust in themselves rather than in God, which the Bible cautions against.

Conversely, winners always ask, *Why not?* They are more worried about missed opportunities than potential embarrassment. Their confidence is in God rather than in themselves or other people, and they are rewarded: "Blessed is the one who trusts in the LORD, whose confidence is in him" (Jeremiah 17:7). Winners are the first ones to get out of the boat and walk on water when God summons them. That's what Peter did when Jesus called him from his fishing boat. The rest of the disciples were terrified of this figure on the water's surface until Jesus said, "Take courage! It is I. Don't be afraid" (Matthew 14:27).

Winners recognize the Lord and find refuge in those words. Whiners are unable—or unwilling—to get beyond their fear. Most whiners have a root of fear operating in their lives, and fear is the opposite of faith. Fear listens to the voice of the Enemy while faith listens to the voice of God and obeys.

When a solution seems impossible, let's reassure ourselves that it will manifest in time. Let's be those who ask, *Why not?* Why not trust God? Why not believe all things are possible through him? Never ask, *What if?* but *Why not?*

VERSES TO DEEPEN YOUR JOY

JEREMIAH 17:5; JOHN 20:29

Go share the joy today!

A Winning Outlook on Setbacks

Commit to the LORD whatever you do, and he will establish your plans.

PROVERBS 16:3

How do you react when things don't go as planned? Some people are derailed by setbacks and struggle to get back on course while others view setbacks as learning opportunities that offer insight for moving forward with greater wisdom. I'm sure you can guess which of these outlooks is that of a whiner and which belongs to the winner. Whiners are easily stuck when failures and disappointments upset their agendas. But when winners fall down, they get back up, dust themselves off, and look to the Lord to move forward.

It's never fun when your hopes go unfulfilled. As Proverbs 13:12 aptly points out, "Hope deferred makes the heart sick, but a longing fulfilled is a tree of life." Grieving a major loss or a failed plan is normal. But once we've dealt with our disappointment, we need to dry our eyes and move on, focusing on the second part of that verse—the eventual fulfillment of our longing. And when the Lord determines our deepest desires, we know he will fulfill them.

Whiners allow failures to become their identity (and often their destiny). But winners understand that failure isn't who they are; failure is a chance to learn and reconsider who they may be. Failure can also consist of neglecting to do what God has told you to do. When we obey God in all things, we will succeed. Winners succeed because they seek God's will and fulfill it with obedient hearts.

VERSES TO DEEPEN YOUR JOY

PSALM 37:4; ACTS 22:10

Go share the joy today!

The Reality of Character Refinement

You have been distressed by various trials, so that the proof of your faith… may be found to result in praise, glory, and honor at the revelation of Jesus Christ.

1 PETER 1:6–7 NASB

We've said that having a winning attitude means you view setbacks as chances to learn and grow. But these moments—the steps God uses to refine our character and strengthen our faith—aren't always fun. In fact, they're usually painful. What if I told you that the often-unpleasant testing of our faith is proof of God's love for us?

A popular quote in Christian circles says, "God loves us just the way we are, but he loves us too much to leave us that way." The fact that God cares so much about us that he calls us his daughters and then endeavors to shape us into the image of his Son, Jesus, blows my mind. And this humbling truth gives us a reason to be happy even in our most challenging times.

When I was a new Christian, having walked with the Lord for no more than a year, I remember going through a tough time. One of my friends, a more mature Christian, tried to comfort me by saying, "It's just a test from God." I thought to myself, *A loving God wouldn't test his children!* How little I knew the Lord at that time. The truth is that while God may not send hardships our way, he does allow us to experience times of discomfort and pain that he can use to promote our personal growth. He wants us to turn to him in these times, drawing closer and yielding to the work his Holy Spirit can do for our ultimate good.

VERSES TO DEEPEN YOUR JOY

JOB 1:6–12; JAMES 1:2–3

Go share the joy today!

Welcome the Pruning Process

"I am the true vine, and my Father is the gardener. He cuts off every branch in me that bears no fruit, while every branch that does bear fruit he prunes so that it will be even more fruitful."

John 15:1–2

Do you like gardening? You don't need to be a master gardener to know that pruning is one of the most important practices for maintaining the health of your plants and flowers. Pruning involves removing dead or living parts from a plant to improve its form or promote the production of fruits and flowers. And it's a process that God, our loving Gardener, uses with his children.

Pruning, in the Christian experience, is the lifelong series of steps that our loving Father takes to make us conform more closely to the image of his Son, Jesus. It's rarely pleasant, yet when we change our perspective and welcome his correction as a sign of love and a show of mercy, we can embrace the process and be transformed more quickly by it.

In today's verses from John, we see that we have two options: be pruned so we can bear better fruit or be cut off entirely. I know which one I'll pick. Again, the process may be unpleasant, but it's preferable by far to be pruned and improved rather than being cut off and discarded. It turns out that being pruned is a great honor.

VERSES TO DEEPEN YOUR JOY

Hebrews 12:5; Revelation 3:19

Go share the joy today!

Pruned to Bear Fruit

"I am the vine; you are the branches. If you remain in me and I in you, you will bear much fruit; apart from me you can do nothing."

JOHN 15:5

In today's verse, Jesus was expanding the image of the vine and the gardener to show that we can't fulfill our potential or reach spiritual maturity on our own. Only by leaning on our heavenly Father and staying rooted in him will we bear the fruit he already sees in our next season.

When we abide in the one through whom all things are possible (Matthew 19:26; Mark 10:27), there's no limit to the God-ordained fruit we can produce. But we must be willing to let our divine Gardener lead the way and call the shots. We must trust his pruning process if we want to produce the fruit he has in mind for our lives.

Are you being pruned? Is God removing some unnecessary parts—sinful attitudes, unhelpful habits, bitterness, resentment? If so, rejoice! He is preparing you to bear better, more bountiful fruit in the future. He is investing in the development of your character so that you can reflect his glory and advance his kingdom on earth. Remember, "For the time being no discipline brings joy, but seems sad and painful; yet to those who have been trained by it, afterwards it yields the peaceful fruit of righteousness [right standing with God and a lifestyle and attitude that seeks conformity to God's will and purpose]" (Hebrews 12:11 AMP).

VERSES TO DEEPEN YOUR JOY

PROVERBS 13:24; HEBREWS 12:7–11

Go share the joy today!

The Fruit of Obedience

"This is to my Father's glory, that you bear much fruit, showing yourselves to be my disciples."

JOHN 15:8

Jesus says that bearing fruit proves that we're following him and brings glory to God. No wonder God wants us to bear fruit. The character qualities we develop through the pruning process—such as love, joy, peace, patience, kindness, goodness, faithfulness, gentleness, and self-control (Galatians 5:22–23)—bring God glory and give us the grace we need for future seasons, be they times of ease or periods of pain.

The fruit we bear on God's behalf is also meant to bring him joy. Following his exhortation for the disciples to remain in him, Jesus said, "If you keep my commands, you will remain in my love, just as I have kept my Father's commands and remain in his love. I have told you this so that my joy may be *in you* and that your joy may be complete" (John 15:10–11).

Bearing fruit and abiding in God's love go hand in hand, bringing joy to us and him. Isn't that amazing? When we remain in him, we "bear fruit—fruit that will last" (v. 16), and that's where we find the only love that conquers all. Let's pursue obedience so that we will bear fruit and bring joy to the Lord and to ourselves.

VERSES TO DEEPEN YOUR JOY

JOHN 15:3–4; GALATIANS 5:22–23

Go share the joy today!

Nip Negativity in the Bud

With God nothing is ever impossible and no word from God shall be without power or impossible of fulfillment.

LUKE 1:37 AMPC

Maybe today you're being pruned severely. Perhaps you feel as if you're being stripped of every last bud and blossom. Or maybe you feel the heavenly Gardener has neglected you, as if he doesn't care what becomes of you. Maybe you're thinking, *God could never use me to do anything great*, or *God has surely forgotten me*. Maybe you feel like a nobody. You don't feel worthy of growth and great things. If any of these scenarios is true for you, let me assure you that you're just the type of person God wants to grow, prune, and use.

God loves to demonstrate his power and might by accomplishing major feats through weak, inexperienced, flawed, and unlikely people. And attitudes of unworthiness and feelings of limitation are some of the aspects he delights in pruning away from our hearts so that growth can occur in their place. All plants in God's garden can bear great fruit under his tender care and expert pruning. No shrub is so far gone that he can't nurse it back to health and life. No flower is too wilted for him to restore it to its former beauty. So sit back and let the pruning process prepare you for God's great plans for your life.

VERSES TO DEEPEN YOUR JOY

JEREMIAH 29:11; MARK 10:27

Go share the joy today!

Smallness Doesn't Limit Significance

"The kingdom of heaven is like a mustard seed...
This is smaller than all the other seeds, but when it is fully grown,
it is larger than the garden plants."

MATTHEW 13:31–32 NASB

It's a biblical principle that God does big things with small resources—including small, weak, unqualified people who consider themselves nobodies. In the gospel of Matthew, Jesus compares the kingdom of God to a mustard seed, saying, "This is smaller than all the other seeds, but when it is fully grown, it is larger than the garden plants and becomes a tree, so that the birds of the sky come and nest in its branches" (v. 32 NASB).

Maybe you feel like you're the smallest of the small. Perhaps you assume that you'll never amount to anything in the garden of the Lord. If that's the case, then guess what? You qualify as a top candidate for God to nurture and use mightily. Do you feel like the least likely pick? You're probably the Lord's first choice. Your small faith, entrusted to the all-powerful hand of God with an attitude of hopeful expectation, can move any mountain that may be staring you in the face today.

Never judge your prospects based on size—the size of your faith, the size of your resources, the size of your stature. God can use anyone, no matter how small or insignificant, to carry out his purposes.

VERSES TO DEEPEN YOUR JOY

MATTHEW 17:20–21; 1 CORINTHIANS 1:27

Go share the joy today!

Perfect yet Unpredictable

[God] has made everything beautiful in its time.
He has also set eternity in the human heart;
yet no one can fathom what God has done from beginning to end.

ECCLESIASTES 3:11

God's timing of the seasons of our lives may be completely unpredictable to us, but it is always perfect. I have proven this truth time and again through personal experience. I waited years before God opened the door for me to begin an evangelistic television ministry. When he told me it was time, I struggled to believe it. My husband had walked out on me the year before, leaving me as a single mom to a newborn baby, and every day I had to believe God for even the most basic provisions. You can probably understand why I was skeptical when God told me it was time to launch my ministry.

But God's perfect timing and corresponding plans rarely align with what we expect. He operates in unexpected ways so that he gets the glory when the plan is fulfilled. I call this the great setup: God sets up situations and puts us in them so that we might grow in our faith and learn to trust him more fully. He does things in such a way and at such a time that we couldn't try to take the credit for ourselves even if we wanted to. His ways are higher than our ways, and his timing is perfect, however unpredictable it may be.

VERSES TO DEEPEN YOUR JOY

PSALM 31:15; HABAKKUK 2:3

Go share the joy today!

Illogical Instructions

The foolishness of God is wiser than human wisdom,
and the weakness of God is stronger than human strength.

1 Corinthians 1:25

Plenty of people in the Bible received seemingly illogical instructions from God that, when followed in obedience, brought about a major victory or propelled them to a new level of faith. Other people may have called them crazy and questioned their sanity, but these individuals knew who was giving them orders, and they knew better than to doubt him. For example, God told Naaman to wash himself seven times in the Jordan River to be cured of the leprosy that afflicted him (2 Kings 5:10). He instructed Joshua to lead his soldiers around the city of Jericho seven times, and then the walls crumbled (Joshua 6:2–5). He called a teenage virgin named Mary to give birth to the Savior of the world (Luke 1:26–28).

More often than not, God's instructions will sound illogical to our minds. Even so, we must walk in obedience, trusting him to guide us to the fulfillment of his great plans. The guidance of God doesn't need to make sense. It doesn't have to seem sound or logical. Humans prize such things, but the wisdom of God confounds human wisdom. His strength surpasses ours by incalculable amounts. And we're wise to obey him no matter what.

VERSES TO DEEPEN YOUR JOY

Isaiah 7:14; 1 Corinthians 1:27

Go share the joy today!

One Obedient Step at a Time

The LORD makes firm the steps of the one who delights in him; though he may stumble, he will not fall, for the LORD upholds him with his hand.

PSALM 37:23–24

It was obvious to me and to everyone who knew me that God alone was responsible for opening the door for my TV ministry. I was given prime-time air on a major Christian network that any large ministry would have been thrilled to secure, yet God had given it to me—a single mom living so modest a life that I had to believe God daily for diapers and baby food.

Talk about humble beginnings! As I started filming episodes in my living room, I stood against the backdrop of a royal-blue bedsheet I'd bought at Bed Bath & Beyond and behind a pulpit I had rented. I had to swallow my pride and listen for God's voice as he led me one small step of obedience at a time.

Yet humility is a hallmark of true believers. And humility is a character trait that Jesus embodied perfectly even though he was the Son of God. We don't need to have all the answers. We don't have to receive full instructions leading up to our destination. We just need to humble ourselves and seek the heart of God.

VERSES TO DEEPEN YOUR JOY

2 CHRONICLES 7:13–14; PHILIPPIANS 2:7–9

Go share the joy today!

Obedience Demands Humility

Humble yourselves in the presence of the Lord,
and He will exalt you.

JAMES 4:10 NASB

As I listened to the Lord each day, taking small step after small step in obedience to what he was telling me to do, his call on my life continued to unfold. There was hardly room for pride. God alone was responsible for getting me to where I was and for the salvation of so many souls as people watched my TV show. That's why we should never despise small beginnings but always embrace God's gifts and seek to follow his lead with teachable hearts. We need to cultivate an attitude of humility that acknowledges God's sovereignty and our dependence on him to fulfill our every need.

Of the opposite attitude, the Bible has this to say: "Pride goes before destruction, and a haughty spirit before stumbling" (Proverbs 16:18 NASB). If we run too fast or too far and we get ahead of God's will, we are likely to fall, but when we take small steps of obedience in continual succession, our heavenly Father will hold us up and usher us forward.

We are ready to obey when we've acknowledged just how much we need God. When we've faced up to our own inadequacies and incompetencies, we're ready for the Lord to use us in big ways. Obedience demands humility, and humility makes it possible for us to obey. Are you ready?

VERSES TO DEEPEN YOUR JOY

ZECHARIAH 3:7; 1 PETER 5:6

Go share the joy today!

Flawed yet Fruitful

Not that we are competent in ourselves to claim anything for ourselves, but our competence comes from God.

2 CORINTHIANS 3:5

I certainly did not get into television ministry due to my own expertise. As I've tried to convey throughout this devotional, I hardly knew the first thing about filming, let alone producing a show and putting it on the airwaves. But my heart was humble, and my desire to see souls saved was earnest, and God blessed me.

Please understand what I'm *not* saying. It isn't that God rewarded me for being saintly. I'm a sinner just like everyone else. He can use anyone whose heart is yielded to him and whose sins are covered in the blood of his Son, Jesus. That's right. God can use even the worst of sinners to achieve his ends. His blood has the power to cleanse all sin, not just some sins but all. Turn to him today in confession and repentance, and he will use you mightily no matter what you may have done.

You don't have to be flawless to be fruitful. In fact, none of us can be flawless in our own strength. We're eternally flawed unless the blood of Jesus has covered and cleansed us. And when we're faithful to invoke the blood, God is faithful to direct and bless us—his flawed children made faultless by his Son.

VERSES TO DEEPEN YOUR JOY

LUKE 18:13–14; 1 JOHN 1:7

Go share the joy today!

A Harlot Turned Heroine

Was not even Rahab the prostitute considered righteous for what she did when she gave lodging to the spies and sent them off in a different direction?

JAMES 2:25

Consider Rahab, a prostitute who lived in Jericho. Joshua had sent two spies to scope out the city and surrounding lands, and when the king of Jericho found out about the spies, he started a search for them. Rahab did not betray the spies but put herself in great danger by hiding them in her home, covering for them, and helping them escape the city unharmed.

Yes, God used Rahab, a worldly woman, to accomplish his work. Because of her bravery and obedience, Rahab's name and occupation are recorded in the Faith Hall of Fame in the book of Hebrews: "By faith the prostitute Rahab, because she welcomed the spies, was not killed with those who were disobedient" (11:31). James also commended her in today's verse, and we know that Rahab's long list of descendants includes the Lord Jesus Christ.

Isn't it amazing that God can use us despite, and sometimes even because of, our flaws? Don't let feelings of guilt or inadequacy keep you from fulfilling God's wonderful plans for your life. Don't hold back because you feel too flawed. Yield your heart to him, sins and all. There's no guilt he can't cover and no person he can't use for his glory.

VERSES TO DEEPEN YOUR JOY

ISAIAH 1:18; 1 JOHN 1:9

Go share the joy today!

Unlimited Resources

My God shall supply all your need
according to His riches in glory by Christ Jesus.
PHILIPPIANS 4:19 NKJV

When God calls you to do something, it means that all the necessary provisions are in place even if you can't see them at the moment. Too many people talk themselves out of fulfilling their callings and pursuing their dreams because they look at their natural resources and abilities and get discouraged. All we must do is step out in obedience, trusting God to supply all our needs.

God called the children of Israel out of bondage in Egypt and ordered them to cross over into the promised land, far away from the scope of their sight and far outside the bounds of their abilities. They couldn't see it; they couldn't touch it; they didn't know the details of their escape. But they trusted God.

When we set out to reach the next place God has called us to, we have to trust that his provision is already in place. If we could see it, touch it, or read the financial report ahead of time, our obedience wouldn't require faith. If we're going to surpass every perceived limit, we need to know from the get-go that God's got this. The details have already been worked out; our needs have been met. All we need to do is move forward in faith.

VERSES TO DEEPEN YOUR JOY

PSALM 24:1; EPHESIANS 3:20

Go share the joy today!

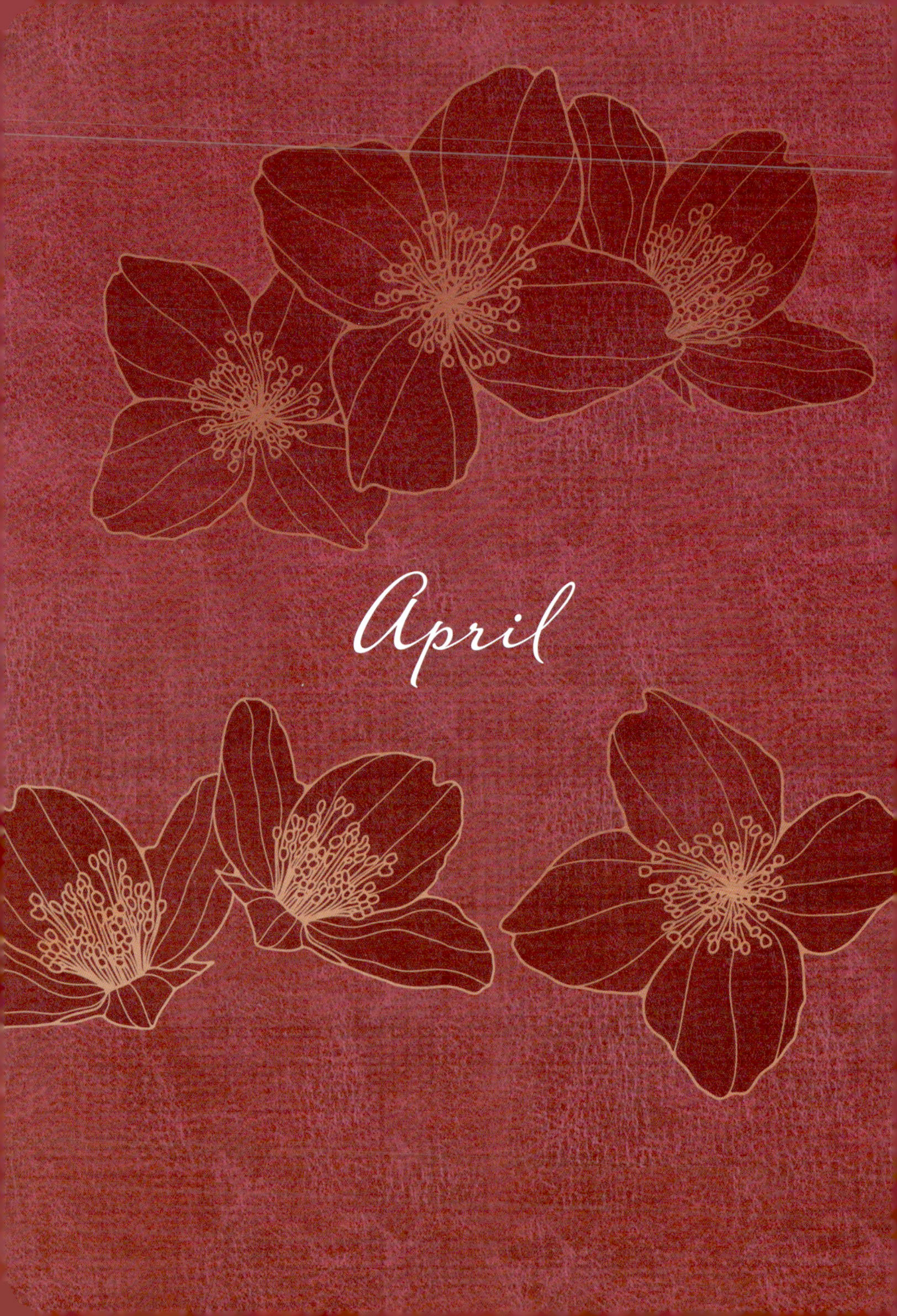

April

Promise of Financial Provision

"The heavens and the highest of heavens belong to the LORD your God, the earth and all that is in it."

DEUTERONOMY 10:14 AMP

Financial provision should not be a worry for those who are in the Father's will. It shouldn't be a big issue in our minds because God always provides where he guides. So don't be afraid to think like God thinks. Think big! Keep expectation and determination alive in your heart as you press forward in his call on your life.

What is money to the Lord? He owns it all. We should never base our decisions strictly on our financial situation. Instead, we must make every decision according to the leading of the Holy Spirit, who guides us in all truth. As Jesus said in John 16:13, "When He, the Spirit of Truth, comes, He will guide you into all the truth [full and complete truth]" (AMP). Remember that God's provision is already in place. He's simply waiting for you to obey and answer his call.

Jesus addressed the topic of money more than almost any other subject he dealt with in his earthly ministry. It's an area that takes a lot of our energy and requires a lot of trust to surrender to God. We aren't to trust in our bank accounts or investments; we're to trust God, who can make our scant resources more than sufficient for the tasks he has called us to.

VERSES TO DEEPEN YOUR JOY

LUKE 6:38; HEBREWS 13:5

Go share the joy today!

Work Out Your Willingness

I am willing to endure anything if it will bring salvation and eternal glory in Christ Jesus to those God has chosen.

2 TIMOTHY 2:10 NLT

Plenty of people say they are willing until it comes to walking in obedience and carrying out the seemingly illogical or inconvenient instructions that God has given them, especially regarding their finances. Yet Jesus assured us, "With God all things are possible" (Matthew 19:26).

Willingness to work for God is one thing. Being obedient to the Holy Spirit's promptings is altogether different. This is especially true when obeying means stepping outside your comfort zone and being generous when your bank account suggests that stinginess would be a wiser practice. But if you're going to "eat the good things from the land," you need to be both willing and obedient.

Have you surrendered your bank account and financial budget to the Lord? Hardly any other area of our lives will demand more trust when God gives us instructions that seem illogical. But if we are diligent to obey him, he will bless us. Pray that God will give you open hands of gratitude and generosity with your financial resources. Look for ways to obey him with your giving, whether by increasing your offerings to the church or seeking out charitable organizations to support. When we trust God with our finances, we've trusted him about as much as we can. If you remind yourself continually that all you have comes from God, you'll probably have an easier time trusting him to guide and bless your spending and saving.

VERSES TO DEEPEN YOUR JOY

GENESIS 22:1–14; PSALM 25:1–5

Go share the joy today!

Trust Your Provider

Some trust in chariots and some in horses,
but we will remember and trust in the name of the LORD our God.

PSALM 20:7 AMP

The book of Exodus shares how God tested the children of Israel for several reasons, primarily to see whether they would respond in obedience and whether they had the proper heart attitude toward daily provision. It was a setup to see if they would trust in God and rely on him to provide for their daily needs.

And provide he did! God gave food to the Israelites while they were fleeing Egypt and for many years afterward. This food came in the form of manna, which fell daily from heaven. "The LORD said to Moses, 'Behold, I will cause bread to rain from heaven for you; the people shall go out and gather a day's portion every day, so that I may test them [to determine] whether or not they will walk [obediently] in My instruction (law)'" (Exodus 16:4 AMP). It also came in the quail that God provided.

Yet the Israelites persisted in grumbling and somehow questioned God's ability to provide for them (Numbers 11). It's easy for us to marvel at their unbelief, but would we have responded any differently? We need to maintain our trust in our heavenly Provider and silence all the doubts that threaten our peace of mind.

VERSES TO DEEPEN YOUR JOY

JOHN 6:32; PHILIPPIANS 4:19

Go share the joy today!

Our Daily Bread

"'Give us each day our daily bread.'"

LUKE 11:3

For the Israelites to receive a passing score of obedience as they camped out in the wilderness, they would have to have trusted fully in the true Provider, not in their provision. And this is a test that each of us must pass.

Sometimes we get so used to trusting in our provision—our paycheck, our savings accounts, our inheritance, for example—that we lose sight of the one from whom it came. We just cruise along without realizing that our trust has shifted from the source of everything to our salaries. When this happens, our faith in God may weaken to the point where, if we lose a job, go through a divorce, make an unwise investment that goes sour, or face an overwhelming situation that causes financial strain, we find it hard to hang on because the thing we've trusted in is slipping through our fingers.

Our heavenly Father promises to supply our daily bread—all our needs. Matthew 6:32–33 says, "The Gentiles eagerly seek all these things; for your heavenly Father knows that you need all these things. But seek first His kingdom and His righteousness, and all these things will be provided to you" (NASB). But we can't plead his promises if we aren't living by faith in him. We can't expect his provision if we're walking in blatant disobedience. One covenant benefit of being a child of God is having the confidence that he will supply whatever we need. We need to rest in that.

VERSES TO DEEPEN YOUR JOY

EXODUS 16:9–14; ROMANS 8:32

Go share the joy today!

Confidence in His Covenant

I have been young and now I am old, yet I have not seen the righteous (those in right standing with God) abandoned or his descendants pleading for bread.

PSALM 37:25 AMP

When you go to the doctor for a checkup, the receptionist may ask to see your insurance card. So you pull that card out of your wallet and hand it over with confidence because you know you have benefits. You don't say, "I have insurance benefits, but I'll just go ahead and pay for this visit out of pocket." That would be foolish. And it's the same when it comes to our covenant benefits as children of the King.

We can pull out our list of benefits—a long list that is recorded throughout the pages of the Bible—and see a detailed compilation of all the covenant blessings that belong to us as the adopted daughters of God. Those blessings far surpass financial provision to include joy, peace, protection, and wisdom, to mention just a few. Heaven doesn't have any bread shortages, so don't walk around with your head hanging low. Hold your head high and stand boldly on the Word—your benefit book—as you trust God to give you your daily bread.

Your means of provision may change, but your Provider is the same yesterday, today, and forever, as Hebrews 13:8 assures us. Don't worry. God has never forsaken the righteous, and he isn't about to abandon you. Never will you need to beg for bread. You may need to exercise your faith in him to receive your daily bread, but that's a great place to be because your intimacy with the Father grows as you rely on him more and more.

VERSES TO DEEPEN YOUR JOY

PSALM 37:18–19; MATTHEW 7:11

Go share the joy today!

Just Enough Is Still Enough

The Israelites did as they were told; some gathered much [manna], some little. And when they measured it…, the one who gathered much did not have too much, and the one who gathered little did not have too little. Everyone had gathered just as much as they needed.

EXODUS 16:17–18

When the children of Israel were crossing over from the land of "not enough" (Egypt) to the land of "more than enough" (the promised land), they had to walk through the land of "just enough" (the desert). In the desert, they received just enough provision for each day. They didn't lack, yet they didn't have an abundance of food or provisions. They had just enough—their daily bread, or manna, from heaven. They weren't supposed to collect more manna than they needed for each day, or it would spoil.

Similarly, when Jesus commissioned the twelve apostles, he gave them the following instructions: "Take nothing for the journey except a staff—no bread, no bag, no money in your belts. Wear sandals but not an extra shirt" (Mark 6:8–9).

Whenever we cross over to a new place or ascend to a higher level of spiritual maturity, we pass through a period in which we have to rely on our daily bread, God's daily provision for our needs. Why is this period necessary? Because the next step in our journey with the Lord will require an increase in our faith and trust in God.

VERSES TO DEEPEN YOUR JOY

DEUTERONOMY 8:18; MATTHEW 6:33

Go share the joy today!

Belief for the Next Step

"In their hunger you gave them bread from heaven and in their thirst you brought them water from the rock; you told them to go in and take possession of the land you had sworn with uplifted hand to give them."

NEHEMIAH 9:15

The Lord is faithful to lead us to the next level and to take possession of the "land" he has promised us when we trust in him. The key is believing that he will do what he has promised. The key is having faith for the next step.

Over the years, each time our ministry has outgrown its office space and relocated to a larger facility, the cost increased, meaning we had to believe that God would give us the extra monthly funds. We never had any extra money, but we always had just enough to meet the payment. It was as if God were doling out our daily manna during these seasons of crossing over to the next phase of ministry. We had to walk through the land of just enough and trust God as never before.

The "daily bread" stage stretches our faith and matures our Christian character. This season is rarely comfortable to the flesh because it's designed to rid us of all waste and excess. Our flesh has to be disciplined if we are going to climb to a higher level. And a higher level is where God wants to take us.

VERSES TO DEEPEN YOUR JOY

PSALM 34:10; 2 CORINTHIANS 9:8

Go share the joy today!

Small Resources, Big Results

*"I am the Lord, the God of all mankind.
Is anything too hard for me?"*

Jeremiah 32:27

Throughout the Bible, we see so many examples of God doing big things with small resources. He rarely does big things with the plentiful resources contributed by an individual or group. This means that we have to abandon any excuses we make, such as, "But I have so little!" and "I don't have enough money/resources/knowledge to accomplish what God is asking of me!" It's tempting to hold back from answering God's call or pursuing our God-given dreams when we're focused solely on our lack—on what we don't have. "I don't have the money," we say. "I don't have enough power"; "I don't have the time." None of that matters when God is in the mix.

If we have abundant resources at our disposal, it's easy to forget that we need God. It's easy to think that we're capable, deserve the credit, and don't need to rely on him. But when we're in a position where God *has* to show up for something to happen, that's when he can work his "super" through our natural circumstances and get the glory. Let's stop looking at our lack and start using what we have, however limited or small it may be, and expecting God to show up. And then let's watch as our resources multiply and miracles unfold.

VERSES TO DEEPEN YOUR JOY

Genesis 18:14; Matthew 6:31–32

Go share the joy today!

A Lesson in Multiplication

The eyes of all look to You [in hopeful expectation],
and You give them their food in due time.
You open Your hand and satisfy the desire of every living thing.

PSALM 145:15–16 AMP

You may be familiar with the story of Jesus feeding the five thousand. With just five loaves of bread and two fish, Jesus prepared a feast for this crowd of five thousand men, plus an unknown number of women and children, who ate their fill and still didn't polish off the food. How he did it perfectly illustrates that we should entrust scant resources to the Lord and let him do his miraculous work.

First, Jesus took the food and "[looked] up to heaven" (Matthew 14:19). He didn't look down but looked up to the Lord. Like Jesus, we need to simply take what we have and look up to the Lord, invoking our faith and trust.

Next in verse 19, Jesus "gave thanks and broke the loaves." It's critical to thank God for what he has given us. Stop complaining about what you lack and start praising God for what he has given you. A grateful heart is always a forerunner for increase. If you aren't thankful for what you already have, why would you expect God to give you more?

Finally, Jesus "gave [the loaves and fish] to the disciples, and the disciples gave them to the people" (v. 19). Although he had only five loaves and two fish, Jesus started distributing that food to the crowd. Talk about a step of faith. When we step out in faith and start doing what we know God has asked of us, the necessary provision will always be there.

VERSES TO DEEPEN YOUR JOY

MATTHEW 14:20–21; LUKE 12:22–26

Go share the joy today!

Natural Eyes Are Inadequate

Faith is confidence in what we hope for
and assurance about what we do not see.

HEBREWS 11:1

Have you been fixated on the scarcity of your resources or the size of your bank account? Have you been listening to the Enemy's intimidating whispers that you'll never have enough? Intimidation and fear that are grounded in our perception of our natural circumstances can stifle our expectation that God's supernatural hand will intervene. Yet expectation invites the supernatural. All we need to do is have faith the size of a mustard seed.

Never forget that God loves using scant resources and frail people to accomplish big feats. He delights in using a little to produce a lot. Don't look at the little you have and let the Enemy steal your hopeful expectation. When you give your limited resources over to the Lord, you can expect major results. When God is in your plans, the results are always big, powerful, and supernatural. All you have to do is keep expectation alive in your heart. Are you expecting God to do big, powerful things in you, through you, and for you?

Ask God to transform your vision so that you can have his perspective on things. Forget what your circumstances tell you and listen instead to what your unstoppable, all-powerful God has told you. He has the final say.

VERSES TO DEEPEN YOUR JOY

1 SAMUEL 16:7; JAMES 1:5

Go share the joy today!

Keep Expectation Alive

Hope that is seen is no hope at all. Who hopes for what they already have? But if we hope for what we do not yet have, we wait for it patiently.

ROMANS 8:24–25

Expectation can work powerfully for us, kindling our hope and keeping us on a path of progress toward the fulfillment of God's promises. Yet it can also work just as powerfully against us if we succumb to negative thinking and low expectations based on the scarcity of our resources.

When we maintain God-inspired expectation and trust in his ability to provide, we can usher in the supernatural. We need to continually remind ourselves of God's all-sufficient provision and infinite power. We need to follow the exhortation of the apostle Paul in Colossians 3:1–2: "Since you have been raised to new life with Christ, set your sights on the realities of heaven, where Christ sits in the place of honor at God's right hand. Think about the things of heaven, not the things of earth" (NLT).

The Living Bible translates Colossians 3:2 in this way: "Let heaven fill your thoughts; don't spend your time worrying about things down here." When you "let heaven fill your thoughts," God-inspired expectation follows. Your mind should be filled with expectations that line up with the Word of God. Then you can keep expectation alive and be encouraged continually.

VERSES TO DEEPEN YOUR JOY

1 SAMUEL 17:45–47; ROMANS 12:2

Go share the joy today!

Big, Bold Expectations

Let us therefore come boldly to the throne of grace,
that we may obtain mercy and find grace to help in time of need.
HEBREWS 4:16 NKJV

God wants us to expect big, bold things of him and to be confident of his ability and desire to fulfill our requests above and beyond our wildest dreams. And we can ask boldly only when we're aligned with his will and, therefore, expect a favorable response.

Scripture assures us that his promises and provisions are ours for the asking. First John 5:14–15 says, "We are confident that [God] hears us whenever we ask for anything that pleases him. And since we know he hears us when we make our requests, we also know that he will give us what we ask for" (NLT). Maybe you need to raise your level of expectation today. Maybe you need to be bolder and to ask for bigger blessings and responsibilities. God wants to release the supernatural in you, through you, and for you. He wants to take whatever resources you have—however scant or flawed—and transform them into something big. But you have to expect him to do that.

Don't let the Enemy dampen the flames of your faith. Don't let him quash your sense of hopeful anticipation or sow seeds of pessimism and doubt in your heart. Many people expect disaster, lack, sickness, defeat, and even death. Don't expect the negative but expect and anticipate that God's supernatural power will meet and even exceed your every need.

VERSES TO DEEPEN YOUR JOY

PSALM 34:4; HEBREWS 10:35–36

Go share the joy today!

Far-Reaching Faith

Faith comes by hearing,
and hearing by the word of God.
ROMANS 10:17 NKJV

Expecting big things is easier when we have strong faith and divine favor. Asking for these big things starts by allowing God to stretch our faith in him and his promises, which come from the Word of God in the first place.

As we expose ourselves to the written Word of God, the Bible, and receive God's revealed (*rhema*) words, which always align with his written Word, we get what I like to call a faith lift. The words that we hear, read, and remember greatly impact the strength and scope of our faith. That's why it's so important to steep ourselves in Scripture. Daily Bible reading and Scripture memorization are two powerful techniques for filling yourself with God's Word.

Just as the words of the Lord increase our faith, the words of the devil decrease our faith and stir up doubt, which erodes our faith even further. That's why we need to be selective about what we're listening to. Even seemingly innocuous amounts of gossip, slander, and other ungodly speech can seep into our hearts and tear down our spirits. So be on guard! Don't leave the Word within you exposed and vulnerable to the devil's destructive tactics. Guard the Word in your heart and mind, where it will empower you, strengthen you, and lift you to new heights of faith.

VERSES TO DEEPEN YOUR JOY

ACTS 3:16; 1 CORINTHIANS 16:13

Go share the joy today!

Fill up with the Word

My child, pay attention to what I say. Listen carefully to my words. Don't lose sight of them. Let them penetrate deep into your heart, for they bring life to those who find them, and healing to their whole body.

PROVERBS 4:20–22 NLT

Even when we're full, we often continue eating when we would do better to show some self-restraint and stop. When it comes to the Word of God, the opposite is often true: we take a little nibble, then push away our plate, the Bible, as though we are full.

Yet we can never have too much of God's Word in us. It is impossible for Scripture to penetrate too deeply into our hearts. We should devour the Word hungrily rather than pretend we're full after just a little taste. The more time we spend in the Word, the more the Word gets into our spirits and influences our thoughts, words, and actions. The Word within us is one way that God can live through us, guiding us by his precepts and prompting us to say and do those things that advance his kingdom in our personal sphere of influence.

Again, we can never have too much of God's Word in us. Keep feeding on the Word, and your faith will grow. Read the Bible in the morning. Listen to it as you're driving in your car or doing projects around the house. Steep yourself in the Bible, and you'll see a major difference in your outlook and level of faith. Anyone else need a "faith lift" today?

VERSES TO DEEPEN YOUR JOY

PSALM 119:11; PROVERBS 7:1–3

Go share the joy today!

Rock Solid

"Everyone who hears these words of mine and puts them into practice is like a wise man who built his house on the rock."

MATTHEW 7:24

Jesus wants us to have rock-solid faith. The key is knowing his Word and living according to it. Jesus said, "Everyone who hears these words of mine and puts them into practice is like a wise man who built his house on the rock. The rain came down, the streams rose, and the winds blew and beat against that house; yet it did not fall, because it had its foundation on the rock" (vv. 24–25). A rock-solid foundation of the Word gives us a platform of faith that has the power to thrust us into a lifestyle of asking and expecting big things from God. When we ask for big things, we will see God do miraculous things in us, through us, and for us.

Don't miss out by falling short in your faith. Don't make the mistake of giving up when you grow weary but press forward in faith. God is ready to bless you if you'll just hang in there and expect it. Build on the rock and say, "Bring it on!" to the wind and waves.

Are you ready to go deeper in your faith? God's ready to take you there; you simply need to ask for it. Then buckle up and trust him all the way there.

VERSES TO DEEPEN YOUR JOY

PSALM 1:1–2; JAMES 1:23–24

Go share the joy today!

Avenging the Locusts

"I will compensate you for the years that the swarming locust has eaten."

JOEL 2:25 NASB

Many people grow bitter when they feel they've been robbed of an opportunity, treated unfairly, or deprived of rights and resources that should have been theirs. When the "locusts" come and pillage their harvest, they get discouraged and hold grudges. If you sometimes feel this way, take heart! God promises to repay all that the Enemy has stolen from you. The key is looking to him rather than to other people to replenish your resources.

Turning to other people for repayment of hurts, wounds, or financial losses is an act of unforgiveness. No one but Christ can truly repay us for our losses. And when he repays us, he does so in a way that far exceeds our expectations. He repays us what we're due plus supernatural interest.

Think about Job. God allowed the devil to subject him to every kind of loss imaginable—loss of family, fortune, and health, to name a few examples (Job 1:6–22). But in the end, "The LORD also restored the fortunes of Job when Job prayed for his friends, and the Lord increased double all that Job had…The LORD blessed the latter days of Job more than his beginning" (Job 42:10, 12 NASB).

If we'll just keep our mouths shut and our hearts right, as Job did, God will reward our hopeful expectation of his recompense. Trust him to avenge the locusts in your life.

VERSES TO DEEPEN YOUR JOY

JOB 42:10–17; ISAIAH 62:11

Go share the joy today!

Running Out

"Test me in this," says the LORD Almighty, "and see if I will not throw open the floodgates of heaven and pour out so much blessing that there will not be room enough to store it."

MALACHI 3:10

With God, we can never expect too big or too much. There's no such thing as too lofty a dream or too large a request. Nothing is too difficult for him to accomplish. But we can expect too little. That's what happened to a widow—whose story is recorded in the fourth chapter of 2 Kings—until the prophet Elisha came along and taught her an important lesson that all of us would be wise to learn.

The widow was fixated on the certainty that her sons would be dragged off to debtor's prison because she had no money left. None of her possessions would have amounted to enough value to satisfy her debts. "Your servant has nothing [at home] at all," she told the prophet Elisha, "except a small jar of olive oil" (2 Kings 4:2). The prophet instructed the woman to go to all her neighbors and gather as many empty jars from them as she could. Then he had her start pouring the oil from her own jar into all the empty jars she had collected. What happened next was amazing.

VERSES TO DEEPEN YOUR JOY

2 KINGS 4:1–7; PSALM 84:11

Go share the joy today!

Running Over

"If you believe, you will receive whatever you ask for in prayer."

MATTHEW 21:22

After Elisha offered to help the widow who faced a financial crisis in 2 Kings 4, she went door-to-door as he instructed, gathering as many empty jars as she could. And when she went home again, the oil she had continued flowing until no jars were left to contain it. If only she'd found a hundred or a thousand jars or even a few large vats to fill. The amount of oil she received was limited only by the space she prepared to contain it.

Elisha's instructions required the widow to ask for and expect big things. She never could have guessed just how important it would be to expect bigger than ever before.

Sometimes we find ourselves in need and fail to ask God for a miracle. Or if we ask for his help, we ask for the bare minimum. We need to take the limits off our thinking because God has no limits. Our "oil" will go from running out to running over when we expect God to make it so.

Where have you been holding back belief? In what areas have you been too uncertain to ask God for big things? It's time to start collecting empty jars and expecting God to fill them to the brim—even to overflowing.

VERSES TO DEEPEN YOUR JOY

MATTHEW 14:31; LUKE 7:9

Go share the joy today!

Prepare for Increase

You do not have
because you do not ask God.
JAMES 4:2

When you're expecting a baby, you prepare. You decorate and furnish the nursery. You childproof the house. You purchase all the necessary supplies. You brainstorm baby names and painstakingly select one for your precious newborn. You'll never give birth to something you aren't expecting, and the first step to giving birth, or receiving, is *preparing* to receive it.

We can't afford to be like the people to whom James wrote those sobering words: "You do not have because you do not ask God." Let's not fail to receive because we've failed to ask. We need to ask and then prepare to receive whatever we have asked for. The more we expect, the bigger the miracle we can receive. We just need to trust God to come through for us even when our resources seem insufficient or if his instructions sound illogical.

I expected my daughter for nine months before I gave birth to her. And prior to conceiving, I expected a child from God for many, many years. What are you expecting today? If you're expecting defeat, that's what you'll get. If you're expecting victory in the name of Jesus, how are you preparing for it? When you expect big things from God, you set the stage for him to set his "super" on your natural circumstances, ushering in the unlimited resources of heaven.

VERSES TO DEEPEN YOUR JOY

PSALM 34:4; JAMES 4:7–8

Go share the joy today!

Enriched for a Reason

A generous person will prosper;
whoever refreshes others will be refreshed.
PROVERBS 11:25

The Lord wants to bless us in radical ways—to go above and beyond meeting our needs—but we often fail to understand the bigger purpose behind this blessing. He bestows financial riches upon us for the fulfillment of kingdom purposes.

Yes, Father God meets all our needs and can give us the desires of our heart, but he will not settle for any position but first place in our hearts. Exodus 34:14 commands us, "You shall not worship any other god, because the LORD, whose name is Jealous, is a jealous God" (NASB). When the Lord is our first love, the foremost desire of our heart is to see his kingdom grow. Our desire to reach the lost becomes so strong that we don't mind how deep we need to dig into our pockets to do our part.

Some of our most prized resources include our time, energy, and finances. When God blesses us with an excess of resources, we are supposed to sow them into the work of the kingdom. Our excess is not for ourselves but for others. When you have an excess of time, invest it in the lives of others. Sow your time in prayer for others or find someone who's lonely or needs encouragement. When you have an excess of income, invest in the kingdom of God.

VERSES TO DEEPEN YOUR JOY

GENESIS 12:1–3; PROVERBS 19:11

Go share the joy today!

Blessed to Be a Blessing

You will be enriched in every way so that you can be generous on every occasion, and through us your generosity will result in thanksgiving to God.

2 CORINTHIANS 9:11

If the Lord has given us an excess of money, resources, gifts, talents, or other blessings, he has done so for the benefit of others, not for our selfish spending. The apostle Paul makes it very clear in today's verse that God blesses us financially so that we "can be generous on every occasion." We have been blessed so that we can be a blessing to others.

Sometimes we misinterpret the "so that" in this verse. We think that God blesses us with extra finances "so that" we can spend it on more clothes, more shoes, expensive vacations, and the like. When you think about it, you can really wear only so many pairs of shoes, and some of your best vacations were probably those you spent at home having quality time with your family. If we blow our excess income on ourselves, we have wasted it.

When we find ourselves with extra resources, let's not automatically assume that we owe ourselves some special treat or another but let's go to God in prayer and ask for direction for how we should allocate them. It just may be that he has someone specific in mind for us to bless.

When we sow it, we invest it. Remember, sow it; don't blow it!

VERSES TO DEEPEN YOUR JOY

PROVERBS 22:9; LUKE 16:11

Go share the joy today!

Loving Money Is Misplaced Love

The love of money is a root of all kinds of evil. Some people, eager for money, have wandered from the faith and pierced themselves with many griefs.

1 TIMOTHY 6:10

In the Lord's Prayer, following the request that says, "Give us today our daily bread," it says, "Forgive us our debts, as we also have forgiven our debtors. And lead us not into temptation, but deliver us from the evil one" (Matthew 6:11–13). Immediately after praying for our daily bread, we are to pray that we will not fall into temptation. That's because we are often most tempted regarding our daily bread and the money we use to get it.

Wealth management is an area in which the devil has a field day, tripping God's children and trapping them in greed. We need to keep our eyes on God with hearts of gratitude for the financial blessings he bestows upon us.

When God blesses us financially, let's be grateful. And let's show our gratitude by using our resources for the benefit and blessing of others, as an act of worship and obedience to our heavenly Father. Let's never forget that everything we have comes from him. We're to love our Provider, not our provision. As long as we remember the proper order rather than giving our pocketbooks misplaced praise, we can love our Provider and spend money in ways that glorify him.

VERSES TO DEEPEN YOUR JOY

MATTHEW 19:24; LUKE 12:15

Go share the joy today!

No Harvest from Hoarding

"Watch out and guard yourselves against every form of greed; for not even when one has an overflowing abundance does his life consist of nor is it derived from his possessions."

LUKE 12:15 AMP

Sometimes we are tempted to hoard up our *daily* bread for years to come. We create a sense of security—a false sense of security, I might add—by setting aside a huge stash of provisions. When we amass reserves of stuff, it reveals a fearful spirit and a lack of trust in God. Instead of trusting the Lord with all our heart, as we are told to do in Proverbs 3:5, we rely on our own abilities and trust in the provisions that we've stored up for ourselves.

Don't get me wrong. I'm not saying that we shouldn't save money. Some people fail to plan for tomorrow because their flesh is caught up in the lusts of the moment. But it's wrong to hoard up today's manna for selfish reasons. Saving money as an aspect of prudent fiscal management is different from hoarding.

An easy way to determine whether we are saving or hoarding is to look at our response when God asks us to dip into our stash for his kingdom purposes. The attitude with which we give to God and his people is a good gauge of our heart condition and an indicator of whether we are saving or hoarding. And hoarding never produces a harvest in God's kingdom.

VERSES TO DEEPEN YOUR JOY

LUKE 12:15–21; JOHN 4:34–38

Go share the joy today!

Honor God with Your Firstfruits

Honor the LORD with your wealth, with the firstfruits of all your crops;
then your barns will be filled to overflowing,
and your vats will brim over with new wine.

PROVERBS 3:9–10

We are told in today's verses to honor God with our "firstfruits." What does that entail? Basically, we give God our firstfruits when we commit to giving to him and his kingdom the best, first portion of whatever we earn or make. It also implies giving him the highest position—first place—in our hearts.

The first person to offer firstfruits to God was Abel, the son of Adam and Eve. While Abel's older brother, Cain, "brought *some* of the fruits of the soil as an offering to the LORD" (Genesis 4:3), Abel "brought an offering—fat portions from some of the *firstborn* of his flock" (v. 4).

Do you see the difference? Cain brought just "some" of his crops without ensuring they were the first he had harvested or that they were of the highest possible quality. Abel, on the other hand, sacrificed some of his firstborn animals—an act that indicated Abel trusted God to meet all his needs. He wasn't stingy, and because of his generosity toward God, "the LORD looked with favor on Abel and his offering" (v. 4). Let's strive to be like Abel and give of our firstfruits to the Lord.

VERSES TO DEEPEN YOUR JOY

PROVERBS 11:4; LUKE 6:38

Go share the joy today!

Firstfruits, Not Final Fruits

He chose to give us birth through the word of truth, that we might be a kind of firstfruits of all he created.

JAMES 1:18

I love this picture from the book of James that paints us believers as the firstfruits of God's creation. We are the finest example of his workmanship. Remember that, when God created the world, the crowning act was his fashioning of the first man and woman.

The Lord honors us by making us his firstfruits—those he saves and redeems. And we should do the same, giving him the best of what we have rather than tossing him the leftovers or the discards. As we honor the Lord with the firstfruits of our income, our resources, and our time, we will overflow with the blessings of the Lord.

God doesn't want our "final fruits," like Cain gave him. No, he wants our firstfruits, as he wanted Abel's, as an indication that we're giving him first place in our hearts. When we prize God above what we perceive to be security, financial or otherwise, he takes us to a place we couldn't have accessed ourselves. He rewards us with blessings that no amount of money can buy. He grants us favor and promotion that we couldn't have earned on our own. God truly blesses us with an overflow when we give him our firstfruits.

VERSES TO DEEPEN YOUR JOY

GENESIS 22:1–18; 1 CORINTHIANS 15:20

Go share the joy today!

The Firstfruits of Your Time

Because of the LORD's great love we are not consumed, for his compassions never fail. They are new every morning; great is your faithfulness.

LAMENTATIONS 3:22–23

I believe that God not only wants the firstfruits of our income but also desires the firstfruits of our day. What do I mean by that? I mean that if we get nothing else done in a day, it doesn't really matter as long as we've given time to our heavenly Father. Spending time with him—in the early morning, throughout the day, and at night—is a critical practice to observe if we're going to deepen our relationship with him and strengthen our devotion to him.

I like to get up early to read the Bible and pray. But some people prefer to dedicate time to these activities before bed. Whatever works best for you is what you should do. No time that we've spent with the Father is wasted.

Jesus modeled this kind of behavior, beginning and ending his days with prayer. Mark 1:35 says, "Early in the morning, while it was still dark, Jesus got up, left [the house], and went out to a secluded place, and was praying there" (AMP). Sometimes he even pulled all-nighters praying. "Jesus went off to the mountain to pray, and He spent the whole night in prayer to God" (Luke 6:12 AMP).

However you schedule your day, be sure to prioritize time with God.

VERSES TO DEEPEN YOUR JOY

PSALM 5:3; ISAIAH 5:11

Go share the joy today!

APRIL 27

Prioritize the Sabbath

"Remember the Sabbath day by keeping it holy."

Exodus 20:8

The Lord also wants us to keep the Sabbath day holy, setting aside time from toil to worship him and enjoy the rest he gives us. Hebrews 4:9 says, "There remains a [full and complete] Sabbath rest for the people of God" (AMP). When we observe the Sabbath, we give God the firstfruits of our week, consecrating to him precious time and energy that are pleasing to him.

When we give God the firstfruits of our week, rather than the leftovers, we are blessed in countless ways. We supernaturally accomplish more than we could have done if we worked nonstop from dawn to dusk. When we devote the first part of each day and all the Sabbath to our heavenly Father, things just fall into place, and our responsibilities and duties are fulfilled in record time.

Don't let your schedule control you. So many people are driven by to-do lists. They panic if they're approaching a deadline and feel as if they won't finish everything they need to do in the time they've set aside to do it. As long as you devote time to God first, everything else will fall into place, and you will be blessed rather than stressed. How might you reorient your calendar to prioritize the Lord? Starting this week, seek out ways to give God the firstfruits of your week and see how he blesses you accordingly.

VERSES TO DEEPEN YOUR JOY

Psalm 88:13; Isaiah 58:13–14

Go share the joy today!

Tithe and Thrive

"'All the tithe (tenth part) of the land,
whether the seed of the land or the fruit of the tree, is the LORD's;
it is holy to the LORD.'"

LEVITICUS 27:30 AMP

Regardless of our financial situation, we are expected to tithe a tenth of our income to the Lord and his work. The instructions on tithes and offerings in today's verse from the book of Leviticus give us ample encouragement.

The word *tithe* actually means "one-tenth" or 10 percent. Some people tithe 3 percent and think they're covered, but they're mistaken. Tithing entails giving 10 percent (or more) of your income. Some Christian teachers will tell you to start where you are and do what you can. But 3 percent obedience doesn't cut it. God requires us to obey 100 percent.

Remember, the one who guarantees to bless our obedience is the Lord Almighty. He never runs out of resources. When we trust him with our money, we are sure to prove his faithfulness time and again.

If you've been tithing faithfully, that's fantastic. And if not, it's never too late to start. Take a close look at your income and figure out how much would constitute 10 percent (or more, if you're so inclined). Then take whatever steps are necessary to ensure that your tithe reaches your local church. Pray that the Lord will settle any anxiety you may have about this process. He's just waiting to bless your obedience.

VERSES TO DEEPEN YOUR JOY

DEUTERONOMY 26:12; MALACHI 3:8–10

Go share the joy today!

Disobedience Brings Debt

Fear the LORD and turn away from evil.
It will be healing to your body and refreshment to your bones.
PROVERBS 3:7–8 NASB

Some people neglect to tithe because they look at their bank accounts and believe that they can't afford to give away 10 percent. Little do they realize that they can't afford *not* to give 10 percent of their income to the Lord's work. That's because obedience brings a blessing while disobedience brings debt.

Just before issuing the command to "bring the *whole* tithe into the storehouse" in Malachi 3:10 (NASB), God had said, "Would anyone rob God? Yet you are robbing Me! But you say, 'How have we robbed You?' In tithes and offerings. You are cursed with a curse, for you are robbing Me, the entire nation of you!" (vv. 8–9 NASB). I don't know about you, but I surely don't want to be accused of robbing God.

When we fail to give God our tithe and offering (an offering is anything above and beyond our 10 percent to advance his kingdom and support his church), we find ourselves under a financial curse because we are basically robbing God. I learned a long time ago that we shouldn't try to rewrite the Book. We can't ignore Scripture passages we don't like and focus only on the ones we do. If we want to be blessed and prosperous, we need to accept and embrace God's Word in its entirety.

VERSES TO DEEPEN YOUR JOY

DEUTERONOMY 26:12; LUKE 6:38

Go share the joy today!

Seed for the Sower

He who supplies seed to the sower and bread for food will also supply and increase your store of seed and will enlarge the harvest of your righteousness.

2 CORINTHIANS 9:10

When God talked about opening the "floodgates of heaven" in Malachi 3:10, he meant what he said. He isn't going to open the windows just a smidge so that a few stingy blessings trickle out. He is going to throw open the floodgates and pour out such a blessing that you won't be able to store it all. In other words, you'll have plenty to share with others.

God is the God of more than enough, and when we are faithful stewards of all that he has given us, he gives us even more so that we can bless the lives of those around us. If we're short on finances, the last thing we should do is stop sowing into the Lord's work. Sow faithfully no matter your situation, and God will faithfully supply above and beyond your needs.

Malachi 3:10 always reminds me of the tomato patch on the farm where I grew up. Every time we planted tomato seeds, even though we sold for a profit a portion of the harvest at our farm stand, we always ended up with so many tomatoes at the end of the season that we had to give many of them away. That's how it is with God. The more you sow into his kingdom, the more you have to keep on sowing.

VERSES TO DEEPEN YOUR JOY

2 CORINTHIANS 9:6; GALATIANS 6:7

Go share the joy today!

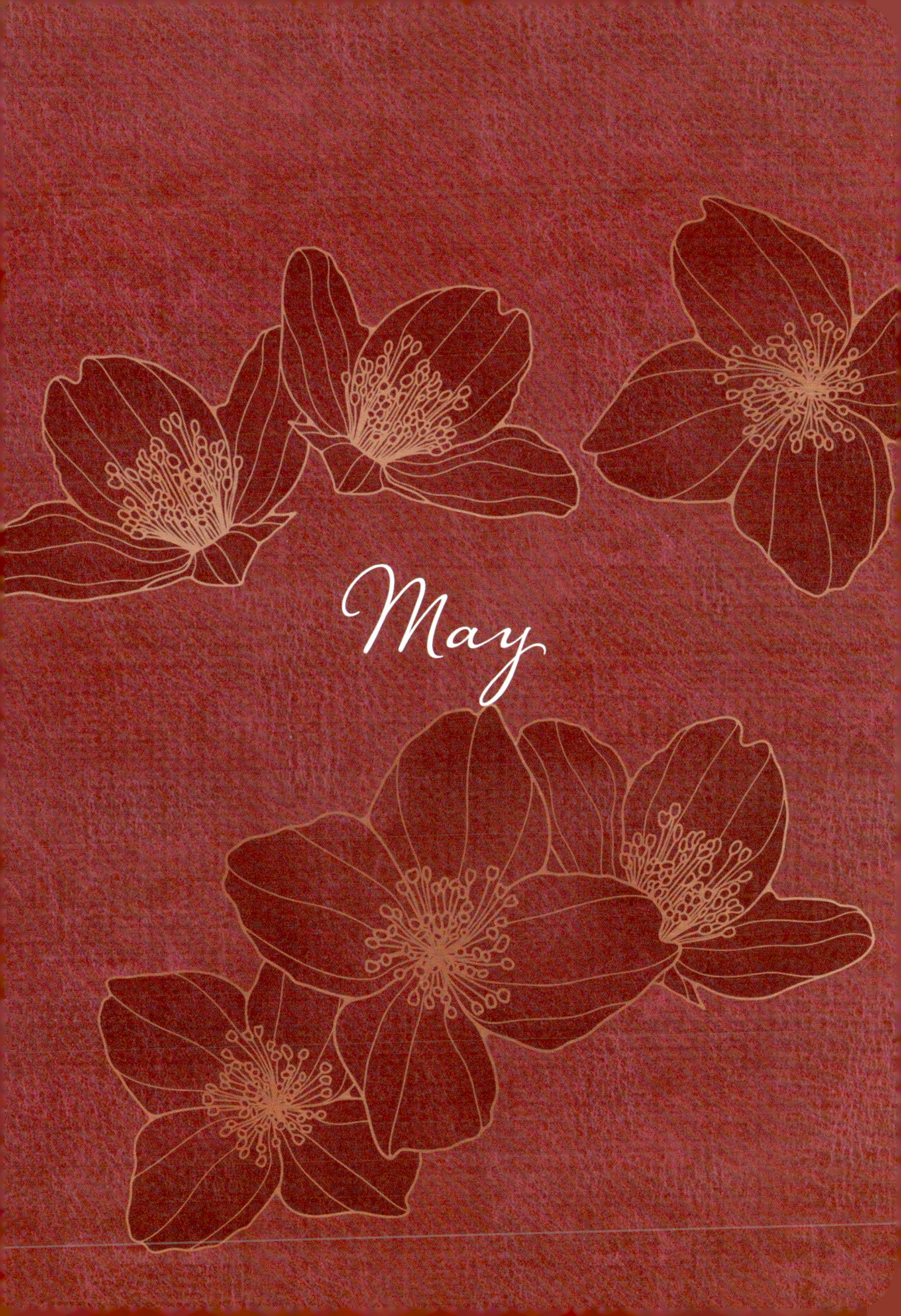
May

Give without Grumbling

Each of you should give what you have decided in your heart to give, not reluctantly or under compulsion, for God loves a cheerful giver.

2 Corinthians 9:7

When we give—whether of our time, talents, or treasure—we must be sure to give generously and not begrudgingly. We should give cheerfully, with grateful hearts, not while grumbling or feeling resentful.

The ultimate example of a generous giver is, of course, God himself. He is never stingy or sparing in his giving, nor should we be. As Paul put it, "He who did not spare his own Son, but gave him up for us all—how will he not also, along with him, graciously give us all things?" (Romans 8:32). Jesus Christ was a priceless gift that God did not withhold from us. Why would we be reluctant to give our very best to him and to those he puts in our path?

In "sowing" his Son by sending him as a sacrifice for our sins, God reaped a family: you, me, and the whole body of Christ. Could anyone else be so generous? Could we ever be more blessed?

Whatever season we find ourselves in—whether we're rolling in the dough or believing God for our next paycheck—we need to keep sowing generously with a smile on our face, for "whoever sows sparingly will also reap sparingly, and whoever sows generously will also reap generously" (2 Corinthians 9:6).

VERSES TO DEEPEN YOUR JOY

Leviticus 19:9–10; Proverbs 11:24–25

Go share the joy today!

Seed Your Need

It goes well for a person who is gracious and lends.

PSALM 112:5 NASB

Growing up on a farm, I would help sow tomato seeds every year. My family didn't wait until we were hungry to get started. Looking ahead, we sowed our seeds because we knew we would need a harvest to support ourselves later. And then, when harvesttime arrived, we reaped more than enough juicy tomatoes to help support our business.

When we find ourselves in great need, that's certainly a great time to sow a seed. But I don't believe in waiting to sow until we have a need but rather in sowing through all seasons, even those of extreme scarcity. That's because sowing seed secures our future and eventual overflow.

In God's economy, we can give our way to blessings. Proverbs 11:25 says, "A generous person will be prosperous, and one who gives others plenty of water will himself be given plenty" (NASB). According to God's Word, the more we give, the more we are blessed—as long as we are sowing in good soil for which God has given his stamp of approval. And as we support others, we are refreshed and blessed.

The outcome is quite different for those who hoard their wealth. Proverbs 28:22 says, "A person with an evil eye hurries after wealth and does not know that poverty will come upon him" (NASB). God's economy and the world's economy operate with opposite methods and values. The world tells us to hold on to everything we can so that someday we can have it all. But in the kingdom of God, we're told to give it all so we can have eternal life. Now that's cause for celebration!

VERSES TO DEEPEN YOUR JOY

PROVERBS 19:17; LUKE 12:33–34

Go share the joy today!

Rewards for Generosity

Whoever is kind to the poor lends to the LORD,
and he will reward them for what they have done.
PROVERBS 19:17

During my most difficult financial struggles, I learned the importance of giving to the poor. I wasn't giving to get; I gave out of a heart of compassion.

Before that time, I had never known what it was like not to have food. I had never known what it was like not to have money to provide for my child or to afford basic necessities like toilet paper. Finding myself in extreme financial straits, I developed a heart of compassion for those who had long been familiar with that struggle, so I would share groceries—and the gospel—with single moms living in subsidized housing nearby.

It was amazing. As I gave out of my own scarcity, I found that all my needs were supernaturally taken care of every month. It never worked on paper, but it was working in my life. I never lost my house, I never went hungry, and my daughter's needs were always met. God brought us to a place of overflowing where we always had more than enough.

If you find yourself in a period of scarcity and lack, there's no better time to walk by faith and give generously from the little you have. The Lord delights in rewarding our generosity, especially when it requires great faith.

VERSES TO DEEPEN YOUR JOY

MATTHEW 25:40; ACTS 4:33–35

Go share the joy today!

Charity Reciprocated

Those who give to the poor will lack nothing,
but those who close their eyes to them receive many curses.

PROVERBS 28:27

During the time I learned to "seed my own need," the Lord showed me today's verse. When I read that portion of Scripture, the Lord said to me, *Danette, you lack nothing because you have given to the poor.* I was shocked! I hadn't been familiar with that verse, yet I had been living it out and was being radically blessed as a result.

God loves it when we have hearts of compassion for those who are in need. Whatever the nature of need that you perceive in those whom God puts on your path—whether financial, emotional, relational, physical, or something else—if God nudges you to meet that need, consider yourself blessed that God appointed you for the task. You can bet that abundant blessings will be on the other side of your obedience.

What God has done for me he can do for you. Get your eyes off yourself, keep your eyes on your Provider, and obey him every step of the way. Seasons of financial strain pass. Just keep pressing your way forward, and before you know it, you may be in a new day of overflowing.

VERSES TO DEEPEN YOUR JOY

DEUTERONOMY 16:17; LUKE 6:38

Go share the joy today!

The Danger of Complacency

Do you put off the day of punishment, yet cause the seat of violence to come near?...Therefore, they will now go into exile with the first of the captives, and the cultic revelry and banqueting of those who lounge around [on their luxurious couches] will pass away.

AMOS 6:3, 7 AMP

Our fallen flesh prefers the familiar. We grow comfortable with what we know, preferring what's familiar to the point where we don't feel much like moving when God calls us on a journey to a better place outside our comfort zones. This type of complacency and inertia can prove devastating to our spiritual health and growth.

Manna and quail for the Israelites were temporary provisions. God didn't plan for his people to remain in the desert dining on manna for the rest of their lives. These items were to be their provision while they traveled to the promised land—the land of more than enough. The Israelites could have completed the transition in a matter of eleven days, but in the face of the unfamiliar, they grumbled and complained—and took forty years to reach the place of promise. Let's not make the same mistake by doubting and despairing. We can trust God to meet our needs above and beyond our greatest expectations if we just step out in faith and follow where he leads.

Don't be complacent and camp out in the familiar. Trust the Lord to lead you beyond the confines of your comfort zone to the unfathomable future he has planned for you.

VERSES TO DEEPEN YOUR JOY

GENESIS 12:1–3; 1 PETER 1:14–17

Go share the joy today!

From Complacency to Crossover

"I will lead the blind by ways they have not known, along unfamiliar paths I will guide them; I will turn the darkness into light before them and make the rough places smooth. These are the things I will do; I will not forsake them."

ISAIAH 42:16

When you feel blinded as to where your provision will come from because your "manna" begins to dry up, it doesn't mean that you are going backward. It means that you are going forward into the land God has promised you by way of the "unfamiliar paths" that the Lord will guide you along.

Exodus 16:35 says, "The Israelites ate manna forty years, until they reached an inhabited land; they ate the manna until they came to the border of the land of Canaan" (AMP). The Israelites received manna until they crossed over to the destination to which God had been leading them all along. Once they were nearing the place of crossover, their temporary source of provision ran dry because there was another one waiting for them.

In my life and in the lives of many others, I have seen the manna begin to dry up just as I was on the brink of accessing a divinely ordained destination. At that point, the flesh screams out, "Don't mess with my manna!" That's when we need to silence the flesh's desires and follow the Spirit's leading to move from complacency to crossover. We can't cross over until we leave comfort and complacency behind.

VERSES TO DEEPEN YOUR JOY

JEREMIAH 33:3; MATTHEW 16:24

Go share the joy today!

Working for Wealth

Lazy hands make for poverty,
but diligent hands bring wealth.
PROVERBS 10:4

The book of Proverbs is filled with wisdom, and you may be surprised by how much of that wisdom has to do with fiscal management. I want to challenge you to read and meditate on the book of Proverbs regularly and see its positive impact on how you manage your resources.

For example, Proverbs 28:19 says, "Those who work their land will have abundant food, but those who chase fantasies will have their fill of poverty." Get-rich-quick schemes never work, and they run the risk of driving you into debt.

Meanwhile, hard work brings abundance. Proverbs 12:11 echoes the previous verse by affirming, "Those who *work their land* will have abundant food." It's wise to work hard. After all, the first thing God ever gave to Adam in the garden of Eden was a job.

Yes, we have to work for our resources. Most of us aren't going to come into a great fortune overnight, such as by winning the lottery or finding ourselves the unsuspecting benefactors of a deceased loved one. Yet the toil and tears we put into earning our paychecks somehow make them more of a reward. God wants us to give our best effort toward earning a living and to work industriously in all that we do with hearts of gratitude for our ability to earn wealth.

VERSES TO DEEPEN YOUR JOY

GENESIS 3:19; COLOSSIANS 3:23–24

Go share the joy today!

Hard Work

All hard work brings a profit,
but mere talk leads only to poverty.

PROVERBS 14:23

Even if you don't immediately see the benefit of your hard work or obtain prosperity, it's a biblical principle that *all* hard work is profitable. It may be that the profit of your hard work is not entirely monetary but more along the lines of character development or a rewarding sense of satisfaction from a job well done.

I grew up on a farm, where my dad raised us kids to be hard workers. Young people today seem largely to lack the work ethic we learned. Unfortunately, many people today don't know how to work hard at physical labor and then don't get to see the rewards of such efforts. The truth is that those who prosper have diligent, hardworking hands coupled with a heart of obedience.

When it comes to accumulating wealth, serious self-discipline is required, especially if you're starting out on a shoestring budget. Establishing a budget and sticking to it is a key to getting out of debt and staying that way, but a budget isn't any good if you aren't disciplined enough to stick to it. This is another type of hard work we often overlook.

Pray that the Lord will show you any areas of your finances where a stricter budget might be helpful. And commit your labors to him, knowing that he is ultimately the one you are working for.

VERSES TO DEEPEN YOUR JOY

PROVERBS 13:22; ROMANS 13:8

Go share the joy today!

Biblical Budgeting

Go to the ant…; consider its ways and be wise!
It has no commander, no overseer or ruler,
yet it stores its provisions in summer and gathers its food at harvest.
PROVERBS 6:6–8

A lot of people view *budget* as a bad word. But a budget doesn't prohibit you from purchasing anything for the purpose of enjoyment. It only helps you bring your flesh under the control of your spirit and discern when to spend and when to save. The practice of budgeting can be liberating and life-giving because it releases you from being in bondage to debt.

A lack of discipline can prove deadly according to Proverbs 5:23: "For lack of discipline they will die, led astray by their own great folly." Discipline is an important practice that affects countless areas of our lives. Budgeting is a form of discipline that may hurt the flesh for a season, but it always brings great rewards in return.

Taking on debt and letting it go unpaid are quick ways of reaping a harvest you haven't earned. And this is a dangerous method. The Word tells us to "owe no one anything except to love one another" (Romans 13:8 NKJV). I'm not sharing this verse in a spirit of condemnation but as an offering of wisdom. Embrace budgeting, live within your means, and reap the rewards.

VERSES TO DEEPEN YOUR JOY

PSALM 31:19; PROVERBS 13:22

Go share the joy today!

Deeper Than the Wallet

God is able to make all grace overflow to you, so that, always having all sufficiency in everything, you may have an abundance for every good deed.

2 Corinthians 9:8 NASB

I was preparing to preach at a miracle service when the Lord spoke to me. He said the people coming that evening believed they needed a breakthrough in their finances alone but that they really needed a breakthrough in their minds, in their faith, and in their flesh.

At the start of the service, I asked for a show of hands from those who needed a breakthrough in their finances. Almost every person raised a hand. I went on to share Scripture passages to prove that their finances weren't the real problem, according to the Lord. I helped them understand that some of them needed a breakthrough in their minds because they were filled with the fear that their needs would not be met. Others needed a breakthrough in their faith because they really didn't believe God would supply their needs. And others needed a breakthrough in their flesh because their financial problems were rooted in excessive spending driven by fleshly desires.

That night, the Holy Spirit put his finger on the root of the real problem in each person's life. The Word says that the truth will set you free (John 8:32). People were set free when they learned the truth about their situations. It isn't enough to treat the symptoms. We need to address the root of the problem, which may or may not be the state of our bank accounts or the size of our wallets.

VERSES TO DEEPEN YOUR JOY

Isaiah 55:1–2; 1 Timothy 6:9, 11–12

Go share the joy today!

Defeat Financial Fear

"Do not fear, little flock, for it is your Father's good pleasure to give you the kingdom."

LUKE 12:32 NKJV

The topic of finances awakens a spirit of fear in many people. For some, financial fear started way back in childhood during times of financial hardship. A sense of security—the confidence that all their needs will be met—is extremely important for children, who are influenced significantly by their parents' attitudes. When they grow up without the confidence that their basic needs will be met, they may develop a sense of insecurity that can open the door to the spirit of fear.

The Lord once showed me that I was filled with fears that were deeply rooted in my childhood. He said, *If you are going to fulfill the call I have on your life, you must doubt your doubts and face your fears.* I was filled with so much doubt—doubt that I could continue to minister as a divorced single mom with a newborn daughter, doubt that we could make it financially. And those were just a couple of my doubts.

He then reminded me that the devil is a liar and the Father of Lies (John 8:44). Therefore, everything he had been telling me was the opposite of the truth. The Lord said again, Y*ou need to doubt those doubts.* Whenever a doubt would come into my mind, I would simply say out loud, "I doubt that! I know God is going to provide." Or "I doubt that. I know God is going to fulfill his call on my life." It worked. Faith began to grow in my heart, and the doubts slowly faded.

VERSES TO DEEPEN YOUR JOY

PROVERBS 18:21; 2 TIMOTHY 1:7

Go share the joy today!

Peace in His Promises

He who did not spare his own Son, but gave him up for us all—how will he not also, along with him, freely give us all things?

ROMANS 8:32 NET

After I learned to doubt my doubts, I had to face my fears, starting with the fear that my needs would go unmet. While I was growing up, my mother struggled to provide for my brothers and me. She was very open about our family's financial woes, and I grew up worrying a lot about money. We also did not yet know God or trust him as our Provider.

Then, one day, many years later, when I knew the Lord and was having to trust him to provide for my daughter and me, I began to pray about our financial situation. I was shocked when the Lord responded, *It's nothing for me to take care of your little girl, your little house, and your little self.* It was reassuring to know that it was nothing for my great big God—the God of the universe—to provide for us.

The years that followed were exciting as I witnessed firsthand my Father's miraculous provision and began to conquer my fear of going hungry. Of course, the adventure was exciting instead of overwhelming only because of my daily decision to walk in faith. We have the choice, you know! Choose the peace that Jesus alone can offer—the peace that prevents our hearts from being troubled and afraid.

How about you? Are you allowing your heart to fill with worry and fear, or are you enjoying the Father's promised peace and provision?

VERSES TO DEEPEN YOUR JOY

JOHN 14:27; PHILIPPIANS 4:6

Go share the joy today!

Faith over Fear

"'Do not fear [anything], for I am with you; do not be afraid, for I am your God. I will strengthen you, be assured I will help you; I will certainly take hold of you with My righteous right hand [a hand of justice, of power, of victory, of salvation].'"

ISAIAH 41:10 AMP

We have no need to fear, whether regarding our finances or any other area. Never forget that fear and discouragement don't come from the Lord. They are some of Satan's favorite schemes to use against us, but they never come from our heavenly Father.

"God has not given us a spirit of fear, but of power and of love and of a sound mind" (2 Timothy 1:7 NKJV). If God is never the source of your fear, then you know that the Enemy is the one who has brought it upon you. Satan will try to cripple you with fear—fear of rejection, fear of failure, fear of other people, fear of loss, fear of the unknown. Yet God has given you all power and authority in the name of Jesus.

Jesus told his followers, and he tells us today, "I give you the authority to trample on serpents and scorpions, and over all the power of the enemy, and nothing shall by any means hurt you" (Luke 10:19 NKJV). Don't relinquish your power by succumbing to a spirit of fear. Resist the devil's deceptions and never forget the power that is yours in Christ Jesus.

VERSES TO DEEPEN YOUR JOY

PSALM 27:1–5; JOHN 14:12

Go share the joy today!

Affirm the Lord's Ability

God…is able, through his mighty power at work within us, to accomplish infinitely more than we might ask or think.

Ephesians 3:20 NLT

When I was in college, a lot of my fellow students would go out for dinner during the week at decent local restaurants, and on the weekends, they would travel to other cities—often out of state—to attend Christian conferences. My experience was a lot different. When I was growing up, we rarely went out to dinner. We might have stopped at McDonald's a time or two, but I have no childhood memories of restaurant meals. Our family budget didn't allow for restaurant dining; plus, we lived on a farm and raised a lot of our own food, so we mostly cooked at home.

One day, some of my college friends announced that they were going to Tulsa, Oklahoma, for a conference. I immediately said, "I'll never have the money to do that." Right after I spoke those words, the Holy Spirit said something in my spirit that really shook me: *You never will have the money if you keep saying you won't.*

That was the first time I truly realized the power of spoken words, and the experience totally changed the way that I spoke from that day forward. I started saying things like, *Lord, I thank you for giving me enough money to do everything that you want me to do and to go everywhere you want me to go.* Not long after that, I had enough money to travel to Christian concerts in Tulsa and elsewhere. Don't speak doubt but make positive confessions about God's perfect ability to provide for you.

VERSES TO DEEPEN YOUR JOY

Matthew 6:25–34; Philippians 4:19

Go share the joy today!

Raise Your Voice

When [Bartimaeus] heard that it was Jesus of Nazareth, he began to shout, "Jesus, Son of David, have mercy on me!" Many rebuked him and told him to be quiet, but he shouted all the more, "Son of David, have mercy on me!"

MARK 10:47–48

Even if the situation looks bleak and even if everyone around you is telling you to give up faith and quit pestering God, you need to hang on in hope and keep raising your voice to the Lord. That's what Bartimaeus, who was blind, did. He refused to stop crying out to God in faith for a miracle despite the efforts of those around him to silence him.

All his shouting paid off. Because Bartimaeus refused to stay silent, Jesus stopped and asked him what he wanted. When Bartimaeus simply stated that he wanted to see, Jesus told him, "Go…Your faith has healed you" (v. 52).

Notice what Bartimaeus did next. "Immediately he received his sight and *followed Jesus* along the road" (v. 52). Now that he could see, this formerly blind man could travel with the Lord. And that's what he did, out of a heart of gratitude.

Nothing will be impossible for us if we use our faith. The key is to put it to use—to exercise it by believing God will fulfill his promises to us—whether that means shouting pleas for healing or picking a name for our unborn child. Having faith means acting before and after receiving what we trust God to give us.

VERSES TO DEEPEN YOUR JOY

RUTH 1:16–17; LUKE 18:7–8

Go share the joy today!

Shout the Doubt Out

The LORD said to Joshua, "I have given you Jericho, its king, and all its strong warriors...When you hear the priests give one long blast on the rams' horns, have all the people shout as loud as they can. Then the walls of the town will collapse, and the people can charge straight into the town."

JOSHUA 6:2, 5 NLT

Once the Israelites had obeyed God's initial instructions regarding Jericho, all it took was a shout to send those city walls crumbling down. And it's often the case that we have to shout out the doubt to press our way into the miraculous. Then we "charge straight" and take the land that God has given us. Doubt and fear form a wall that we must dismantle with our words if we expect to possess God's miracles.

Maybe you doubt you'll ever experience financial freedom. Go ahead and shout those walls of doubt right down! When my daughter was an infant, many days I didn't know how I would make ends meet. God often prompted me to shout. I would walk around my little house, shouting praise and glory to God and proclaiming at the top of my lungs that he would supply all my needs. That kind of shouting kindles joy in your spirit, just as it did for Joshua.

Walk in obedience to the voice of the Lord and shout those walls of debt right down. Never doubt God's ability to eliminate your debt and take care of you financially.

VERSES TO DEEPEN YOUR JOY

MARK 11:23–24; 2 CORINTHIANS 3:4–6

Go share the joy today!

Perception Precedes Possession

The Lord *said to Abram, "Look as far as you can see in every direction—north and south, east and west. I am giving all this land, as far as you can see, to you and your descendants as a permanent possession."*

Genesis 13:14–15 NLT

God told Abram that he would give him whatever Abram could see. Abram had to see it before he could possess it, and the same is true for us. If we can't see ourselves living in a season of abundance, we will probably never make it to the land of more than enough. But if we can see it, God will give it to us because he desires to shower us with abundant blessings.

Perception precedes possession. What you see is what you get. If you accept your current season as your destination, it probably will be. Unless you can envision in your mind's eye the next place God is calling you to, you won't reach it.

If you can't see yourself out of poverty, chances are you will remain impoverished. If you can't see yourself free from debt, chances are you never will be. Unless you put on your "spiritual eyes" and see yourself healed and whole, you will remain sick and broken. We must see it, reach for it, and then possess God's promises for every realm of our lives.

VERSES TO DEEPEN YOUR JOY

Romans 15:13; Colossians 1:23

Go share the joy today!

Envision with Eyes of Faith

When your faith is tested, your endurance has a chance to grow.

JAMES 1:3 NLT

Nothing tests your ability to see with eyes of faith quite like seasons of financial hardship. During my season of extreme lack as a single mom, I had to envision myself having arrived in a new season long before I reached it. Even though I had to daily believe God for each diaper and jar of baby food, I was determined that my faith would change the facts and transform my financial situation.

The Lord kept telling me that I needed to see myself in a place of abundance. When you've been living on corn dogs and canned tuna for eighteen months, seeing the pathway out of the wilderness and into the promised land is a little challenging. But that's where my obedience came into play. The Lord put it on my heart to go to the nicest mall in our community to window-shop. I would walk around the mall, saying, *Thank you, Lord, that the day is coming when I will be able to come to this mall and buy anything I want.* At the time, it sounded crazy. I didn't have more than twenty dollars to get us to the end of the month. But I needed to see myself, through faith, in a place of blessing. The atmosphere of the mall gave me a different picture from my surroundings at home, where the cupboards were bare and I even had to ration the toilet paper.

Exercise your imagination today and "see" with your mind's eye what God has in store.

VERSES TO DEEPEN YOUR JOY

MATTHEW 17:20–21; HEBREWS 11:1

Go share the joy today!

Love That Can't Be Lost

I am convinced that neither death nor life, neither angels nor demons, neither the present nor the future, nor any powers, neither height nor depth, nor anything else in all creation, will be able to separate us from the love of God that is in Christ Jesus our Lord.

ROMANS 8:38–39

According to 2 Timothy 1:7, not only has God given you power, but he has also given you love and "a sound mind" (NKJV). And his love is so strong that nothing can separate you from it. Your mind can remain sound when you rest in God's unchanging, unfailing love.

The Enemy likes to mess with your God-given need to give and receive love, perverting its forms and planting seeds of strife in your relationships. Yet you were created to love and be loved because you were designed in the image of God and "God is love" (1 John 4:8, 16). When you are bound up in fear, the Enemy isolates you behind an emotional wall so that your need for love goes unmet. It's like a car without gas or any other energy source; it doesn't get very far.

Never forget your heavenly Father loves you and remember the sound mind that makes it possible for you to maintain your joy. He who lives in you is greater than the Enemy of your soul, and by God's power, you can overcome fear with faith, receive a love that can't be lost, and rejoice in the resulting soundness of your mind.

VERSES TO DEEPEN YOUR JOY

PSALM 136:26; 1 JOHN 4:4

Go share the joy today!

Expose the Enemy's Lies

Whatever is true, whatever is noble, whatever is right, whatever is pure, whatever is lovely, whatever is admirable—if anything is excellent or praiseworthy—think about such things.

PHILIPPIANS 4:8

Not only has God given us power and love that are stronger than fear, but he has also made provision for each of us to have a sound mind. Of course, the devil would prefer it if the sound of his lies echoed through your mind daily—lies like *Nobody loves you. You're all alone. You're different. You don't have any friends*, and so on. But your heavenly Father has given you a mind capable of standing on his truth about yourself and your situation. By filling your mind daily with God's Word, you won't leave any room for the devil's lies.

A sound mind is not plagued with thoughts of fear because it meditates on things above, not on things below. In other words, it meditates on the truth rather than on the Enemy's deceptions. Don't be deceived into thinking that your problems are outside the scope of God's control. Even if your troubles are outside your control and beyond hope in the natural realm, nothing is too hard for God to handle.

Our greatest battles always begin in our minds. As we renew our minds daily to the truth of God's Word, we can maintain a sound mind amid every challenge life throws our way, whether the challenge is in our finances, our health, our relationships, or another realm.

VERSES TO DEEPEN YOUR JOY

MATTHEW 19:26; COLOSSIANS 3:2

Go share the joy today!

Never Alone

"The LORD himself goes before you and will be with you; he will never leave you nor forsake you."

DEUTERONOMY 31:8

One of the Enemy's favorite lies to get believers to fall for is that they're alone. You may be surrounded by people and still feel all alone if the Enemy has managed to convince you to buy his lies and build an emotional wall around yourself. But when you recognize the impression of isolation as a deceptive lie from the pit of hell, you can combat it with the Word of Truth.

When you are God's child, he is always with you, ready to direct, sustain, encourage, and help in whatever way you need. That's the very reason the Enemy tries to discourage you—to cause you to feel all alone, outnumbered, and defeated. Satan knows you aren't alone. He's fully aware that the God of the universe is on your side, and his only hope is to intimidate you to the point where you throw in the towel and admit that you're alone and defeated. If he can convince you that you're alone, he might just get you to give up.

But there's no way he can win if you refuse to give in to his schemes. God has created you to have fellowship with him first and then with other believers. It isn't good for anyone to go it alone, as we saw in the garden of Eden. As Christian believers, we have to be diligent about getting together and spurring each other on in the faith. That way we'll have a constant reminder that we're never really alone.

VERSES TO DEEPEN YOUR JOY

GENESIS 2:18; HEBREWS 10:25

Go share the joy today!

The Battle for Health

"I am the LORD who heals you."

EXODUS 15:26 AMP

Maybe today you're in a fight for your very life. Battling illness, disease, and chronic health conditions can be spiritually oppressive, physically draining, and emotionally overwhelming if you don't maintain the mind of Christ by meditating on the Word of God.

Several years ago, following my annual mammogram, I was asked to return to the hospital for some additional tests. A spirit of fear seized me for a moment, but I quickly recognized it as a scheme of the Enemy and determined to stand against it. When I returned for the extra tests, I spent most of the day at the hospital. As time went on, I became increasingly nervous, especially as I lay on the table with doctors hovering over me, discussing my test results. My doctor ordered an ultrasound of my lymphoid area, which confirmed the presence of a knot. During this test of faith, God enabled me to experience the solitary, lonesome feeling of those who are waiting in desperation for a miracle.

But we are never alone, even during our battle for health. The Enemy will do whatever he can to get us to think things are worse than they really are. He's good at painting pictures of doom and gloom as he tries to get us to give up hope. Yet our God can handle any trick the Enemy throws our way. If he chooses, God can also heal any disease and restore any injured body part to full function. Don't let the Enemy convince you otherwise.

VERSES TO DEEPEN YOUR JOY

PSALM 41:3; ISAIAH 57:18–19

Go share the joy today!

The Cure for Every Condition

He Himself brought our sins in His body up on the cross, so that we might die to sin and live for righteousness; by His wounds you were healed.

1 Peter 2:24 NASB

If you need a total turnaround in your health, you're in good company. Millions of people today are searching for physical healing or improved health. I want to challenge you not to accept the status quo. Stop agreeing with the report of people and receive instead the report of the Lord.

I have experienced the overwhelming fear and frustration of negative reports from doctors or other medical professionals. I also know the overwhelming joy and humility that result from witnessing a miracle from the hand of the Lord—and especially from receiving one in my own body. Take heart. What the Lord has done for me, he can do for you, for he is "no respecter of persons" (Acts 10:34 KJV). His favor is for all of us, and the healing power of Jesus can cure every illness.

One day, I was praying that the Lord would reveal the cure for cancer. The Lord immediately answered, *I already have revealed the cure for cancer—I AM!* For years, I had known that the Lord is the healer, the great physician, the answer for everything. Yet the fresh revelation I received that day really shook me. The Lord has the power to cure all cancer and sickness and disease. Even though we don't always see complete physical healing in this life, there is no problem he can't solve, no sickness he can't heal. And he is ready to intervene on your behalf today.

VERSES TO DEEPEN YOUR JOY

Psalm 6:2; Malachi 4:2

Go share the joy today!

Curses Reversed

The Lord your God…turned the curse into a blessing for you, because the Lord your God loves you.

Deuteronomy 23:5

The Enemy will try to hire people, situations, and circumstances to pronounce a curse on you. But God is the God of total turnaround. The Lord, who loves us, can flip 180 degrees any evil scheme or ill-meaning attempt, as the book of Deuteronomy tells us.

King Balak hired a man named Balaam to pronounce a curse on God's people, but God turned the attempted curse into a blessing out of his love for his people. "They did not come to meet you with bread and water on your way when you came out of Egypt, and they hired Balaam son of Beor from Pethor in Aram Naharaim to pronounce a curse on you. However, the Lord your God would not listen to Balaam but turned the curse into a blessing for you, because the Lord your God loves you" (vv. 4–5).

God turned around the curse that Balaam tried to bring, and God can turn around any curse of sickness that the Enemy tries to bring you. God can take Satan's attempts to curse you and turn them into huge blessings for your life—all because of his great love for you! Yes, God can and will use for your good what Satan means for evil.

VERSES TO DEEPEN YOUR JOY

Genesis 50:20; Zephaniah 3:9

Go share the joy today!

Protected from Plague

Surely he will save you from the fowler's snare
and from the deadly pestilence.
PSALM 91:3

The love of God and his hand of protection on his children continually amaze me. Take the Israelites, for example. Every time God brought a plague to Egypt while the Israelites were in bondage there, his children were untouched.

The Lord told Moses exactly what he ought to say to Pharaoh every time God sent a different plague. God followed up that demand with an explanation of the particular plague that would befall the Egyptians if Pharaoh did not listen.

In one instance, before sending the plague of flies, the Lord said to Pharaoh through Moses, "On that day I will deal differently with the land…where my people live; no swarms of flies will be there, so that you will know that I, the LORD, am in this land. I will make a distinction between my people and your people" (Exodus 8:22–23). God always makes a distinction between his people and the people of the world.

Maybe you need a turnaround today in your finances or your health. Believe that God is at work in this situation. Yes, the people of God sometimes suffer but never without purpose. God can save us from any harm that befalls us.

VERSES TO DEEPEN YOUR JOY

PSALM 91:5–8; JEREMIAH 17:14

Go share the joy today!

Believe the Right Report

Don't put your trust in mere humans.
They are as frail as breath. What good are they?
ISAIAH 2:22 NLT

The world is filled with noisy voices, so it's difficult to know what to believe about our circumstances. But when you have a relationship with the Lord and cultivate a powerful prayer life, you have union and communion with the Holy Spirit. It's this relationship of intimacy that allows you to hear the prophetic voice of the Lord regularly. That is, we can hear and understand what God is saying to us today. Then if we receive a negative report from people—be it regarding our health or another aspect of our lives—we may discern in our spirit what God's report says and believe him.

One way we foster a relationship with God is by reading his Word. But if someone teaches or studies his Word without having a prophetic ear to hear what the Lord is saying today, even that discipline can be flat and lack anointing. You don't teach from the Bible like you would instruct students enrolled in a math class. You don't study the Bible like a textbook. God's Word speaks to us today.

The Lord's report will always align with his written Word, the Bible, which tells you that the price for your salvation was paid more than two thousand years ago by the Son of God, Jesus Christ, "by whose stripes you *were healed*" (1 Peter 2:24 NKJV). Notice the use of the past tense in this verse. Your spiritual healing has already been taken care of! All you must do today is simply receive your healing by faith. And faith comes by hearing the Word (Romans 10:17).

VERSES TO DEEPEN YOUR JOY

ISAIAH 55:9; ROMANS 4:17

Go share the joy today!

Build Faith for Healing

"'I will restore health to you and I will heal your wounds,' says the Lord."

Jeremiah 30:17 AMP

God wants to build your faith, but you need to take an active role in the process. Faith comes by hearing the Word of God (Romans 10:17) while doubt comes by hearing the word of the Enemy. You must choose to hear the Word of the Lord.

The tougher your battle, the more of the Word you need. You need to be meditating on the Word minute by minute to stand in faith through every minute of your life. Always remember that the battle is not yours but the Lord's—even if you're battling for your life moment by moment!

What have you been declaring about your health? Even when the doctors declare sickness and disease over us, we must get in agreement with God and declare what he declares. The Word doesn't deny that we will experience sickness and other physical challenges. But it does declare that God can restore us to health and heal our wounds. Sometimes this restoration comes on earth, and other times it takes place in heaven.

We see in today's verse from Jeremiah that God himself declares health and healing over us. Let's make sure we echo the declarations of God over our own situations. Build your faith by reading God's Word and letting it seep into your soul. The spiritual healing will be immediate.

VERSES TO DEEPEN YOUR JOY

Luke 17:5; 2 Corinthians 5:7

Go share the joy today!

Forget Not His Benefits

Bless the Lord, O my soul, and forget not all His benefits:
who forgives all your iniquities, who heals all your diseases,
who redeems your life from destruction.

Psalm 103:2–4 NKJV

We need to be in agreement with God and praise him in all situations. If we aren't careful, we can begin to find fault with God. I like the way the *Amplified Bible, Classic Edition* translates Philippians 2:14: "Do all things without grumbling and faultfinding and complaining [against God] and questioning and doubting [among yourselves]." We should praise God for all that he has already done, for this practice helps us cultivate hearts of gratitude. Thinking only of what we wish he would do fosters a spirit of anger, bitterness, and self-pity.

If we dwell in the Lord's presence, we can dwell on the fact that he will take care of everything. As Psalm 91:1 assures us, "He who dwells in the shelter of the Most High will abide in the shadow of the Almighty" (ESV). If we stop dwelling in his presence, we may begin to question God in a way that brings about anger at God and resentment in our hearts—and that's the last thing we need.

When we are dwelling in the Lord, we can rest on our knowledge of what is true about him. Through our words and thoughts, we can internalize our belief that the Lord is taking care of us and protecting us. Then we can confidently say, like the psalmist, "He is my refuge and my fortress" (v. 2 ESV).

VERSES TO DEEPEN YOUR JOY

Psalm 91:3–16; 1 Thessalonians 5:18

Go share the joy today!

Hang On to Hope

Hope does not disappoint, because the love of God has been poured out in our hearts by the Holy Spirit who was given to us.

ROMANS 5:5 NKJV

You have the power to stand and the power to persevere as long as you have hope. Get a strong grip on God's rope of hope—his Word—and don't allow anything to loosen your grip.

The devil comes to steal, kill, destroy, and otherwise wreak havoc in your life (John 10:10). If he manages to steal your hope, sending you negative diagnoses and dire medical reports, you may be tempted to give up believing for your miracle. You'll likely be robbed of joy and peace. Don't let the devil steal your hope!

If the devil can't manage to steal your hope, he'll try to get you to stake your hope on something other than God—something that will let you down. Don't fall for this tactic either. Instead, hope in the only one who will never let you down. "Put your hope in the LORD, for with the LORD is unfailing love and with him is full redemption" (Psalm 130:7). Don't merely hope in God; let him be your hope: "You are my hope, O Lord GOD; You are my trust from my youth" (71:5 NKJV).

When your hope is the Lord, you will be filled with joy and peace to the point of overflowing. "May the God of hope fill you with all joy and peace in believing, that you may abound in hope by the power of the Holy Spirit" (Romans 15:13 NKJV).

VERSES TO DEEPEN YOUR JOY

ISAIAH 45:17; ROMANS 9:33

Go share the joy today!

Inexhaustible Strength

Those who hope in the LORD will renew their strength.
They will soar on wings like eagles;
they will run and not grow weary, they will walk and not be faint.

ISAIAH 40:31

Hope in God trumps the facts of any situation. In the person of Abraham, we see a great example of someone who knew this, someone who, "against all hope,...believed and so became the father of many nations, just as it had been said to him, 'So shall your offspring be'" (Romans 4:18). Even though he and his wife were "as good as dead" (v. 19)—meaning both he and his wife were well beyond their childbearing years—Abraham believed that God would fulfill his promise. And the Lord did, all because Abraham hung on to hope without giving up.

The truth of God always trumps the facts—and so does our hope when we're hoping in God and his Word. The fact of his age didn't cause Abraham's faith to weaken or his hope to dwindle. Don't let your faith or hope diminish in the face of the facts either. Like Abraham, be "fully persuaded" (v. 21) that God has the power to do what he has promised no matter what the facts may suggest.

Allow the power of the Holy Spirit to overflow your hope into the lives of those around you. Share your rope of hope with them. That rope has limitless length, so go ahead and throw them a lifeline.

VERSES TO DEEPEN YOUR JOY

PSALM 119:114; ROMANS 4:20

Go share the joy today!

Alive Again

God told [Abraham], "I have made you the father of many nations." This happened because Abraham believed in the God who brings the dead back to life and who creates new things out of nothing.

Romans 4:17 NLT

At a miracle service, I witnessed a lady who had been diagnosed with breast cancer receive a creative miracle. She had had one breast surgically removed to prevent the spread of cancer, but during that service, the Lord supernaturally grew her a new one! At other services, I have seen the Lord cause legs to grow out that were inches shorter than the other leg. I have seen people who could not walk jump out of wheelchairs as the power of God hit them. God can turn any situation around.

No matter how "dead" your situation looks, God can breathe his prophetic voice into it so that new life comes forth. He is the God who "brings the dead back to life and who creates new things out of nothing." God is the God who gives life. He is all-powerful. He can call something healed, healthy, and whole even when it's dead. All healing comes in his presence, whether on this side of heaven or the other.

We can also be Jesus' hands of healing. Jesus said to his disciples, "Truly, truly I say to you, the one who believes in Me, the works that I do, he will do also; and greater works than these he will do; because I am going to the Father" (John 14:12 NASB). We are supposed to be doing even greater works than the Lord did, including in the realm of healing.

VERSES TO DEEPEN YOUR JOY

Psalm 30:2; Mark 16:17–18

Go share the joy today!

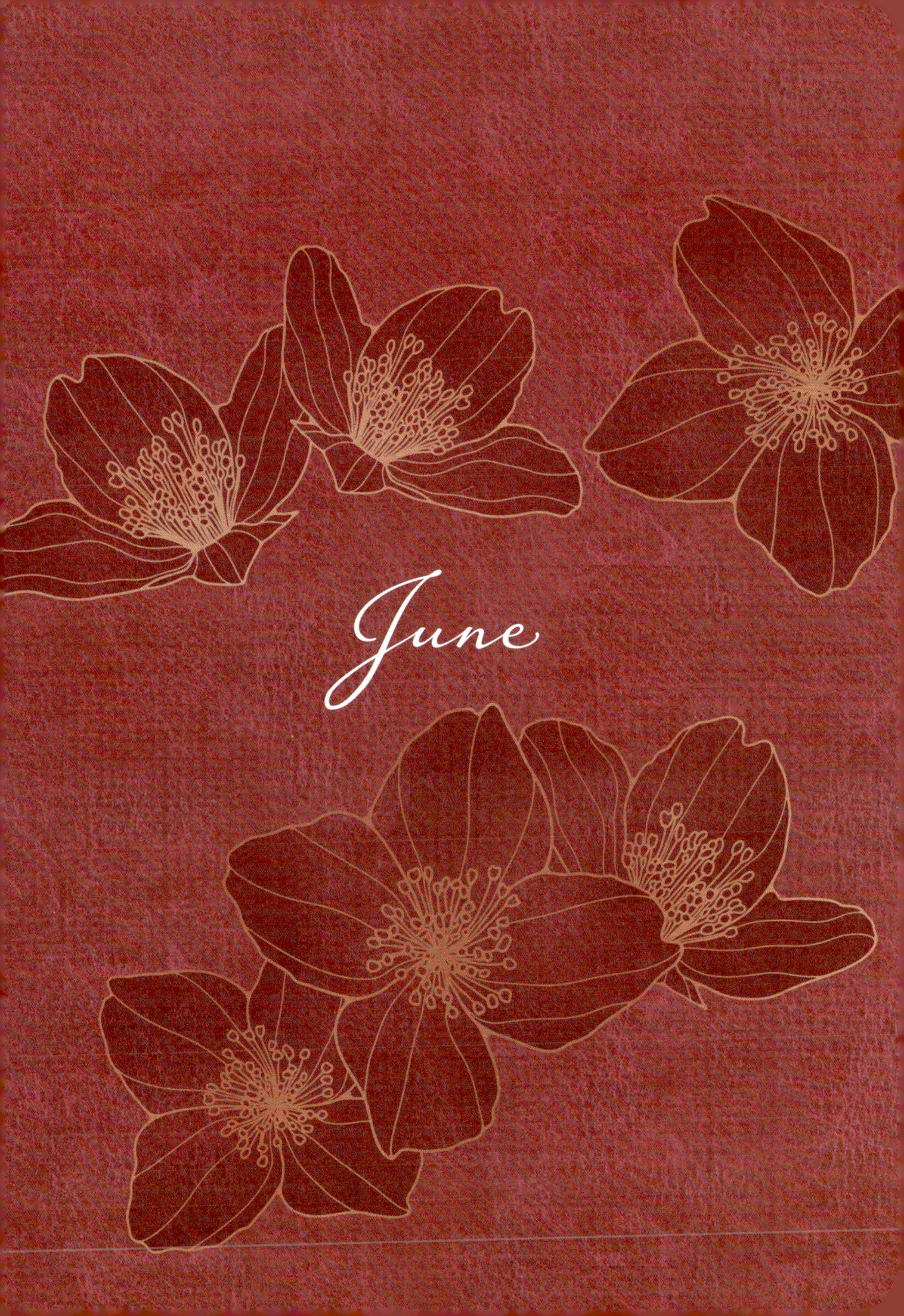
June

Breathe on Dry Bones

"Prophesy to these bones and say to them, 'Dry bones, hear the word of the LORD! This is what the Sovereign LORD says to these bones: I will make breath enter you, and you will come to life.'"

EZEKIEL 37:4–5

The prophetic voice of God has the power to turn any situation around. The prophet Ezekiel dramatically experienced this power. As he prophesied according to the Lord's direction to a valley filled with dry, dead bones, those bones "came to life and stood up on their feet—a vast army" (v. 10). The bones weren't just dying; they were as dead as they could get. Yet God turned things around through the power of his prophetic word by breathing life into the dry bones.

Jesus did the same thing as he ministered to people during his earthly life. He "went throughout Galilee, teaching in their synagogues, proclaiming the good news of the kingdom, and healing every disease and sickness among the people…People brought to him all who were ill with various diseases, those suffering severe pain, the demon-possessed, those having seizures, and the paralyzed; and he healed them" (Matthew 4:23–24).

Many Christians today have the teaching and the preaching down, but what about the miracles? Let's never forget that Jesus healed every disease and sickness. God is pouring out his Spirit, and today is the day of miracles! Jesus is the same yesterday, today, and forever. Jesus healed people in the Bible, and he still heals people today. We simply need to receive his healing.

VERSES TO DEEPEN YOUR JOY

EZEKIEL 37:6–9; HEBREWS 13:8

Go share the joy today!

Faith Changes the Facts

It is impossible to please God without faith.
Anyone who wants to come to him must believe that God exists
and that he rewards those who sincerely seek him.

HEBREWS 11:6 NLT

Facts, such as a doctor's diagnosis, exist in the natural realm. But faith exists in the supernatural realm, and faith changes the facts. Let me repeat: your faith in the Lord's report—in his Holy Word—can change the facts. The supernatural realm is far more powerful than the natural realm. Don't deny the facts but pray over them with faith.

We shouldn't dismiss the reports of doctors altogether. Their diagnoses and expert opinions are useful in that they indicate how we ought to pray. I don't believe that we're supposed to live in a state of denial. However, if you have received a diagnosis, don't view it as an unavoidable destination; use it as an aid to formulate detailed prayers to the Lord, who heals. Be specific as you make requests and petitions to God.

It's easier to fight when you know your enemy. When you have a name for the thing that is attacking your body, you can take it to the Lord in prayer and turn the battle over to him. Denial won't get you anywhere, but neither will fear. So don't fear the doctor's diagnosis. Simply stand in faith that God has the power to turn it around.

VERSES TO DEEPEN YOUR JOY

PROVERBS 18:21; JOHN 10:27

Go share the joy today!

Receive Your Miracle Healing

Cast your burden on the LORD [release it] and He will sustain and uphold you; He will never allow the righteous to be shaken (slip, fall, fail).

PSALM 55:22 AMP

God wants to bless you with your miracle today, and receiving is the first step. Healing, like salvation, is a gift. You can't earn it. Maybe you find yourself in need of healing today. However, perhaps to be healed, you first need to believe you are worthy of God's blessing.

Some people believe that God will heal everyone else while they themselves feel unworthy of his healing touch. But it has nothing to do with merit. Know that the Lord wants you to receive his gift of healing. Don't think for a minute that God loves anyone else more than he loves you. None of us deserve anything good from the Lord, yet he showers us with the blessings of salvation, wholeness, health, and more—not because we deserve them but because he loves us so much.

His Son, Jesus, was the only one who was worthy of receiving eternal life, and he passed along that blessing to all humankind by paying the ultimate price—his very life. "He who did not spare [even] His own Son, but gave Him up for us all, how will He not also, along with Him, graciously give us all things?" (Romans 8:32 AMP). God gives generously "for us all," and that includes you.

VERSES TO DEEPEN YOUR JOY

PSALM 73:26; JAMES 1:17

Go share the joy today!

Worship While You Wait

The Pharisees went out and conspired against Him, discussing how they could destroy Him. Being aware of this, Jesus left there. Many followed Him, and He healed all of them [who were sick].

MATTHEW 12:14–15 AMP

Jesus healed *all* the sick. He didn't pick favorites. God wants to heal everyone, and physical healing was a major part of Jesus' earthly ministry. Even when the Pharisees were trying to kill Jesus, he continued reaching out and healing others.

Today's Scripture passage indicates that we should follow Jesus' example by keeping our eyes off ourselves and on the Lord. I have learned that one key to healing is taking every opportunity to pray for others to receive their miracle.

We can also practice the habit of praise, dwelling on the good and minimizing the bad. Have you ever noticed how fast bad news spreads? But when Jesus was traveling around healing people, the news also traveled fast: "News about Him spread throughout all Syria" (Matthew 4:24 AMP). Don't be overwhelmed or discouraged about the quick spread of bad news but spread the good news in every moment.

Throughout your life, you will hear many medical reports—some positive and others discouraging. Shout joyfully and worship God at every good report! Spread news of every victory along the way. Even if you are in the middle of a health crisis, don't hold back from celebrating a good report just because you aren't totally out of the woods yet. Praising God with every step deepens your faith and gives you strength.

VERSES TO DEEPEN YOUR JOY

PSALM 150; JAMES 5:13

Go share the joy today!

Physicians as God's Hands and Feet

"It is not the healthy who need a doctor, but the sick."

MATTHEW 9:12

Jesus himself never dismissed the profession of physicians. He acknowledged their purpose in helping the sick, as we see in today's verse. And Luke, who wrote the book of Acts and the gospel named after him, was himself a doctor (Colossians 4:14). The truth is that God often works miracles through medical professionals. The idea is for doctors and specialists to serve as the Lord's hands and feet.

My prayer is the same for all doctors across the nation: *Lord, heal the sick and grant miracles to all in need!* As you pray for others, standing in faith for their healing as you meditate on the Word of Truth, you should expect to see healings occur in their lives and in yours.

Without the prophetic voice of the Lord, things become lifeless and dead. Without his prophetic insight, you can become overwhelmed and tempted to accept a grim diagnosis with resignation. Stand up and fight in faith. The battle isn't over. When God is on your side, you are not alone or powerless no matter how many foes (or negative diagnoses) may come against you. So don't let others speak death over you. Believe in God and trust him.

Keep believing that a miracle is possible and don't limit God in how that miracle comes to pass. Let God do it his way. Sometimes our miracle can come through a doctor, and sometimes God may work in another way. Regardless, keep your focus on him and know that he is working on your behalf. My prayer is that you will find medical professionals who share your faith in healing.

VERSES TO DEEPEN YOUR JOY

LUKE 4:14–23; COLOSSIANS 4:14

Go share the joy today!

Far beyond Imagining

"My thoughts are nothing like your thoughts," says the Lord. *"And my ways are far beyond anything you could imagine. For just as the heavens are higher than the earth, so my ways are higher than your ways and my thoughts higher than your thoughts."*

Isaiah 55:8–9 NLT

One time, years ago, a cyst appeared on my daughter's face. I stood in faith, believing that she would not need surgery. I kept praying the Word over her, and I stood on God's promises for total healing. The longer I stood in faith, the bigger the cyst grew. I didn't understand it. I didn't want my baby girl to have to endure surgery. Plus, I didn't have the money for such a procedure. I just wanted God to work a miracle. I wanted to wake up one morning and see that the cyst had disappeared.

In the end, we went the route of surgery. I nearly passed out when I saw the incision on her face—and again when I saw the bill for thousands of dollars. My daughter, Destiny, had a difficult recovery, too, but today she is totally healed. I tell you all this as proof that God sometimes uses surgery to perform a miracle. He sometimes sends us along the route of medical procedures for the manifestation of our miracles.

Never feel ashamed or condemned for taking medication or undergoing a medical procedure. Just make sure you have a word from the Lord on the matter. Once you have reached a place of peace from the Lord regarding your decision, step forward in faith, trusting him to bring about a fruitful procedure.

VERSES TO DEEPEN YOUR JOY

Hosea 6:1; Matthew 8:1–4

Go share the joy today!

Trust God above All

"If we are thrown into the blazing furnace, the God we serve is able to deliver us from it, and he will deliver us…But even if he does not,…we will not serve your gods or worship the image of gold you have set up."

DANIEL 3:17–18

When I was nineteen years old, a cousin of mine was killed in a snowmobile accident. I was a new Christian at the time, and I questioned God on the matter. I couldn't understand why the Lord would allow such a tragedy. Then, one day in prayer, the Lord directed me to Proverbs 3:5–6:

> Trust in the LORD with all your heart
> and do not lean on your own understanding.
> In all your ways acknowledge Him,
> and He will make your paths straight. (NASB)

I never questioned God again—regarding that situation, at least. When we stop leaning on our own understanding and start trusting God instead, we can have peace in every storm.

When you are standing in faith for a total turnaround in your health, you don't always understand the things God does or why or how. Fortunately, you don't have to understand his ways. You simply have to trust him. When we try to figure God out, we can easily get angry, frustrated, and discouraged. We must not grumble against God or fault him for what's happening in our lives. It's not wrong to question, but it is wrong to allow our questions to cause a gap or a wedge to develop between us and the Lord.

VERSES TO DEEPEN YOUR JOY

JOB 1:21; PSALM 34:1–3

Go share the joy today!

Draw Close to the Healer

People brought all their sick to [Jesus] and begged him to let the sick just touch the edge of his cloak, and all who touched it were healed.

MATTHEW 14:35–36

The Word tells us that all who touched Jesus were healed. We must get close enough to touch the Lord. How do we do that? We touch the Lord by our faith, in our worship, and by drawing close to him through a personal relationship. We can't get close to him through other people. Yes, other believers can teach us about Jesus and show us how to get close to the Lord. But we can't hang on to other people's coattails as they touch the Lord. That isn't enough. We must develop that relationship for ourselves. We must recognize who he is: the miracle Man. The Healer. The Son of God, who took the stripes on his back for our healing.

When we recognize who Jesus really is, we then realize we don't have to beg him to heal us because healing is part of his nature. He *wants* to heal us. And he has already paid the price for our healing; we simply need to receive it and unwrap the bows and paper from this beautiful, free gift.

Doubt and unbelief prevent many people from touching the Lord. Don't let the devil's deceptions steal your hope. Reach out by faith and touch the Lord. He is passing your way today! Reach out in prayer. Reach out in worship. Reach out in faith, determined to touch him.

VERSES TO DEEPEN YOUR JOY

PSALM 145:18; JAMES 4:8

Go share the joy today!

Near Enough to Touch Him

When she heard about Jesus, she came up behind him in the crowd and touched his cloak, because she thought, "If I just touch his clothes, I will be healed." Immediately her bleeding stopped and she felt in her body that she was freed from her suffering.

MARK 5:27–29

The woman with the issue of blood in Mark 5 had suffered for twelve years. She had consulted every doctor and spent every dollar, only to become progressively worse. She was desperate for a miracle. And a state of desperation isn't always a bad place to be.

Sometimes we don't get serious about touching God until we are desperate. In her desperation, this woman was determined to touch the Lord. She had tried everything else and exhausted every other option. She pressed her way through many obstacles, distractions, and challenges just to touch the hem of Jesus' garment. And in an instant, she was healed.

You may need to press your way through the "crowd" of negative medical reports, grim prognoses, and dire outlooks. You may need to press your way past pain and fear. But if you persevere in faith, you will touch the Healer.

In most cases, healing is a progressive process. On rare occasions, it may happen instantly, as it did for this woman. Immediately her bleeding stopped, and her suffering ended. It was God, not the doctors, who received the glory from her healing. The medical professionals couldn't do a thing for her, but God came through. And he deserves the glory for your healing as well. Draw close to him and have faith.

VERSES TO DEEPEN YOUR JOY

DEUTERONOMY 4:29; MATTHEW 11:28–30

Go share the joy today!

Faithful Father

He Himself has said, "I will never leave you nor forsake you." So we may boldly say: "The LORD is my helper; I will not fear. What can man do to me?"

HEBREWS 13:5–6 NKJV

It's wonderful to have friends. It's good and necessary to engage in fellowship with other believers. But the only one who can be with us always is God. He is the only one we can confidently say will never leave us nor forsake us.

When Jesus was preparing to ascend into heaven following his resurrection, he told his disciples that he was going to be with the Father and that he would send them the Comforter—the Holy Spirit—so his presence would always be with them (John 14). The Holy Spirit is omnipresent, meaning he can be with everyone everywhere, all at the same time. He is the power of God, fulfilling the will of the Father on earth, and he is with you today as you're reading this book. He goes with you into battle, whatever the struggle may be that you're facing.

We should never be in a rush when we spend focused time with the Lord. Let's not take his presence for granted but bask in it and be saturated by it. Most of us consent to sit in the waiting room at the doctor's office for what seems like hours, yet we aren't willing to wait in God's presence for more than a few minutes. Be patient as you fellowship with the Father who never forsakes you and remember that he is right by your side, ready to help you in whatever battle you're facing.

VERSES TO DEEPEN YOUR JOY

PSALM 27:14; LAMENTATIONS 3:25–26

Go share the joy today!

Speak the Word

"This Book of the Law shall not depart from your mouth."

JOSHUA 1:8 NKJV

Father God has given us instructions in his Word for overcoming fear and finding success. It's up to us to carry out those instructions with fidelity and faith.

He has clearly told us how to be prosperous and successful—by speaking his Word, a process that internalizes his truths into our hearts and helps us preserve a sound mind. We are not to let his Word depart from our mouths, meaning that we shouldn't get lazy and let the Enemy fill our minds with his garbage. No one can choose for you. You must decide for yourself that you will speak the Word daily and that you will meditate on it so that your words will reflect what God has said and recorded in his Word.

Remember the power that God has given you? A lot of that power is right under your nose—on your tongue! "Death and life are in the power of the tongue" (Proverbs 18:21 NKJV). With your words, you speak either life or death to your faith, your emotions, and your outcomes. Start speaking the Word over yourself and your circumstances. Speak the Word over the people around you. Deny what the devil says and affirm what the Lord has spoken, and faith will arise in your spirit.

VERSES TO DEEPEN YOUR JOY

PROVERBS 17:4; JAMES 4:7

Go share the joy today!

Do the Word

"Meditate on it day and night, so that you may be careful to do everything written in it. Then you will be prosperous and successful."

JOSHUA 1:8

Not only are we supposed to speak the Word daily, but we are also to meditate on it day and night so that we may do what is written in the Word—in other words, live according to what it says. One thing that helps me to meditate on the Word is to print out verses and put them in various places in my home. I have Scripture passages hanging throughout my bedroom, in my office, and on my bathroom mirror. When I surround myself with the Word, I can focus on what God says throughout my day.

It is similar to following a recipe to prepare a special dish. You'd better review the instructions thoroughly before getting started to ensure you have all the necessary ingredients and kitchen tools on hand. In the same way, if you're preparing to live by the Word, you'd better get closely acquainted with what it says so you'll know what's expected of you.

When you regularly speak the Word, think the Word, and do the Word, fear and discouragement will depart from you. Your greatest battles always begin and end in your mind. As you renew your mind daily by the truth of God's Word, you can maintain a sound spirit, a firm faith, and an unshakable confidence despite every obstacle you encounter.

VERSES TO DEEPEN YOUR JOY

JEREMIAH 31:34; HEBREWS 8:11

Go share the joy today!

Defeat the Spirit of Depression

Why are you in despair, O my soul? And why have you become restless and disturbed within me? Hope in God and wait expectantly for Him, for I shall again praise Him for the help of His presence.

PSALM 42:5 AMP

Depression is closely related to a spirit of fear. When we entertain and internalize fear for almost any length of time, it can easily turn into depression. If you have struggled with a spirit of depression and any related symptoms, you may never have recognized that fear is the root of your problem.

Don't allow undetected fear to turn into a cloud of depression. Ask the Holy Spirit to show you whether an underlying spirit of fear has caused you to get into a deep pit of despair. If this has happened, you know what to do: dig your way out of the pit by speaking, thinking, and living by the Word of Truth. Tell your soul, as the psalmist did in today's verse, to resume trusting God and praising him in all circumstances.

If you know someone who is struggling with depression, the approach is the same. You can pray for that person, either privately or in their presence, asking God to reveal himself to them in a powerful way that removes the potency of their fear. Share with them as many Bible verses as you can that demonstrate God's faithfulness to save, heal, redeem, and restore. Deliverance is possible through the power of God.

VERSES TO DEEPEN YOUR JOY

PSALM 143:7–8; ISAIAH 61:1–3

Go share the joy today!

Rest, Don't Despair

It is vain for you to rise early, to retire late, to eat the bread of anxious labors—for He gives [blessings] to His beloved even in his sleep.

PSALM 127:2 AMP

Regardless of your situation in the natural realm, remember God operates in the supernatural realm, and nothing is impossible for him. All that exists is under his power. When you internalize that truth, you can rest and relax, knowing that he has it all covered. There's no need to despair.

As 1 Chronicles 29:11 tells us, God owns it all: "Yours, O LORD, is the greatness and the power and the glory and the victory and the majesty, indeed everything that is in the heavens and on the earth; yours is the dominion and kingdom" (AMP). Nothing lies beyond the scope of his sovereign power and boundless mercy. So there's no need to despair over any aspect of your life, whether it be the state of your relationships, the amount in your bank account, the condition of your health, or something else. Put your hope in God and praise him.

As you seek God, he will never forsake you. He is your stronghold in troubled times (Psalm 9:9–10). Nothing can remove you from God's presence or disqualify you from his protection. Rest in the comfort of this confidence today, rejoicing that the Almighty covers you and your all-powerful Redeemer keeps you safe.

VERSES TO DEEPEN YOUR JOY

PSALM 9:10; 2 CORINTHIANS 1:3–4

Go share the joy today!

The Power of Perfect Love

There is no fear in love. But perfect love drives out fear, because fear has to do with punishment. The one who fears is not made perfect in love.

1 JOHN 4:18

Father God loves his children unconditionally—today, tomorrow, and forever (Hebrews 13:8). His love does not depend on our bank accounts, our abilities, or our record of mistakes and misdeeds. Never confuse the love of your heavenly Father with human love, which is fickle and, despite our best intentions, conditional, at least to some degree.

People are inconsistent. They may say that they love you one day, with actions to back it up, and then the next day, they may express something entirely different, depending on their mood. But God isn't like that. He "is not man, that he should lie, or a son of man, that he should change his mind" (Numbers 23:19 ESV).

Because we can be completely confident in the Father's love for us, we can trust in his good intentions and refresh ourselves with his companionship in every season. No matter how our human relationships may be going, God the Father is the only one who is capable of loving us perfectly and without strings attached.

Have you been putting too much stake in your human relationships? Have you been nursing hurts and disappointments? Turn to the best friend you will ever have—the only one who won't let you down.

VERSES TO DEEPEN YOUR JOY

ZEPHANIAH 3:17; 1 JOHN 3:1

Go share the joy today!

When Human Love Falls Short

The hearts of the people are fickle.

Hosea 10:2 NLT

We've all experienced imperfect, unhealthy love, such as in dysfunctional relationships, broken covenants, and codependent unions. This kind of "love," more accurately labeled as situational affection, nurtures anxiety and distrust. But perfect love drives out fear in all its forms. And perfect love is what our Father God demonstrates to us. Because he has chosen us and has not rejected us, as he tells us in Isaiah 41:9–10, we don't have to fear.

Thank the Lord that his love is constant! We don't have to wonder how God feels toward us. We can be confident in his love and care. We can trust that he understands, accepts, and pardons us when we make mistakes and repent of our wrongdoing. He doesn't hold our sins against us but lovingly invites us back with open arms.

Invite the Holy Spirit to reveal and uproot any fear from your life so that you can operate fully by the power, love, and sound mind that God has provided for you to enjoy. The Lord wants you to be free to love and to be loved, but you can love others in a healthy, godly way only according to the measure that you let yourself experience love—not only from God and other people but also from yourself. Then you will have a sound mind that isn't plagued with thoughts of fear and rejection.

VERSES TO DEEPEN YOUR JOY

Psalm 27:10; Proverbs 23:6–8

Go share the joy today!

Embracing the You God Made

I praise you because I am fearfully and wonderfully made;
your works are wonderful, I know that full well.

PSALM 139:14

We've discussed that you can love others in healthy ways only once you accept and love yourself. But this assumes that you know yourself. Who is the true you—the person God has made "fearfully and wonderfully" in his image yet uniquely one of a kind?

That question is becoming harder to answer in a society that offers many causes to cling to and titles to claim but few meaningful ways of actually defining oneself. The media says that we can invent our identity, and this so-called freedom has left many people unmoored and aimless, unsure of even the most foundational aspects of their identity.

Identity is vital, but when we search within for its source, we are lost. Our true identity is found in our almighty God, the one who fashioned and formed us for his glory. When our identity is firmly established in him and what he has said about us, we can stay the course and weather every storm that threatens to knock us off our path.

You don't need to invent your own identity, thank God. You don't have to heed the competing voices that would cause you to question who he made you to be. At its heart, your identity is as a daughter of the Most High God. Your heavenly Father has adopted you into his family and made you his precious, blood-bought child.

VERSES TO DEEPEN YOUR JOY

PSALM 107:2–9; ISAIAH 43:1

Go share the joy today!

Whose Are You?

You belong to Christ,
and Christ belongs to God.

1 CORINTHIANS 3:23 NLT

When we anchor our identity in the Lord, we can withstand every storm. Where can we discover the details of our identity as his children? The answer is in his Word—the rope of hope he has provided to pull us out of every pit, whether physical, emotional, mental, or spiritual. Health in these areas comes from knowing who we are and *whose* we are. When we are confident of our identity in Christ, we can maintain hope and joy even when others mistreat us, reject us, or try to reinvent our identity.

The Word of God empowers us to take anything that isn't part of our true identity and leave it at the foot of the cross. It won't happen overnight, but when we renew our minds to the Word and allow the Holy Spirit to change our thinking, we can internalize our true identity and gain unshakable self-confidence from knowing what God says about us. To know who you are, look no further than the mirror of God's Word.

As we speak God's Word and internalize it in our heart, we renew our mind. Out with the old lies and in with the truth. I like to daily reinforce the truth of who—and whose—I am by repeating to myself Scripture verses pertaining to my identity in Christ. Once you speak the truth long enough, it becomes a part of you. The Word of Truth gets into your heart, your mind, and your spirit.

VERSES TO DEEPEN YOUR JOY

JOHN 10:27–28; ROMANS 14:7–8

Go share the joy today!

Rehearse the Word

"I know the plans I have for you," declares the LORD, "plans to prosper you and not to harm you, plans to give you hope and a future."

JEREMIAH 29:11

There's no end to the beautiful assurances the Bible gives us about who we are and whose we are. We are children of the King of kings. Don't let anyone steal your identity or try to redefine who you are. To God alone belongs the privilege of creating you and calling you. He has made and equipped you to carry out the amazing plan he has for your life.

The following are a few of my favorite verses that remind me of my identity in Christ. I encourage you to memorize these verses and then search the Bible for others that you can stand on when you feel unmoored and buffeted by the contradictory voices shouting at you from all sides.

- "[God] hath made us accepted in the beloved" (Ephesians 1:6 KJV).
- "God has said, 'Never will I leave you; never will I forsake you'" (Hebrews 13:5).
- "The LORD your God is with you, the Mighty Warrior who saves. He will take great delight in you; in his love he will no longer rebuke you, but will rejoice over you with singing" (Zephaniah 3:17).
- "See what great love the Father has lavished on us, that we should be called children of God! And that is what we are!" (1 John 3:1).
- "[Jesus said,] 'All those the Father gives me will come to me, and whoever comes to me I will never drive away'" (John 6:37).

VERSES TO DEEPEN YOUR JOY

1 CORINTHIANS 6:19; 2 CORINTHIANS 1:21–22

Go share the joy today!

Remember Who Fights for You

"The Lord who saved me from the paw of the lion and the paw of the bear, He will save me from the hand of this Philistine."

1 Samuel 17:37 NASB

When David was preparing to fight the giant Goliath, many people weighed in with advice. And King Saul suggested that David abandon his plan altogether. This was his gloomy forecast: "You are not able to go against this Philistine to fight him; for you are only a youth, while he has been a warrior since his youth" (v. 33 NASB).

But David knew better. He gave the king an abbreviated résumé of his experiences: "'Your servant has killed both the lion and the bear; and this uncircumcised Philistine will be like one of them, since he has defied the armies of the living God.' And David said, 'The Lord who saved me from the paw of the lion and the paw of the bear, He will save me from the hand of this Philistine'" (vv. 36–37 NASB). Talk about some divinely backed swagger! David had confidence in his ability to defeat Goliath because he trusted God to give him victory and rescue him, just as the Lord had when David previously fought against such wild beasts as bears and lions. I don't know about you, but I'd like to have that kind of confidence.

When we place all our trust in God, we can be confident in our identity as children of the King of kings—and we can be sure he will never abandon us to our enemies or leave us to face our struggles alone.

VERSES TO DEEPEN YOUR JOY

Exodus 14:14; 2 Corinthians 10:4

Go share the joy today!

Be True to Yourself and God

We are God's handiwork, created in Christ Jesus to do good works, which God prepared in advance for us to do.

EPHESIANS 2:10

The king agreed to let David fight Goliath but not without once again imposing his "advice" by telling David what he ought to wear: "Saul dressed David in his own tunic. He put a coat of armor on him and a bronze helmet on his head" (1 Samuel 17:38).

Sometimes other people will try to tell you how to do something, and they don't even realize they're doing it. Anyone can offer "expert" advice from a heart that means well, but even our best intentions don't guarantee that advice is necessary, desired, or helpful.

Although David was open to hearing Saul's advice because he was a teachable, humble servant, David was confident enough to speak up and say he would accomplish the task in the way God had equipped him to do it. David knew that he would prevail against Goliath only if he went into battle as himself. If he had tried to be someone else—wearing another person's armor and wielding another man's weapons—the outcome could have been completely different. He would have struggled to fight an adversary while dressed in armor that hindered his mobility. More important was the fact that God had anointed David for the task when David was confident enough to be himself.

Those around you may doubt whether God can use you in a certain role. But if God has given you the direction and the vision, you must be confident that God *can* and *will* use you.

VERSES TO DEEPEN YOUR JOY

EXODUS 4:10–12; 2 SAMUEL 7:8

Go share the joy today!

Fulfilling Your Calling

"You have not chosen Me, but I have chosen you and I have appointed and placed and purposefully planted you, so that you would go and bear fruit and keep on bearing."

JOHN 15:16 AMP

David remained confident that God would use him, even with his small stature and seemingly inadequate weapons, to defeat the enemy. He envisioned nothing ahead but victory over Goliath, despite the pessimism of the people around him. And victory was what David achieved because he remained true to himself, just the way God had created him and called him. We read this in 1 Samuel 17:49–50:

> Reaching into his bag and taking out a stone, he slung it and struck the Philistine on the forehead. The stone sank into his forehead, and he fell facedown on the ground.
>
> So David triumphed over the Philistine with a sling and a stone; without a sword in his hand he struck down the Philistine and killed him.

David used the tools God had given him to accomplish the calling God had given him. David's obedience to the Lord resulted in the defeat of not only Goliath but the entire Philistinian army. And God used this victory to prepare David for another calling God had anointed David for: to be the next king of Israel. "From that day Saul kept David with him and did not let him return home to his family…Whatever mission Saul sent him on, David was so successful that Saul gave him a high rank in the army. This pleased all the troops, and Saul's officers as well" (18:2, 5).

VERSES TO DEEPEN YOUR JOY

1 CORINTHIANS 12:4–11; 1 THESSALONIANS 5:24

Go share the joy today!

Anointed as Yourself

Now to each one the manifestation of the Spirit is given for the common good...All these are the work of one and the same Spirit, and he distributes them to each one, just as he determines.

1 Corinthians 12:7, 11

I was twenty-one when I started my career as a traveling evangelist. I remember trying hard to emulate other preachers and evangelists I had long admired. It came as a revelation when God told me, *You will be anointed when you are just yourself!* Sure enough, when I was preaching as myself, the glory would fall. If I tried to preach like anybody else, my efforts would fall flat. But when I stepped into my own gifting and used the abilities God gave me, the anointing was strong, and many souls were saved.

Do you find yourself trying to be someone else? Are you attempting to fight wearing someone else's armor? To battle wielding someone else's weapons? Have you been listening to the so-called experts instead of heeding *the* expert, your heavenly Father? Can you say, "I'm free to be me"? Or "I'm free to fulfill my God-given role while being true to myself, to the way God has made me"? Or are you still trying to fit into a mold designed by somebody else?

Just be yourself. God had a reason for making you the way he did.

VERSES TO DEEPEN YOUR JOY

Isaiah 42:6; 1 Corinthians 12:4–6

Go share the joy today!

Carried by the Glory

The anointing which you have received from Him abides in you, and you do not need that anyone teach you; but as the same anointing teaches you concerning all things, and is true, and is not a lie, and just as it has taught you, you will abide in Him.

1 John 2:27 NKJV

When I preached at my first weeklong revival many years ago, I learned a valuable ministry lesson. I was speaking at a little church in Oklahoma, and from the eighth pew, a little old man scowled at me for the duration of my message. At the end of the service, he came forward, his brow still furrowed, and said—I kid you not—"Honey, I ain't never believed in them there woman preachers!" He went on to tell me, "Although I ain't never believed in them there woman preachers, there's just something about you, honey. You just keep on preaching!"

Through this man's roughly worded change of heart, the Lord taught me that nobody can argue with God's anointing on your life. When you're anointed, everyone knows it. They may not like it, but they won't be able to argue with the fact that you are a carrier of God's presence. And when you carry the glory of God's presence, the glory carries you.

It's impossible to fake the anointing. God's glory falls where the anointing is genuine, and you can't be genuinely anointed when you're trying to be somebody else.

VERSES TO DEEPEN YOUR JOY

Isaiah 10:27; 1 John 2:20

Go share the joy today!

Kindle the Fire of Anointing

"Watch therefore, for you know neither the day nor the hour in which the Son of Man is coming."

MATTHEW 25:13 NKJV

Today's verse comes from Jesus' parable of the ten virgins. Of ten virgins who went out to meet the bridegroom (representing Jesus), five wisely brought along extra oil for their lamps while the other five failed to plan ahead and ran out of fuel. As a result, the unprepared virgins missed the bridegroom's arrival and didn't get to share in the wedding banquet.

In this parable, the oil can represent the anointing of the Holy Spirit, which we receive by dwelling in God's presence. We tap into the anointing, or the "Holy Spirit oil supply," by remaining in the presence of the Lord. When we maintain a powerful prayer life, we also maintain our oil supply. When we worship God, whether privately or in a corporate setting, such as at church, we get a download of extra oil from heaven. When we meditate on God's Word, we are saturated with the oil of his presence.

How is your oil supply these days? If it's running a little low, you need to run to the Lord's presence for a fresh fill-up of the anointing. As we kindle the fire of God's presence in our lives, it fuels our fight against sin and strengthens us for every battle we face.

VERSES TO DEEPEN YOUR JOY

PSALM 132:17; 2 TIMOTHY 1:6–8

Go share the joy today!

Trim Your Wick

"Every branch in Me that does not bear fruit, He takes away; and every branch that continues to bear fruit, He [repeatedly] prunes, so that it will bear more fruit [even richer and finer fruit]."

JOHN 15:2 AMP

The wise virgins in Jesus' parable from Matthew 25 took care of their lamps by trimming the charred ends of the wicks and adding fresh oil to the reservoirs. They had specific tasks to tend to in order to prepare for the coming of the bridegroom.

We are responsible for the same tasks, albeit in a spiritual sense: we must add oil to our lamps daily, filling up with the Lord's presence, and we must also trim our "charred ends," cutting away the influence of the flesh in our lives and trimming the aspects of our hearts that aren't pleasing to God.

If we don't trim our wicks regularly, we hinder the fire of God from burning at maximum capacity in our hearts. Trimming our wicks is similar to having our branches pruned, as Jesus discussed in John 15. To keep the fire of the anointing burning in our lives, we have to be vigilant about working to rid ourselves of fruitless habits, sinful thoughts, negligent words, and so forth. With the Holy Spirit's help, we can have the fresh oil and trimmed wicks we need to keep God's fire burning brighter day by day.

VERSES TO DEEPEN YOUR JOY

JOHN 14:16; 1 JOHN 2:24–25

Go share the joy today!

Tend Your Own Lamp

"Of that day and hour no one knows, not even the angels in heaven, nor the Son, but only the Father. Take heed, watch and pray; for you do not know when the time is."

MARK 13:32–33 NKJV

When Christ returns—at a day unknown to everyone but the Father—each one of us will need to supply our own "oil." We can't rely on anyone else to supplement our anointing or our lack thereof; we can't hang on to anyone's coattails when it comes to the tending of our lamps. Preparedness can't be shared or transferred.

Ultimately, each one of us will stand alone before the Lord and give an account of our lives. That's why it is so important to keep the fire of God burning in our hearts. And we simply can't do that unless we have enough oil. The oil is combustible. It's what ignites the fire and keeps it aflame. We need to add oil to the lamps of our lives daily.

In the parable of the ten virgins in Matthew 25, each virgin had to supply her own oil. If the lamps were bright and the oil burned quickly, the young women may have had to refill them every fifteen minutes. And I think that's a great rule of thumb: every fifteen minutes take a "praise break" and refill your lamp. As you keep your heart and mind focused on the Lord, you can get enough regular fill-ups to keep the fire burning.

VERSES TO DEEPEN YOUR JOY

HEBREWS 4:13; 1 PETER 4:5

Go share the joy today!

Don't Quench the Fire

Do not quench (suppress or subdue) the [Holy] Spirit.

1 THESSALONIANS 5:19 AMPC

The apostle Paul cautioned the readers of his first epistle to the Thessalonians not to quench the Holy Spirit—in other words, not to extinguish his fire. The *Amplified Bible, Classic Edition* adds the synonyms *suppress* and *subdue* to drive home the idea of what it means to "quench" the Holy Spirit.

What have we been allowing to put out our own fire? What are the habits, people, or situations that cause our flames to flicker and fizzle out? Whatever they are, they aren't worth pursuing any longer. We need to surround ourselves with people and involve ourselves in activities that fan the flame of God in our hearts.

I fear that the fire of God has been quenched in a lot of churches today because they've run out of oil. Why? Because people don't want to pay the price of having the oil of God's presence in their lives. We must pay the price of dying to the flesh through fasting, prayer, reading God's Word, and worship.

My heart's cry is *Lord, let your fire fall!* May he cause his fire to fall in our hearts and our homes, our churches and our communities, all around the world. Let's do all we can to avoid quenching the fire and instead to fan the flames.

VERSES TO DEEPEN YOUR JOY

JOHN 14:17; EPHESIANS 4:30

Go share the joy today!

The Fire Inspires

"God may speak in one way, or in another, yet man does not perceive it. In a dream, in a vision of the night, when deep sleep falls upon men, while slumbering on their beds, then He opens the ears of men, and seals their instruction."

JOB 33:14–16 NKJV

You're probably familiar with the troubles that Joseph encountered when he shared his vivid dreams of fame and power with his brothers (Genesis 37:5–9). Okay, so maybe it isn't always wise to tell other people every detail of our God-given dreams and visions. But it's exciting to realize that when we're dwelling in the secret place and we're anointed by God, he will sometimes give us insights into the future—wonderful visions of what he has planned.

If God decides to give us a glimpse of the future, he doesn't usually include all the details up front because he wants us to stay focused on him as we progress toward the finish line. He wants our God-given dreams and divinely inspired visions to fuel our faith. Any destination that doesn't require faith isn't worth reaching.

How gracious is our heavenly Father to inspire us with dreams and visions! When we carry his anointing, we know that he's smiling along with us, excited to watch our dreams reach their fulfillment. Has God been inspiring your dreams lately? Pay close attention to recurring themes and pray for discernment and understanding.

VERSES TO DEEPEN YOUR JOY

NUMBERS 12:6; ACTS 2:17

Go share the joy today!

Refined by Fire

*"Behold, I have refined you, but not as silver;
I have tested you in the furnace of affliction."*

ISAIAH 48:10 NKJV

Joseph's brothers acted on their jealousy when they put Joseph in a pit and then faked his death and sold him to traders bound for Egypt. When someone hurts us, it's painful, but when the person is a member of our own family, the pain is magnified.

Sometimes the bigger our dreams and the greater our anointing, the more serious our struggles will be and the more severe our pains as we journey toward the fulfillment of God's promises to us. Along the way, God desires to refine our character so that we increasingly resemble his Son, Jesus.

When God tests and challenges our humanness, it's often a setup for us to improve. He sets us up and gives us opportunities to build us up and take us upward. When you and I endure hardships as Joseph did, we have a chance to undergo character refinement, grow our faith, and draw closer to God.

Wherever you find yourself today—living large or languishing in the "furnace of affliction"—God can use you for his glory. None of us have it all together, and we won't until we reach heaven. But when we let God purify us through our experiences, we can rejoice in helping advance his kingdom and can bring him glory.

VERSES TO DEEPEN YOUR JOY

ZECHARIAH 13:9; MALACHI 3:2

Go share the joy today!

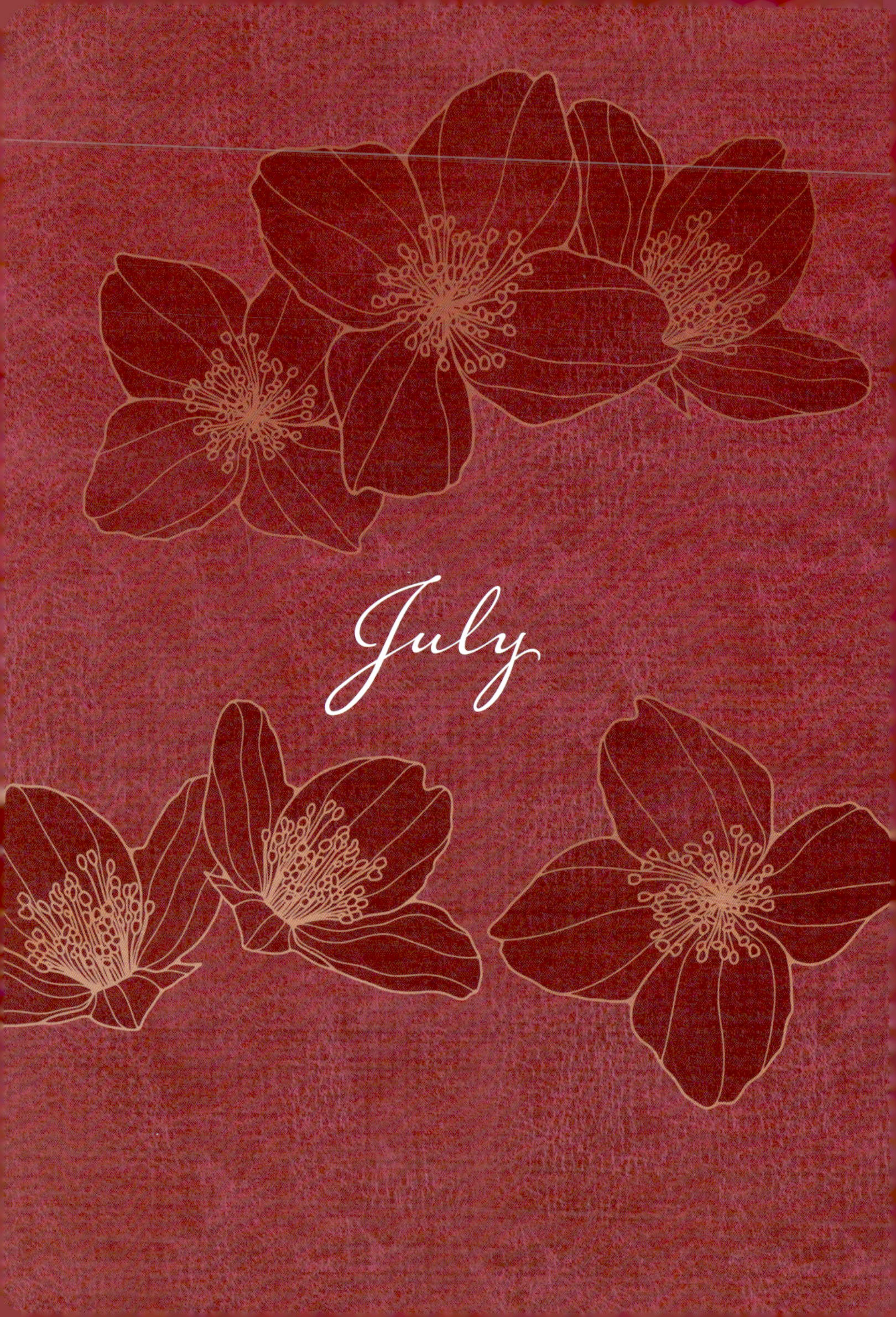
July

Our Guiding Light

Your word is a lamp to my feet
and a light to my path.
Psalm 119:105 NKJV

When Moses and the Israelites were traveling in the wilderness after fleeing the bondage of Egypt, God guided them in the form of a cloud by day and a pillar of fire by night. Exodus 13:21 says, "The Lord went before them by day in a pillar of cloud to lead the way, and by night in a pillar of fire to give them light, so as to go by day and night" (NKJV). Similarly, the fire of God's presence in our lives gives us much-needed guidance. In the night seasons of life, in the difficult times and the struggles, God guides us by his fire.

One area where we desperately need God's guidance is in relationships. Associating with or trusting the wrong people or going to the wrong places can cause major delays in our progress toward fulfilling God's plans for our lives. Certain people and places may thwart aspects of his plan altogether, at least for a time.

But the fire of God leads us and gives us discernment in the night seasons. The fire lights the way so we can clearly see and discern the right people, the right places, and the right timing for our pursuits. Praise God for his faithful guidance!

VERSES TO DEEPEN YOUR JOY

Psalm 32:8; Isaiah 30:21

Go share the joy today!

Fan the Flame

His word was in my heart like a burning fire shut up in my bones;
I was weary of holding it back, and I could not.

JEREMIAH 20:9 NKJV

In today's verse, the prophet Jeremiah likened the Word of God to a fire in his bones that he couldn't contain. If we have the oil of God's presence, it keeps the fire burning in our bones and in our lives. And when the fire of God consumes us, we can live a life of limitless victory.

The fire of God's presence breaks apart obstacles and eliminates hindrances to our pursuit of God's call on our lives. It breaks every chain of bondage. "'Is not My word like a fire?' says the LORD, 'and like a hammer that breaks the rock in pieces?'" (23:29 NKJV).

We ought to be fire starters who cause oil spills everywhere we go. If we're out shopping, we should spill oil on aisle nine or wherever we encounter a person needing the oil of God's presence. As we allow our oil to spill into the lives of others, the fire of God can ignite within them. But sharing oil requires that we have an abundant supply.

How can you fan the flame of God's presence today? The Holy Spirit is ready to help as you dive into the Word, engage in worship, and pray faithfully.

VERSES TO DEEPEN YOUR JOY

MARK 16:15; JOHN 15:12–13

Go share the joy today!

Baptized by Fire

"I baptize you with water. But one who is more powerful than I will come, the straps of whose sandals I am not worthy to untie. He will baptize you with the Holy Spirit and fire."

LUKE 3:16

John gave the explanation in today's verse to the people he was baptizing. It is the Holy Spirit who really keeps the fire burning in our lives. And our baptism in the Spirit is symbolized by fire itself.

When I first came to salvation, the idea of being baptized in the Holy Spirit made me awfully uneasy. I thought people who spoke in tongues were strange. Anything that's unfamiliar to us can seem scary. But now, having been filled with the Holy Spirit, I realize that it's all the stuff I did before that point that was weird and scary.

The first instance of people being baptized in the Holy Spirit is recorded in the book of Acts. The apostles were gathered on the day of Pentecost, and here's what happened: "Suddenly a sound like the blowing of a violent wind came from heaven and filled the whole house where they were sitting. They saw what seemed to be tongues of fire that separated and came to rest on each of them. All of them were filled with the Holy Spirit and began to speak in other tongues as the Spirit enabled them" (Acts 2:2–4).

If you haven't yet been baptized in the Holy Spirit, seek the Lord and ask him to fill you to overflowing. It's impossible to keep your fire burning and maintain your oil supply of anointing without the Holy Spirit's power operating in you every day.

VERSES TO DEEPEN YOUR JOY

JOHN 14:26; ACTS 2:14–21

Go share the joy today!

A Universal Gift

"Repent and be baptized, every one of you, in the name of Jesus Christ for the forgiveness of your sins. And you will receive the gift of the Holy Spirit."

ACTS 2:38

This gift of the fire of God in our lives, through the baptism of the Holy Spirit, is what burns out such impurities as sin, compromise, and unholiness. The fire of God helps us stay separate from the world and consecrated to the things of God.

The baptism of the Holy Spirit is not a gift reserved for a select few believers. It's for every person who calls on the name of the Lord and surrenders his or her life to him. The apostle Peter encouraged the believers of his day to be baptized, assuring them that they would receive the "gift" of the Holy Spirit—a "promise…for you and your children and for all who are far off—for all whom the Lord our God will call" (v. 39).

The only requirements for being baptized in the Holy Spirit are trusting the Lord Jesus as your Savior, confessing your sins to him so that he may forgive them, and surrendering your life to him. If you've met those prerequisites, this gift is yours.

Gifts are freely given and freely received. I hope that you will claim the free gift of salvation today. It's a gift beyond compare and without price.

VERSES TO DEEPEN YOUR JOY

EPHESIANS 4:7; HEBREWS 2:3–4

Go share the joy today!

Patiently Await the Gift

"Do not leave Jerusalem, but wait for the gift my Father promised, which you have heard me speak about. For John baptized with water, but in a few days you will be baptized with the Holy Spirit."

ACTS 1:4–5

When I first became a Christian, I had to learn to wait to fully experience what God could do through me by the Holy Spirit. Waiting wasn't easy because I wasn't very patient back then. I can remember feeling discouraged and worrying that I wasn't a good enough Christian because I hadn't yet received the fullness of the Spirit.

Don't grow impatient and give up on God as you await the filling of the Holy Spirit. Ask the Lord right now to allow you to experience the fullness of the Holy Spirit's power and then yield to him. Be patient and keep on seeking his face and his filling. If you desire something strongly enough, you go for it, even if you have to wait longer than you would prefer.

Growing impatient only makes the process harder than it has to be. The Holy Spirit's filling is a gift that the Father wants to give you. Don't overthink things like I did; only receive. Let the Holy Spirit speak through you in the prayer language he wants to release through you today. It isn't weird, strange, or demonic; it's biblical! The best things are worth waiting for.

VERSES TO DEEPEN YOUR JOY

LUKE 11:3; JOHN 20:21–22

Go share the joy today!

Saturation Brings Sanctification

May the God of peace Himself sanctify you completely;
and may your whole spirit, soul, and body be preserved blameless
at the coming of our Lord Jesus Christ.

1 THESSALONIANS 5:23 NKJV

Being baptized in the Holy Spirit is one aspect of our being consecrated—set apart—to the Lord. This process of consecration propels us toward sanctification, the lifelong process of growing in grace and spiritual maturity until we meet Jesus face-to-face. Consecration to the Lord comes in large part from being saturated with his presence. Countless people live saturated in offense, bitterness, and other sinful attitudes and habits that not only are destructive to their relationship with God but also serve to destroy their well-being.

Let's make sure that we're saturating ourselves with the presence of the Lord through prayer, praise, and meditation on his Word. After all, Jesus said to his Father when praying for his followers, "Sanctify them by Your truth. Your word is truth" (John 17:17 NKJV).

When we are completely saturated in God's presence, we're like a piece of meat that has marinated in seasoning and dressing before being grilled for an amazing flavor. God wants us to be separated, consecrated, and saturated—to marinate in his presence. That way, the nature of God will completely permeate us, and we can reflect his "flavor" in all that we say and do.

VERSES TO DEEPEN YOUR JOY

1 CORINTHIANS 6:11; HEBREWS 10:14

Go share the joy today!

Clean Hands and Pure Hearts

The one who has clean hands and a pure heart…
will receive blessing from the Lord and vindication from God their Savior.

Psalm 24:4–5

Whenever we're expecting company, we clean our houses and strive to keep things tidy, don't we? Well, I don't know about you, but I'm always expecting company—a visitation from the Holy Spirit, that is! I'm also awaiting Jesus' return to the earth at any time. And because I'm expecting this kind of company, I strive to keep my spiritual house clean.

Today's passage from Psalm 24 emphasizes the importance of having clean hands (acting with righteousness) and a pure heart (maintaining a proper attitude) as we prepare to receive the best kind of company: visitations of the Holy Spirit.

There's no limit to the number of Holy Spirit visitations that your heavenly Father wants you to experience. So expect company daily and keep your spiritual house clean. One way you do this is by keeping your mouth shut and your heart right. No matter what anyone else may say or do, you must resist the natural inclination to defend yourself. Those who turn the other cheek, as Jesus taught in his Sermon on the Mount, will be blessed by the Lord when he visits.

When it comes to vindication, God is the only defense we will ever need. He will clear our name of false accusations, uphold our cause, and defend us when others oppose our righteous way of living. So get ready because company's coming!

VERSES TO DEEPEN YOUR JOY

Matthew 5:38–39; Romans 12:19

Go share the joy today!

Set Apart for a Purpose

The word of the LORD came to me, saying, "Before I formed you in the womb
I knew you, before you were born I set you apart;
I appointed you as a prophet to the nations."

JEREMIAH 1:4–5

A realm of God's kingdom needs your exact blend of traits, talents, and experiences. And as all God's faithful servants have done, you must take certain steps to prepare to fulfill your purpose.

In the opening Scripture passage from Jeremiah, we see an important sequence. First, God knew Jeremiah. Second, the Lord formed him. And third, God set Jeremiah apart according to God's purpose for his life—to be a prophet, communicating God's will and Word to the people. It was only after Jeremiah had been set apart that God appointed him to fulfill the purpose he had in mind for Jeremiah's life.

The same three-step process applies to your life and mine. God knew us in his heart. Then he decided what he wanted us to do in his kingdom, and he designed us accordingly. Because God already knew us, he formed us with every gift, talent, preference, priority, and personality trait that we would need to fulfill his purpose for us.

We don't fulfill our purpose automatically, however. The Holy Spirit has a lot of work to do in our hearts and minds to get us ready for our divine destiny. The key to being ready to fulfill our purpose is to go through the steps of preparation—in other words, to run faithfully the course God has set out for us with the Holy Spirit as our divine coach.

VERSES TO DEEPEN YOUR JOY

ISAIAH 41:9; 1 CORINTHIANS 6:19–20

Go share the joy today!

The Season of Get Ready

The Lord said to Joshua…: "Moses my servant is dead. Now then, you and all these people, get ready to cross the Jordan River into the land I am about to give to them—to the Israelites."

Joshua 1:1–2

I love the book of Joshua. On one occasion, God gave me a fresh revelation as I read it. He said, *"Get ready" is a season*. When God told Joshua to "get ready," he was defining the season that Joshua and the Israelites were in. When we find ourselves in the season of get ready, we often think it's going to last a day or two. Yet this season usually lasts a lot longer than we anticipate.

Take Joseph, for example. He had some dreams, got excited about them, and started telling everyone. That didn't go over so well. As a matter of fact, it landed him in the bottom of a pit where his brothers stashed him until they sold him into slavery. Yet God used that empty pit as part of Joseph's season of get ready. And then, when it was go time, Joseph was ready.

Most of us are like my little dog, Mimi. When God says, *Get ready*, we stand by the door, waiting for him to open it. We expect it to swing wide open at any minute, so we just sit and wait. But most of the time, when God says, *Get ready*, it's the beginning of a new season, and there probably won't be a lot of sitting around involved.

VERSES TO DEEPEN YOUR JOY

Joshua 1:9; Jeremiah 23:23–24

Go share the joy today!

Chosen, Not Forgotten

"I have given you every place on which the sole of your foot treads, just as I promised to Moses...Just as I was [present] with Moses, so will I be with you; I will not fail you or abandon you."

JOSHUA 1:3, 5 AMP

In the season of get ready, when we're preparing for the next season God is leading us to, we may be tempted to wonder whether God has forgotten us. We may feel abandoned or overlooked. Yet God has chosen us, not neglected us. That's why he's getting us ready. We are about to experience a total turnaround as we grow in spiritual maturity.

Don't lose sight of the fact that you are in a season of preparation. Otherwise, you won't hang in there through the entire process. If you don't go through the process, you won't be ready when your "suddenly" arrives—your sudden promotion, your sudden arrival, your sudden turnaround. Suddenly, you will be called out of this season and ushered into the next.

God is always more interested in who you are as a person when you get to your new season than he is about the new season itself. We, on the other hand, tend to be far more interested in forging ahead and arriving at our destination. We forget that we must be dressed and prepared. If we aren't first clothed in the character of Christ, we won't be able to handle the pressures and responsibilities of the new season once we get there.

Don't buy the lie that God has forgotten you or overlooked you. Just submit to the season of get ready and be patient until you step into your total turnaround.

VERSES TO DEEPEN YOUR JOY

PSALM 27:14; ISAIAH 64:4

Go share the joy today!

Pursuing Impossible Goals

"Be strong and confident and courageous, for you will give this people as an inheritance the land which I swore to their fathers (ancestors) to give them."

JOSHUA 1:6 AMP

God did not merely suggest but rather commanded Joshua to get the people ready, and then he showed Joshua exactly what they were getting ready for. He explained that their new land would be extensive. In other words, God was preparing them for major feats. All too often, our vision is too limited; our goals are too small. If your goals don't sound impossible to accomplish, chances are you haven't made them big enough.

Hebrews 11:6 says that it is impossible for us to please God if we don't have faith. Our faith prompts us to walk in obedience to the leading of the Holy Spirit, which brings great pleasure to God. It takes faith to do what God tells you to do—to respond to his "illogical" instructions by getting out of the boat and walking on water (Matthew 14:22–29) or speaking to a mountain and telling it to move (Matthew 17:20; 21:21; Mark 11:23).

In the Israelites' season of preparation, God was expanding their vision and showing them details of his plans for them. God's vision for you will always call you out of your comfort zone and into your potential zone. His purpose for you will always be so big—so "impossible"—that you could never achieve it in your own strength. It's a strategic way of requiring you to depend on him to reach your God-given goals.

VERSES TO DEEPEN YOUR JOY

PSALM 32:8; ISAIAH 58:11

Go share the joy today!

Propelled by Faith

[Urged on] by faith Abraham, when he was called, obeyed and went forth to a place which he was destined to receive as an inheritance; and he went, although he did not know or trouble his mind about where he was to go.

HEBREWS 11:8 AMPC

Abraham was a man spurred forward by faith—and his faith stayed strong despite the vagueness of God's instructions to him. All he knew was that God had told him to get up and go. God didn't provide a final destination; he didn't give clear reasons why. Yet Abraham obeyed without question, urged on by his faith.

Don't try to talk yourself out of anything that you've been prompted to do through faith in the Lord. Just go for it! Surround yourself with those who agree with you and your faith because there's great power in agreement. Don't trouble your mind or worry about where you are going; just follow as the Lord leads.

I was just finishing graduate school at age twenty-four when God told me that my ministry would involve television broadcasts and published books. In my natural mind, I never would have imagined either of those things. If I hadn't received my goals from God by faith that day, I might not be writing now. When the land that God has given you to possess looks completely out of reach, that's your first clue that it must be a God thing.

God is more than able to cause us to accomplish anything that he has called us to do. Get in the presence of God and allow him to birth his goals in your heart.

VERSES TO DEEPEN YOUR JOY

PROVERBS 16:3; MATTHEW 17:20

Go share the joy today!

Come What May

"Only be strong and very courageous; be careful to do [everything] in accordance with the entire law which Moses My servant commanded you; do not turn from it to the right or to the left, so that you may prosper and be successful wherever you go."

Joshua 1:7 AMP

The first part of the Israelites' preparation for the promised land was to "be strong and very courageous." This was such an important part of their preparation that the Lord repeated it multiple times. He's trying to get the point across loud and clear.

One definition of *strong* involves having strength of character. Character counts the most. You may have all the gifts and talents in the world, but if you lack character, you will never be ready for what will happen next in your life.

Another aspect of the word *strong* is the ability to resist attack—being able to bear up under the Enemy's assaults. We are engaged in a spiritual battle, and we resist the Enemy's attacks and onslaughts by relying on our strength in the Lord. During the season of get ready, the Lord is preparing us to cross over into a new season of life. If you can't handle the warfare in this season, you won't last long once you have crossed over. The warfare there will be even more intense.

When facing difficult situations, many of us would rather retreat. But when the Holy Spirit dwells within us, we can courageously face our enemies head-on. We can rely on God's strength, not our own limited abilities, to get us through. This is a vital part of our preparation.

VERSES TO DEEPEN YOUR JOY

Psalm 56:3–4; Isaiah 41:10

Go share the joy today!

Tackling Terror

"Have I not commanded you? Be strong and courageous! Do not be terrified or dismayed (intimidated), for the LORD your God is with you wherever you go."

JOSHUA 1:9 AMP

It's never wrong to feel afraid as long as you don't allow your fear to steer you off course from the path God has put you on. You should always be led by the Holy Spirit rather than by fear and discouragement. If you succumb to terror and fear, you won't go forward and possess the land when God says to move. You can't afford to fear failure; you can't afford to fear rejection; you can't afford to fear other people. You must fear only God if you are going to experience a total turnaround in every area of your life and possess all that God intends to give to you.

The Enemy doesn't want you to be confident, and he definitely doesn't want you to be confident in the Lord—certain of what God can do in you and through you. When the Enemy succeeds at stealing your confidence, you feel hopeless, and when you feel hopeless, you lose your confidence. It's a vicious cycle.

Satan will throw obstacles or distractions your way in an attempt to distract and discourage you. When you are distracted from your purpose and place in God, you become easily discouraged. But when you are right where you are supposed to be, doing what you are supposed to be doing, you can withstand his schemes and stop terror in its tracks.

VERSES TO DEEPEN YOUR JOY

PSALM 91:5–6; ISAIAH 54:14

Go share the joy today!

Consecrated unto the Lord

Joshua told the people, "Consecrate yourselves,
for tomorrow the Lord *will do amazing things among you."*

Joshua 3:5

The final preparatory step in the season of get ready is to consecrate yourself. God takes holiness very seriously. Holiness wasn't just for people in the olden days. Whether you are three or ninety-three, God wants you to live a holy life. Holiness never goes out of style. Young people (including me—because I'm young, remember?) like to dress stylishly. That's great, but let's keep it holy. Beauty comes from the inside out, and when you live a holy life, you glow with the glory and presence of the Lord.

Again, Joshua told the people, "Consecrate yourselves." In other words, dedicate yourself to the Lord. He was telling the people to take personal responsibility for their relationship with the Lord and how they were living before him.

Consecrating yourself to the Lord means living separately from worldly desires and training your "appetite" by abstaining from things that aren't glorifying to God. Whatever appetite is the strongest in your life will lead the way and direct your course. When the Holy Spirit leads you because you are separated from the world and what it has to offer and when you are consecrated to God, you will discern his voice and walk in his ways. That's the path to a blessed life of success and fulfillment.

VERSES TO DEEPEN YOUR JOY

Romans 6:13–14; 2 Timothy 2:20–21

Go share the joy today!

Turnaround Time Is Coming

"Still the vision awaits its appointed time; it hastens to the end—it will not lie. If it seems slow, wait for it; it will surely come; it will not delay."

HABAKKUK 2:3 ESV

We read yesterday the Lord's word to Joshua—that "tomorrow" the Lord would do amazing things among the Israelites (Joshua 3:5). Just as it was for the children of Israel, your own turnaround time is drawing near. So keep on preparing yourself, for you don't want to be found unready when God says it's your time.

Joshua 3:5 specifies that "the LORD will do amazing things *among* you." The glory of God is going to fall in our midst. It's a corporate event! I believe we are going to see more miracles among us, the body of Christ, than ever before. God will display his miraculous power not only during our worship services but also at gas stations, grocery stores, airports, and so forth. God is going to show up and show off like never before. So get ready and consecrate yourself. The world and the church are desperate for the healing, power, and presence of the Lord.

God wants your life to be a platform for his glory. That's the reason for every turnaround he orchestrates for you. As you consecrate yourself in his presence and submit to his planning, he will transform your life into a platform for his glory. The whole world is watching because they need a miracle turnaround too. They just don't have any idea how to get it until you and I show them the way.

VERSES TO DEEPEN YOUR JOY

ISAIAH 46:13; ZEPHANIAH 1:14

Go share the joy today!

Get Yourself Ready

"Get yourself ready! Stand up and say to them whatever I command you."

Jeremiah 1:17

Those of us who are mothers have plenty of experience getting ready—getting ourselves ready, of course, but also, maybe even more so, getting others ready. We often have to get everyone else in the household ready for school every morning, for soccer practice on Saturdays, for church on Sundays, for road trips and vacations and doctor's appointments. But until Mom's ready, no one can go anywhere. If you are a mom, you must get yourself ready first before getting your kids ready. If you try to get the kids ready first, you will never have time to get yourself ready. And again, if Momma's not ready, nobody's going anywhere.

Once, when I read today's verse from Jeremiah, the Holy Spirit said to me, *Too many people spend all their time trying to get others ready, and as a result, they themselves are not ready when I need them*. How sobering!

As much as we would like to help others get ready—as much as we'd like to get our loved ones ready for what God has for them—the truth is that we're responsible only for making ourselves available and readying ourselves for doing the work of the kingdom. Let's not lose sight of our own preparation process by focusing solely on the status of those under our care or in our sphere of influence. When it comes to our position before God, we're responsible for ourselves, first and foremost.

VERSES TO DEEPEN YOUR JOY

Proverbs 16:3; Matthew 24:44

Go share the joy today!

Available and Amped

I heard the voice of the Lord saying, "Whom shall I send? And who will go for us?" And I said, "Here am I. Send me!"

Isaiah 6:8

If you spend all your time trying to get your spouse or your children ready to fulfill God's call on their lives, you will never be ready to answer God's call on your own life. Don't spend all your focus getting others ready. You must get yourself ready and make yourself available.

Did you know that God wants to anoint you for a purpose? He has exciting projects planned for you. Ephesians 2:10 says, "We are God's handiwork, created in Christ Jesus to do good works, which God prepared in advance for us to do." And no one else can do the "good works" God has prepared specifically for you. You have the ability and the skills to assist, serve, and otherwise help certain people that no one else could reach in quite the same way.

What are the gifts God has given you? What are the unique traits, talents, and experiences that he might choose to use in the building of his kingdom? They might not be the ones you'd first think of. Remember, God loves to use unlikely people and unexpected things to accomplish his plans.

So get yourself ready. Be available and amped when God calls for someone he can send. Every day in his kingdom is a wonderful adventure.

VERSES TO DEEPEN YOUR JOY

Proverbs 24:27; Ezekiel 38:7

Go share the joy today!

Establish Healthy Boundaries

"All who do evil hate the light and refuse to go near it for fear their sins will be exposed. But those who do what is right come to the light so others can see that they are doing what God wants."

John 3:20–21 NLT

One key to staying focused on getting yourself ready is to establish healthy, well-defined boundaries in your life and relationships. Let the Lord guide you in this area so you can stay focused on your relationship with him and remain committed to the work he has called you to do.

Sometimes the most compelling inspiration for those whom we might be trying to help get ready is for them to see us running hard after God. We can't shake it into them, beat it into them, or even preach it to them if they are unwilling to receive it. But when we live it out for them to see, the Holy Spirit can use our example to inspire them. He can use the power that's released through our prayer times to prompt a total turnaround in their lives.

In many cases, all you can really do is pray. Don't get involved in situations where you're apt to try to take control. It won't work! Entrust your loved ones to the Lord because nobody is more desirous of their salvation than he is.

VERSES TO DEEPEN YOUR JOY

1 Timothy 2:3–4; 1 Peter 3:1

Go share the joy today!

Go the Steps

Physical training is of some value, but godliness has value for all things, holding promise for both the present life and the life to come.

1 Timothy 4:8

I once did a teaching series called "No One Takes the Elevator; Everyone Takes the Steps." The point of the series was that we must take the necessary steps if we want to grow into the people God has called us to be.

In the natural realm, almost everybody prefers pushing a button and taking the elevator—be it literal or figurative—straight to the top. Shortcuts and time-savers are always appealing. When we get sick, we want to be able to pop a few pills and feel immediate relief. Online ordering and curbside pickup have eliminated many literal steps for today's shoppers (although they also eliminate the temptation for me to wander aimlessly down the aisles of the store, so this can be a big plus!).

Yet there is no shortcut to developing Christlike character and becoming the people God desires us to be. There are steps we have to take and experiences we must endure before we're qualified for the next season of our faith in God. It is dangerous when we are promoted to a place where our character cannot keep us. God is building principles in us today that will help us thrive in the next place where he is taking us. We must be patient as we pass through the trials and tests along our journey. When we submit to the steps, we are sure to succeed.

VERSES TO DEEPEN YOUR JOY

Psalm 25:8–9; 1 Corinthians 9:25

Go share the joy today!

Steps to Holiness

Like the Holy One who called you, be holy yourselves in all your conduct [be set apart from the world by your godly character and moral courage]; because it is written, "You shall be holy (set apart), for I am holy."

1 Peter 1:15–16 AMP

We need to take steps to discipline our flesh so that we can be led by a spirit that's surrendered to the Holy Spirit. This process happens through such spiritual practices as prayer, meditation on the Word, fasting, acts of service, and overall self-denial. When we refuse to give in to the impulses of our flesh, we become disciplined and walk in holiness, which paves the way for turnaround in every area.

First Corinthians 10:13 says that when our flesh is tempted, God will always give us a way out. He will never leave us without the ability to stand up against enticement. And it is never God who tempts our flesh but the devil. When we take the path out of that temptation by saying no to it and yes to God's best, we become stronger in every way. If something hinders your walk with the Lord, get rid of it—throw it off! A wise pastor once told me, "When in doubt, do without!"

As we run with perseverance and ignore all interference, our lives can be a platform for the glory of God. By fixing our eyes on Jesus and continually focusing forward, we can enjoy all the covenant benefits that come from living a holy life. And holiness never goes out of style.

VERSES TO DEEPEN YOUR JOY

1 Corinthians 10:13–15; Hebrews 12:14

Go share the joy today!

Jesus Took the Steps

Going a little farther, [Jesus] fell with his face to the ground and prayed, "My Father, if it is possible, may this cup be taken from me. Yet not as I will, but as you will."

MATTHEW 26:39

If anyone thinks themselves immune to the steps God has designed to refine their character and prepare them for their purpose, guess again. Jesus Christ, the Son of God, had to take the steps and follow the route of obedience—all the way to the cross.

During a trip to Jerusalem as a young boy, Jesus separated from his family to listen to the temple teachers and learn from them (Luke 2:41–52). Later, as he prepared for his earthly ministry, he went into the wilderness for forty days and was tempted again and again by the devil (Luke 4). The purpose of this testing was to develop his obedience to God's Word rather than to human inclinations, such as hunger, thirst, and lust for power.

Even though he never sinned, Jesus still had to take the steps and submit his desires to those of his Father. At the appointed time, when his earthly ministry was ending, he was so utterly submitted in obedience to his Father that he shed his blood for the sins of humanity.

If Jesus himself was not spared the steps, why should we think we'll get out of this refining process? These steps are designed by God to mold us into his character and likeness. What an honor that he considers us worth investing in!

VERSES TO DEEPEN YOUR JOY

LUKE 2:52; 1 CORINTHIANS 10:13

Go share the joy today!

Chastened as Beloved Children

"The Lord disciplines the one he loves,
and he chastens everyone he accepts as his son."
HEBREWS 12:6

Most of us are not likely to have our obedience tested to the point of death. As the writer of Hebrews put it, "In your struggle against sin, you have not yet resisted to the point of shedding your blood" (12:4). But we can rejoice when God leads us through steps that are meant to refine our character and cleanse our souls. He's treating us as the children he loves.

The author of Hebrews went on to say, "The Lord disciplines the one he loves, and he chastens everyone he accepts as his son" (v. 6). I know that discipline doesn't feel good at the time we experience it. Even the author of Hebrews acknowledged, "No discipline seems pleasant at the time, but painful. Later on, however, it produces a harvest of righteousness and peace for those who have been trained by it" (v. 11).

The discipline we endure as we're trained in obedience to God's voice and his ways may not be pleasurable at the time, but the ultimate aim is for us to share in his holiness. A "harvest of righteousness and peace" is about the best outcome I can think of for any believer. Aren't you excited that it can be yours?

VERSES TO DEEPEN YOUR JOY

JEREMIAH 46:28; 2 CORINTHIANS 9:10

Go share the joy today!

Steps to Blessing

Boaz replied, "I've been told all about what you have done for your mother-in-law since the death of your husband—how you left your father and mother and your homeland and came to live with a people you did not know before."

RUTH 2:11

When we take the steps God ordains for us, he will abundantly bless us. One person in the Bible who proved this is Ruth. When Ruth was widowed at a young age, her mother-in-law, Naomi, urged her to return to her own family and find a new husband, just as her sister-in-law was planning to do (1:1–14). Naomi encouraged Ruth to do what was smart and right in the eyes of the world—in the opinion of the society where they lived. "Go home!" she insisted. "There's nothing for you here" (v. 15, author's paraphrase).

Naomi's other daughter-in-law did just that, but the Lord ordered Ruth's steps, and the response Ruth gave her mother-in-law is one of the most beautiful expressions of selfless love found in the Bible: "Where you go I will go, and where you stay I will stay. Your people will be my people and your God my God. Where you die I will die, and there I will be buried. May the LORD deal with me, be it ever so severely, if even death separates you and me" (vv. 16–17).

What beauty there is in a life submitted to God! Obediently take the steps God has laid before you today even if they defy worldly wisdom.

VERSES TO DEEPEN YOUR JOY

PSALM 37:5; MATTHEW 16:24

Go share the joy today!

Richly Rewarded by the Lord

*"May the LORD repay you for what you have done.
May you be richly rewarded by the LORD, the God of Israel,
under whose wings you have come to take refuge."*

RUTH 2:12

Ruth continued to take the steps God ordained by following her mother-in-law, Naomi, to her hometown of Bethlehem, where Ruth made sure to secure Naomi's permission before going to glean in the fields (2:2). It was in the fields where she met Boaz, a wealthy and widely respected man, whose hand in marriage was eventually her blessing. He recognized the servant heart of Ruth and was himself part of the Lord's rich reward toward her.

And here is the best blessing of all: Ruth got to be in the bloodline of Jesus Christ. She is one of the few women named in the genealogy of the Savior of the world (Matthew 1:1–16). What an honor! Ruth set aside her own agenda and humbly submitted to what was best for those around her. As a result of these gifts, she was blessed beyond belief.

God rewards us when we follow his path for us. Whatever steps the Lord is asking you to take today—to surrender something to him, to serve someone in a selfless manner, to fast or pray for some person or event—you can trust that blessings will result from your faithfulness.

VERSES TO DEEPEN YOUR JOY

RUTH 3:14–15; PROVERBS 31:10–31

Go share the joy today!

Trust the Lord to Order Your Steps

The Lord directs the steps of the godly.
He delights in every detail of their lives.

Psalm 37:23 NLT

When we believe that God has a plan for our lives and we trust his leading, we are sometimes surprised by the gifts he uses or the traits he turns into opportunities to showcase his glory.

When I was a young Christian, I told the Lord I didn't know how he could possibly use me because I didn't seem to have any distinctive gifts. Several years later, he revealed to me that I had the gift of *determination*. Until that time, such a trait wasn't something I would have considered to be a "gift." But God went on to assure me that he had given me just what I would need to fulfill his call on my life.

As if to convince me of this, he began asking me questions. He said, *Do you remember when you worried how you would pay for your college tuition, but you were determined to go anyway? Do you remember when other people were telling you that women couldn't preach, but you obeyed my voice anyway?* He went on in this way, reminding me of situations and scenarios in which I had overcome some obstacle because of my determination. I came to see that determination was a priceless gift—one that had gotten me to the place God led me.

I'm so glad I submitted to the step of letting God show me my gift! He will do the same for you if you'll open your heart to him.

VERSES TO DEEPEN YOUR JOY

Psalm 119:133; Romans 12:6

Go share the joy today!

Sit at Jesus' Feet

As Jesus and his disciples were on their way, he came to a village where a woman named Martha opened her home to him. She had a sister called Mary, who sat at the Lord's feet listening to what he said.

LUKE 10:38–39

Getting ready for God's service means coming to the place where you are supposed to be. When you are running hard after God and his purposes for your life, you have to sit more than ever. Sounds paradoxical, doesn't it? Yet running and sitting go together.

What do I mean? The harder we are running after God and his will for our lives, the more we need to sit at his feet in prayer. Sometimes when we are running hard, we rush right past the place of sitting. That's how we end up tripping and falling! To get ourselves ready, we must sit at God's feet daily.

We see the importance of sitting at Jesus' feet in the scene from Luke's gospel in which Jesus visits the sisters Martha and Mary. Mary sat at Jesus' feet, listening. All the things that she needed to do could have distracted Mary. Or perhaps she could have caved to the pressure to please her sister, who complained that Mary wasn't helping with the preparations. Instead, Mary was doing the most important thing: learning from Jesus. Mary fixed her focus on Jesus.

What are you focused on today? Have "good" things taken you away from the best thing, which is sitting at the feet of Jesus? When we take the time to sit at Jesus' feet, everything else in our lives will experience the overflow.

VERSES TO DEEPEN YOUR JOY

EXODUS 33:14; ISAIAH 30:15

Go share the joy today!

Avoid Frenzied, Fruitless Action

Martha was distracted by all the preparations that had to be made... "Martha, Martha," the Lord answered, "you are worried and upset about many things, but few things are needed—or indeed only one. Mary has chosen what is better, and it will not be taken away from her."

LUKE 10:40–42

Sometimes we get caught up in the idea of acting—and it isn't the kind of action God has in mind. We run ourselves ragged trying to do this and that, all to please the Lord. But unless the Lord has ordained this and that, our efforts may not produce the fruit we think they will.

Martha got bent out of shape over the demands of hospitality when Jesus came for a visit, and she became annoyed with her sister for failing to help her out. Jesus responded by telling Martha that Mary's kind of "action"—sitting at his feet—was the most important kind.

It seems that our natural tendency is to be out of balance. We either have too much action or not enough. Or we have too much of the wrong type of action, which is what Mary struggled with. Sitting at the Lord's feet in prayer and listening to the Lord's voice as we abide in his presence are the most important actions. We should do these things daily even if others perceive these actions as inaction. For it's at his feet where we receive our marching orders for every moment.

VERSES TO DEEPEN YOUR JOY

PSALM 46:10; PROVERBS 8:34

Go share the joy today!

When God Says It's Time

Faith by itself, if it is not accompanied by action, is dead.

JAMES 2:17

Once we've sat at the feet of Jesus long enough to know his will for us, we are ready to take action. James tells us that faith without works is dead. In other words, having faith is good as long as we have the action that goes along with it. We know our faith is authentic when it prompts us to act on God's behalf to serve others and advance his kingdom.

"Faith comes by hearing, and hearing by the word of God," according to Romans 10:17 (NKJV). When God speaks to us with a revelatory word, faith rises up within us. It's up to us to respond in faith by taking the necessary action. Sometimes—probably most of the time, in fact—the action God demands will take us far outside our comfort zones. But I have learned that if we don't leave our comfort zones, we will never achieve our potential.

Action is great when it's accomplishing the plans God gives us. It's an essential aspect of living out our faith. But we shouldn't take action aimlessly. Again, we need to sit at Jesus' feet long enough to receive our marching orders from him. That way we'll know that our actions are purposeful and follow God's plans.

VERSES TO DEEPEN YOUR JOY

EZEKIEL 3:22; JAMES 2:18–20

Go share the joy today!

The Right Place at the Right Time

"Who knows but that you have come to your royal position for such a time as this?"

ESTHER 4:14

We see a great example of faith in action modeled by Esther, a woman in the Old Testament who got herself ready in the strictest sense of the phrase. When she went to the palace to compete for the honor of being queen to King Xerxes, with the ultimate motive of saving the Jewish people from annihilation, she had no one to help bear the burden of risks. She had no contract to guarantee her safety or success once she left her comfort zone. She had to take the required action, by faith, to position herself correctly for the ultimate preservation of her people (Esther 2:7–8).

Guided by the Holy Spirit, Esther proceeded to the palace and, by force of character, caught the eye of the man in charge of the harem. Esther went for it. She took the required action to get herself ready for her royal destiny. And because her action took her to the right place, at the right time, amid the right people, she experienced favor.

When we get ourselves to the place where we're supposed to be, God puts us in the best position possible to be recipients and conduits of his blessings. Just get where you're supposed to go and be who you're supposed to be. A key to positioning ourselves for God's favor is to pray about the decisions that we make. Don't just choose what seems to be the best decision; pray and ask God to guide you. He knows things we do not know, and his leading will position us for a future even greater than we could plan for ourselves.

VERSES TO DEEPEN YOUR JOY

EXODUS 33:12–14; JOHN 16:13

Go share the joy today!

Divine Beauty Treatments

Before a young woman's turn came to go in to King Xerxes, she had to complete twelve months of beauty treatments prescribed for the women, six months with oil of myrrh and six with perfumes and cosmetics.

ESTHER 2:12

Esther wasn't ready to present herself to the king until she had completed the required beauty treatments. Part of getting ourselves ready to fulfill God's purposes is submitting to a series of divinely ordained "beauty treatments." As we sit at the Lord's feet, we are saturated with the oil of his presence, and in the Lord's presence, we're transformed into the people he desires us to be. Our hearts, our attitudes, and even our very countenances transform.

I thank the Lord for makeup—foundation, eyeliner, blush, mascara. But it's the inside that causes the outside to glow with the presence of the Lord. True beauty really does come from within. When God heals us of bitterness, hurt, and other negative emotions and scars, our outward appearance reflects our newfound sense of inward refreshment.

We humans are triune: we are spirits, have a soul, and inhabit a natural body. Since we are spirit beings, our spiritual state causes even our natural, external appearance to change. I always say, "Sin makes us ugly, but the presence of the Lord makes us beautiful!" Don't forgo the beauty regimen our heavenly Father has made available. Nothing is more radiant than a heart surrendered to him.

VERSES TO DEEPEN YOUR JOY

1 SAMUEL 16:7; PROVERBS 31:30

Go share the joy today!

August

With the Right People

One who walks with wise people will be wise.

Proverbs 13:20 NASB

Esther succeeded in her quest to become queen and save her people not only because she was in the right place at the right time but also because she was among the right people. We must do the same by pursuing those relationships that the Lord has ordained. When we position ourselves in the right place, at the right time, with the right people, God will take care of the rest.

Esther met all three of these conditions, and she blew the competition away. Even so, she acted with humility; she wasn't out to win it all. She wasn't focused on herself, and she asked for nothing more than what the man in charge of the harem advised while continuing to follow Mordecai's instructions (Esther 2:15, 20). By surrounding herself with wise people and following their advice, she stepped into the position God prepared for her and proceeded with his favor.

As we pursue the Lord's favor and seek to obey his Word, we need to surround ourselves with the right people—faithful Christ followers who have our best interests at heart and who prize the ways of God above the ways of others. Their example will encourage us to seek God's will and obey him in all circumstances, and hopefully, we can do the same for them. Ask the Lord also to show you those relationships that you should cultivate to secure a position of favor with him and an opportunity to help build his kingdom.

VERSES TO DEEPEN YOUR JOY

Proverbs 18:24; 1 Corinthians 5:11

Go share the joy today!

Discern Unwise Associations

A companion of fools will suffer harm.

PROVERBS 13:20 NASB

Some dangerous people were in the palace when Esther arrived. However, the king was not aware of them until the righteous lifestyle of Esther and her cousin Mordecai exposed those people who had manipulated their way into the king's palace.

We read of two such individuals in the following passage: "During the time Mordecai was sitting at the king's gate, Bigthana and Teresh, two of the king's officers who guarded the doorway, became angry and conspired to assassinate King Xerxes. But Mordecai found out about the plot and told Queen Esther, who in turn reported it to the king, giving credit to Mordecai" (Esther 2:21–22).

Just as God exposed the ill-intentioned people and their evil schemes to the king, he wants to expose unwise associations in our lives as well—those who would harm us or derail us from fulfilling our God-given purpose. Once he has shown these to us, we need to distance ourselves from those who stand opposed to the Lord's purposes because they can keep us from advancing God's kingdom and hinder our spiritual growth.

Pray that God will give you discernment in your relationships and that he shows you those you should pursue and those you should either limit or stop altogether. He will sharpen your discernment as you trust in him.

VERSES TO DEEPEN YOUR JOY

JOB 15:34; PROVERBS 4:23

Go share the joy today!

Find Favor with God

The King was attracted to Esther more than to any of the other women, and she won his favor and approval more than any of the other virgins. So he set a royal crown on her head and made her queen instead of Vashti.

ESTHER 2:17

The Lord has to see us to extend his favor to us. When the Father sees us as those who are faithfully committed to following his plan, who have the heart we're supposed to have, and who respond with obedience when the King calls upon us (even when seemingly inconvenient), his favor will propel us closer to his calling for us.

When we have the favor of God, we often also have the favor of people. God has favor waiting for us. All we have to do is show up in the right place, at the right time, with the right people. Then we will find favor with our heavenly Father as well as with some of our fellow humans.

The favor of God never ceases to amaze me. My ministry—an overtly Christian organization—has received generous donation checks from professing atheists. When we have nonbelievers sending money to our Christian ministry, that's nothing but God showering his favor on us because we're doing what he has told us to do in the place he has told us to do it.

VERSES TO DEEPEN YOUR JOY

PSALM 90:17; PROVERBS 8:12–35

Go share the joy today!

The Anyway Blessing

Let the [gracious] favor of the Lord our God be on us;
confirm for us the work of our hands—
yes, confirm the work of our hands.

PSALM 90:17 AMP

God establishes the work of our hands for us when we have his favor. King Xerxes was attracted to Esther's obedience, and the King of kings is attracted to our obedience. God's stamp of approval will get you anywhere and everywhere you need to go.

Having God's favor means that you get what I call the anyway blessing. When other people slander your character and spread lies about you, God blesses you anyway. When coworkers and neighbors falsely accuse you, God blesses you anyway. The anyway blessing trumps every attempt by the Enemy and those in his sway to stop you in your tracks.

We see several great examples in the Bible of individuals who had the anyway blessing. I think, in particular, of Joseph, who, despite a series of plots by multiple people to end his life or extend his prison sentence, found favor with everyone and worked his way from the prison to the palace (Genesis 39–41). The anyway blessing was his, and it's a blessing that's ours for the taking today. When we have the favor of God, nobody can stop our success or preclude our promotion.

VERSES TO DEEPEN YOUR JOY

PSALM 5:12; PROVERBS 3:1–4

Go share the joy today!

Irrevocable Favor

God's gifts and His call are irrevocable. [He never withdraws them when once they are given, and He does not change His mind about those to whom He gives His grace or to whom He sends His call.]

ROMANS 11:29 AMPC

The favor of God is irrevocable, meaning nothing and no one can alter it. There's no revoking, no reneging, no retracting it.

Joseph's brothers envied the exceptional favor Joseph had. In their covetous spirit, they attempted to quash that favor by tossing Joseph in a pit and then selling him into slavery. But their schemes had no effect on God's favor toward Joseph—favor that followed Joseph wherever he went. It didn't matter who liked it and who didn't; Joseph was covered with the favor of God.

For a short time, it looked as if Joseph's brothers had stripped him of favor—literally, of course, but figuratively too. They tore his beautiful coat to shreds, and soon they had sold him to some merchants traveling to Egypt, and he was far from home. But his brothers couldn't strip away Joseph's God-given mantle, calling, or vision. They couldn't revoke that which he had received from his heavenly Father.

When it comes to the favor of God on your life, nobody can take that away. Regardless of who opposes you, God will provide for you, promote you, and bless you.

VERSES TO DEEPEN YOUR JOY

LUKE 1:30; ACTS 7:9–10

Go share the joy today!

Unexpected Paths to Promotion

Trust in the LORD with all your heart,
and lean not on your own understanding;
in all your ways acknowledge Him,
and He shall direct your paths.

PROVERBS 3:5–6 NKJV

When you have the favor of God, his blessing puts you on unexpected paths to promotion and success. Suddenly people start making exceptions for you. On your own, you wouldn't qualify to advance or secure a higher position, but God steps in and supernaturally makes it possible for you to meet demands that would otherwise remain unreachable. For example, maybe you haven't attained the degree of education a prospective employer said you needed, but God blesses you anyway with your dream job. Your anyway blessing takes you all the way to the top.

Joseph's brothers were going to kill him, but then, at the last minute, they made a sudden exception and spared his life instead, throwing him in a pit before selling him to some Midianite merchants. That pit became the first part of a route to the pharaoh's palace.

In many cases, the Lord is preparing us for our position in the palace, and all we can see is the pit that we're in. That's why it's crucial to have a heavenly perspective. God knows everything, sees everything, and ultimately orchestrates everything. Keep trusting him, even in the pits and prisons. He will not revoke his favor but will be faithful to put you on the proper path.

VERSES TO DEEPEN YOUR JOY

PSALM 119:105; ISAIAH 30:21

Go share the joy today!

Favor's Universal Effect

The LORD was with Joseph so that he prospered, and he lived in the house of his Egyptian master. When his master saw that the LORD was with him and that the LORD gave him success in everything he did, Joseph found favor in his eyes.

GENESIS 39:2–4

The favor of God is the key to every blessing because favor influences everything. Its effects are universal in scope. After Joseph was thrown into a pit and then sold into slavery, his anyway blessing—when God blesses us despite our circumstances—shined on him through every subsequent trial and trouble. He couldn't help but prosper.

Likewise, when the Lord is with you, his favor will help you thrive, flourish, and succeed in everything you set your hand to do. That kind of prosperity affects every area of your life in a way that no one can suppress. Remember, it's irrevocable.

Joseph found favor with everyone in every situation. While he was in prison, "the LORD was with him; he showed him kindness and granted him favor in the eyes of the prison warden" (v. 21). Prison wardens aren't known for being exceedingly merciful toward or trusting of their wards, yet this warden gave Joseph full authority (v. 23). The warden could tell that there was something special about Joseph, and that caused him to trust Joseph with his responsibilities.

Even as a prisoner, Joseph found favor with God and people. That's because God's favor extends its effects without limitation.

VERSES TO DEEPEN YOUR JOY

EXODUS 3:21; GALATIANS 1:10

Go share the joy today!

Favor Follows God's Timing

You will arise and have compassion on Zion,
for it is time to be gracious and show favor to her;
yes, the appointed time [the moment designated] has come.

Psalm 102:13 AMP

Through all the pitfalls he encountered on his path to the palace, Joseph maintained his faith and trust in the Lord. Yet I'm sure there must have been times when he wondered if God had forgotten him, just as his fellow prison inmate, the cupbearer, did after being released (Genesis 40:14–23).

Joseph knew he was not guilty of any wrongdoing. I'm sure he wondered to himself what God was doing and why he had allowed Joseph to suffer enslavement, wrongful accusation, and imprisonment. Have you ever felt forgotten or abandoned by God? If so, you're in good company.

God was awaiting the time he had appointed to clear Joseph's name and secure a position of influence that would enable Joseph to safeguard the lives of his family and, ultimately, the people of Israel when famine struck. At the appointed time, things turned around dramatically for Joseph. When God's appointed time comes, nothing can stop your promotion. No one can forget about you even if they want to. No false accusation, personal attack, or evil agenda can stand against what God has in store for you. Trust him to work out his favor according to the divinely ordained timetable.

VERSES TO DEEPEN YOUR JOY

Genesis 18:14; Exodus 9:5

Go share the joy today!

Favor Invites Exponential Increase

"'Well done, good and faithful servant. You have been faithful and trustworthy over a little, I will put you in charge of many things; share in the joy of your master.'"

MATTHEW 25:21 AMP

The favor of God on Joseph's life was not only irrevocable; it also grew exponentially. It resulted in Joseph regaining with dramatic increase what his brothers had taken. Genesis 41:42 says, "Pharaoh took off his signet ring from his hand and put it on Joseph's hand, and dressed him in [official] vestments of fine linen and put a gold chain around his neck" (AMP). His brothers stole his robe, but the king gave him robes, plural. That's because Joseph was a faithful steward of God's favor on his life, and to the faithful steward of the gifts he bestows, God says, like the master in the parable of the bags of gold, "Well done, good and faithful servant. You have been faithful and trustworthy over a little, I will put you in charge of many things; share in the joy of your master" (Matthew 25:21 AMP).

Praise the Lord! Just like Joseph, your exponential blessing of favor and promotion is about to manifest if you keep your heart right and abide in the Lord. Trust him to restore to you what he deems appropriate. You will receive back an exponential increase of that which your enemies have taken from you.

VERSES TO DEEPEN YOUR JOY

ISAIAH 40:10; JOEL 2:25

Go share the joy today!

Favor Founded on Relationship

The LORD God is a sun and shield; the LORD bestows favor and honor; no good thing does he withhold from those whose walk is blameless.

PSALM 84:11

The favor of God is key to finding open doors at every turn. But it isn't something you can just drum up on your own. And it isn't a reason for seeking God, as if he were some divine genie who dispenses favor when we "rub" him the right way. The first step is a right relationship with the Lord—one in which you are continually growing, going deeper, and looking increasingly like his Son, Jesus. Striving to earn God's favor without first forming a solid relationship is no use, for you'll be striving in your own strength.

Some people assume God favors them when they have momentary success or when unexpected opportunities present themselves. Yet these types of fortunate events are not a failproof sign of divine favor. True favor comes from the Lord alone to those who hear his voice and follow.

Let's work on keeping our walk blameless, and we will find favor with our heavenly Father. As we live our lives surrendered to his purpose, plan, and perfect timing, we'll find ourselves suddenly promoted and supernaturally positioned to bless the world around us as we advance his kingdom on earth.

VERSES TO DEEPEN YOUR JOY

PSALM 89:17; PROVERBS 11:27

Go share the joy today!

Fulfilling God's Commands

"If anyone [really] loves Me, he will keep My word (teaching); and My Father will love him, and We will come to him and make Our dwelling place with him."

JOHN 14:23 AMP

If God commands us to do something—or commands us *not* to do something—we should take him seriously. We should listen closely and endeavor to obey. When God gave Moses the Ten Commandments, he intended them to be just that—commandments. They weren't the ten suggestions. And he blessed the people abundantly when they lived in alignment with those commandments.

Sometimes God commands us to "take the land"—to seize a dream, to overcome an enemy, to surmount a limitation, to pave the way for his message to penetrate the hearts of those who have never heard it before. At other times, he may command us *not* to do something because it saddens him or fails to edify us and others.

We must always keep in mind that the commands that the Lord gives us are motivated by his unconditional, unfailing love for us. God never gives his commands out of anger, hatred, vengefulness, or a desire to rule us with a heavy hand. Rather his commands always come from his heart of love, to protect and guide us along the path that leads us to his very best for our lives.

VERSES TO DEEPEN YOUR JOY

DEUTERONOMY 28:1–14; REVELATION 22:14

Go share the joy today!

Commands and Unfailing Love

The Lord loves righteousness and justice;
the earth is full of his unfailing love.

Psalm 33:5

Have you ever been in a relationship with someone who expected you to meet all their emotional needs? Have you ever known someone who seemed to believe you could read their mind and that you should respond accordingly? Such relationships are totally exhausting and can't be sustained. No human being, no matter how wonderful, can meet all the emotional needs of another human being. Only the Lord and his unfailing love can satisfy the desires of our hearts, and the commands that he gives us stem from his great, all-sufficient love for us.

Again, other people may love us—truly love us—yet their love is liable to fail us or let us down. But God's love is forever unfailing. It never falls short of what we need or want. God's love for us is inexhaustible and ever reliable.

When we hear God's commands, let's keep in mind that each one is motivated by God's heart of unconditional, unfailing love for us. A young child who hears her parent say, "I'm doing this for your own good and because I love you," doesn't usually understand. She is too focused on her immediate desire and the disappointment of not having that desire granted. But when she grows older, she gets it, especially when she has children of her own.

VERSES TO DEEPEN YOUR JOY

Psalm 33:18; Proverbs 20:6

Go share the joy today!

Promoting Productivity

"Very truly I tell you, unless a kernel of wheat falls to the ground and dies, it remains only a single seed. But if it dies, it produces many seeds."

JOHN 12:24

When we are not yet mature in the things of God, we are apt to overlook the times when the Lord is working to produce fruit in our lives through situations that we find unpleasant or undesirable. God's heart of love for us may command us to go in a certain direction or may "plant" us in a certain place that is not appealing to our flesh.

But when we are planted in the right place—the place that God has ordained—we will never fail to bear fruit. When we are successfully rooted, as with any plant, the seeds fall to the ground and die. And when we sense the dying process occurring, our inclination is to get out of there! Our flesh wants to run. But the longer we stay planted, the stronger our root system will grow. The deeper the roots, the greater the fruits. What are we running from? It may be just the thing we need to deepen our faith.

We need to get out of God's way and stand in his will. God's best is always worth whatever price we must pay for obediently following his commands. Remember, each of those commands is motivated by God's heart of unfailing, unconditional love for us. Let's embrace his instructions and let the productivity flow.

VERSES TO DEEPEN YOUR JOY

PSALM 1:1–3; 1 CORINTHIANS 7:20–24

Go share the joy today!

Commands That Guide Our Steps

Establish my footsteps in [the way of] Your word; do not let any human weakness have power over me [causing me to be separated from You].

PSALM 119:133 AMP

Because of their foundation in his great love for us, God's commands are intended to guide our steps in the right direction. Psalm 107, like many passages in the Bible, is an exhortation to praise the Lord for his unfailing love because he hears the prayers of those in need and saves them.

I love the way Psalm 107 captures this idea. Here's an excerpt for you to consider:

> They cried out to the LORD in their trouble,
> and he delivered them from their distress.
> He led them by a straight way
> to a city where they could settle.
> Let them give thanks to the LORD for his unfailing love
> and his wonderful deeds for mankind,
> for he satisfies the thirsty
> and fills the hungry with good things. (vv. 6–9)

God's unfailing love saves us from sin and distress. God's unfailing love rescues, heals, and delivers us. So let us give thanks to him daily. Let's give thanks for his unfailing love, and let's stop complaining that we don't want to do what he commands us to do. It's not about us; it's about him leading us into his best for us. Our steps are secure when they're guided by the Lord and in line with his commandments.

VERSES TO DEEPEN YOUR JOY

PSALM 23:3; PROVERBS 8:20

Go share the joy today!

Commanded to Love

We love, because He first loved us.

1 John 4:19 NASB

Sometimes God's unfailing love is reflected to us through the people around us. At other times, we need to experience God's unfailing love straight from the source because no one else is shining it into our lives. Either way, we should strive to reflect God's unfailing love in our relationships no matter how others may treat us.

It isn't easy to turn the other cheek and return love instead of bitterness, as Jesus commands us to do in Matthew 5:38–41. But when God is our everything, he definitely helps us always respond with love.

Psalm 90 includes this plea to the Lord: "Satisfy us in the morning with your *unfailing love*, that we may sing for joy and be glad all our days" (v. 14). The revelation of God's unfailing love should cause us to sing and be filled with his joy every day, at all times, through all circumstances.

When God's unfailing love satisfies us, we can say, regardless of our circumstances and state of mind, "God's got this!" We can go ahead and get our praise on. We can shout, dance, and rejoice, for God is still on his throne. We must stop acting as if he has fallen off. And Jesus is seated at the right hand of the Father, interceding on our behalf (Romans 8:34). When we're resting securely in his love, we can love others unconditionally instead of only when it suits us.

VERSES TO DEEPEN YOUR JOY

Psalm 143:8; Ephesians 4:2

Go share the joy today!

Salvation Is the Seal

Show us your unfailing love, LORD,
and grant us your salvation.
PSALM 85:7

First John 1:9 says, "If we confess our sins to him, he can be depended on to forgive us and to cleanse us from every wrong" (TLB). God's unfailing love is not a license to sin. It isn't a free pass to do whatever we please without consequence. Rather it gives us a road to bypass sin through his provision of salvation—the evidence, or the seal, of God's unfailing love for us. To receive and cash in on God's unfailing love, we must repent of wrongdoing and then receive his forgiveness. We must acknowledge where we have fallen short, and we must invoke his all-sufficient grace and forgiveness.

Proverbs 28:13 says, "Whoever conceals their sins does not prosper, but the one who confesses and renounces them finds mercy." If we fail to confess our sin or deny that our actions were sinful in the first place, our blessings will be cut off. But when we confess and repent of our sins, God's unfailing love will cause us to thrive, succeed, and flourish.

Prayerfully consider your recent actions and heart attitudes. Have you committed sins you weren't aware of at the time? Turn them over to God in repentance, and he will forgive you freely. Then you can continue walking in obedience and growing closer to him.

VERSES TO DEEPEN YOUR JOY

EXODUS 15:2; 2 SAMUEL 22:3

Go share the joy today!

Restoration of Relationship

Confess your sins to each other and pray for each other so that you may be healed. The prayer of a righteous person is powerful and effective.

JAMES 5:16

After we confess our sins to the Lord, we can experience God's total restoration in our lives. This is true especially when we go beyond confessing our sins to the Lord by acknowledging them to our brothers and sisters in Christ. James 5:16 exhorts us to do this, going even further to point out that it is a key to our healing: "Confess your sins to each other and pray for each other so that you may be healed."

If we've wronged someone, it's appropriate to humbly ask for that person's forgiveness. Remember that God "gives grace to the humble" (James 4:6 NKJV). Pray and ask the Holy Spirit if there's anyone in your life from whom you need to seek forgiveness. If he brings someone to mind, ask him for wisdom in approaching that person with an acknowledgment of your sin and a request for forgiveness.

And while you're in forgiveness mode, don't forget to forgive yourself for all your past mistakes. That can be harder than forgiving others. But the salvation of God has made a way for us to forgive and move on. His salvation is the seal of his love in our hearts.

VERSES TO DEEPEN YOUR JOY

MATTHEW 6:15; 2 CORINTHIANS 5:18–20

Go share the joy today!

Obedience Springing from Love

Whoever despises the word and counsel [of God] brings destruction upon himself, but he who [reverently] fears and respects the commandment [of God] will be rewarded.

PROVERBS 13:13 AMP

I've learned that every time God asks me to do something I *really* don't want to do, that's the very thing that will propel me into the place of abundant blessings. This has happened to me time and time again. And while I can't say that it's made obedience to God all that much easier, I can say that the Lord has a perfect track record of rewarding me for obeying him by faith.

Jesus said to his disciples, "If you [really] love Me, you will keep and obey My commandments…The person who has My commandments and keeps them is the one who [really] loves Me; and whoever [really] loves Me will be loved by My Father, and I will love him and reveal Myself to him [I will make Myself real to him]" (John 14:15, 21 AMP). When we are in relationship with our heavenly Father, it becomes our heart's desire to obey his commands, which, as we've discussed, he gives us with our best interests in mind.

If God has been calling you to do something that doesn't seem appealing, you can be sure that obeying him will bring you closer to his heart and more aligned with his purposes. Pray for an openness to obedience and a willingness to do all his will. And then watch as your will aligns with his.

VERSES TO DEEPEN YOUR JOY

DEUTERONOMY 28:1–12; PSALM 37:4

Go share the joy today!

Blessings of Obedience

"I call heaven and earth to witness against you today, that I have placed before you life and death, the blessing and the curse. So choose life in order that you may live, you and your descendants."

DEUTERONOMY 30:19 NASB

For those who seek to follow God's commands and live by his standards, the rewards are beyond compare. Abundant blessings are always on the other side of obedience. Once we have crossed over to the side of obedience, the blessings of God chase us down and eventually overtake us.

God had great blessings in store for Abraham, but he had to obey when God said, *Go!* The Lord may give you instructions that aren't convenient for your flesh to follow, but do them anyway. God may tell you to do things that seem impossible or don't make any sense. Go for it! Pass the test of obedience. Obedience always brings blessings while disobedience always grieves the Holy Spirit. Our obedience opens the door for blessings just as our disobedience ties the hands of God from releasing the blessings he wants to get to us.

We have to know by faith that blessings are waiting for us on the other side of our obedience, even when we struggle to obey Father God's commands. If we will just faithfully endure for a little while, we will step into the overflow of blessings that waits just across the bridge of obedience.

VERSES TO DEEPEN YOUR JOY

DEUTERONOMY 28:13, 44; JOSHUA 1:8

Go share the joy today!

Willing and Obedient

*"If you are willing and obedient,
you will eat the good things of the land."*
ISAIAH 1:19

It's clear throughout Scripture that God wants his children to have the best. If you have kids, just think of how strongly you desire that they have the best; now multiply the strength of that feeling as many times as you can, and you'll get a sense of how strongly our heavenly Father desires to bless us.

Whether we receive his blessings is up to us. We open or close the door on the blessings of God through our choices. Again, the Word assures us of blessings "if [we] are willing and obedient." If we get successfully past the *if*, then we've passed the first step. Willingness and obedience are the first two requirements for receiving God's best.

Going all the way in obedience is a different matter. Our spirits may be willing, but our flesh may be too weak for us to follow through with true obedience (Matthew 26:41). At times I've prayed, *Lord, I'm willing to be willing. Please help me over this obstacle by the power of your Holy Spirit.*

It's easy to be willing to follow the Lord's guidance; it's much harder to actually obey it. Being willing will take you to a certain level, but obedience will take you all the way into everything the Father has for you. God wants to give us the best there is, but he can do so only if we qualify through our obedience to receive it.

VERSES TO DEEPEN YOUR JOY

2 CORINTHIANS 12:9; JAMES 1:22

Go share the joy today!

Know the Way to Obey

"This is the new covenant I will make with the people of Israel on that day, says the LORD: I will put my laws in their minds, and I will write them on their hearts. I will be their God, and they will be my people."

HEBREWS 8:10 NLT

We won't know what God has told us to do if we don't know him in the first place. That's why it's key to spend time in his Word every day and to record any *rhema* (revealed) words of instruction he gives to us. I keep a daily journal of words from God and insights about his Word to help me remember what he tells me to do.

The parable of the sower in Luke 8 highlights the importance of keeping the Word within us rather than letting the Enemy steal it away. We can't afford to forget what God has said. Satan wants us to forget, to fail to understand, and even to fail to hear what God is saying. That's why recording God's messages to us is so critical. Of course, we should endeavor to *obey* those instructions so that we avoid being hearers of the Word but not doers (James 1:22). That way, we will be sure to know the Father's "good, pleasing and perfect will" (Romans 12:2) that always works to prosper his obedient children.

Don't let anyone or anything keep you from obeying God.

VERSES TO DEEPEN YOUR JOY

2 CHRONICLES 31:21; JAMES 1:23–25

Go share the joy today!

Full Obedience

If you fully obey the Lord your God and carefully follow all his commands I give you today, the Lord your God will set you high above all the nations on earth. All these blessings will come on you and accompany you if you obey the Lord your God.

Deuteronomy 28:1–2

God desires our full obedience at all times, not just when it's convenient or suitable to our preferences. Partial obedience doesn't cut it either. King Saul found that out the hard way: he went from being anointed as king to being rejected (1 Samuel 15:1, 26) because he failed to fully obey God's instructions.

King Saul did carry out God's instructions when it came to attacking the Amalekites but not *fully*. God instructed him to "utterly destroy all that they have" (v. 3 NKJV), sparing nothing. "But Saul and the people spared Agag and the best of the sheep, the oxen, the fatlings, the lambs, and all that was good, and were unwilling to utterly destroy them" (v. 9 NKJV).

God immediately expressed his regret to Samuel that Saul hadn't performed all his commandments (v. 11). Saul tried to save face, protesting, "I have obeyed the voice of the Lord, and gone on the mission on which the Lord sent me" (v. 20 NKJV). He tried pinning the wayward pillage on other people, but Samuel (and God) knew better.

We don't have to understand why God is telling us to do something; all we need to do is obey *fully* and *completely*. When we miss the mark, our Father is there with open arms, ready to forgive when we acknowledge our failed attempts at full obedience.

VERSES TO DEEPEN YOUR JOY

1 Samuel 15:30–31; Ephesians 1:7

Go share the joy today!

Acknowledge God-Ordained Authorities

Let everyone be subject to the governing authorities,
for there is no authority except that which God has established.
The authorities that exist have been established by God.

ROMANS 13:1

According to today's verse, our loving, heavenly Father is the one who has established all authority figures. Thus anyone who rebels against the authorities that God has established is rebelling against God himself. Let's not incur judgment by rebelling against that which God has instituted, for the Word likens rebellion to the sin of witchcraft. It says in 1 Samuel 15:23, "Rebellion is as the sin of witchcraft, and stubbornness is as iniquity and idolatry" (NKJV).

We don't want to dally with spiritual witchcraft by speaking against those in authority, especially those in spiritual authority. God says, "Touch not mine anointed" (1 Chronicles 16:22 KJV). Let's not "touch" them with negative words. Let's keep our minds and mouths clean and clear from negative comments and backbiting. This doesn't mean that we excuse sin in the lives of our leaders, but speaking against them with a rebellious spirit reveals sin in our hearts that will hinder our relationship with God.

If you've harbored a poor attitude toward someone in authority, ask God to reorient your allegiance and soften your heart. Start praying for that person, and I think you'll find your attitude shifting and your heart being humbled.

VERSES TO DEEPEN YOUR JOY

PROVERBS 29:2; MATTHEW 28:18

Go share the joy today!

Pray for Those in Authority

I urge, then, first of all, that petitions, prayers, intercession and thanksgiving be made for all people—for kings and all those in authority, that we may live peaceful and quiet lives in all godliness and holiness.

1 TIMOTHY 2:1–2

Sometimes those who have been abused by an authority figure, such as a teacher or pastor, develop a mindset of rebellion against anyone in authority. But past abuses of power don't negate God's principle of authority. God can use even fallen leaders to bring about his ends. One of our greatest keys to stepping into everything that God has for us is to acknowledge, respect, and submit to those in positions of authority over us. We do this by honoring them, listening to them, obeying them, and praying for them.

Sadly, many believers today lack respect for spiritual authority. They forget that authority is for their protection—that God established it with their best interests in mind. When we are under authority, we sit beneath an umbrella of protection that God has provided for our own well-being. According to Romans 13:4, "The one in authority is God's servant for your good."

Let's be faithful to pray for our leaders and lift them to the Lord for guidance and blessing. God will honor our efforts and bless our leaders in response.

VERSES TO DEEPEN YOUR JOY

PROVERBS 21:1; 1 TIMOTHY 2:3–4

Go share the joy today!

Disqualified by Disobedience

Walk by the Spirit, and you will not gratify the desires of the flesh.

Galatians 5:16

Disobedience is a detour that can derail you from fulfilling the purpose God has for you. We should never flirt with detours when we've received directions from God, whether in his Word or by a *rhema* (revealed) word. Don't buy the Enemy's lies when he whispers, *This little sin won't hurt. No one will ever know.* Satan comes to steal, kill, and destroy (John 10:10).

Our decisions can disqualify us from receiving God's blessings and favor. It isn't worth losing our job, family, or ministry over one impulsive decision, no matter how seemingly insignificant. Esau sold his birthright to his younger brother, Jacob, for a bowl of stew—how silly! Many people do the same thing, selling their "birthright"—their anointing and God-ordained position—for a quick fix of the flesh. Esau's fleshly satisfaction lasted only a few moments, just long enough for him to fill his belly. Then he got up and left—with his birthright forfeited forever (Genesis 25:33–34; Hebrews 12:16).

Was it really worth it? Is a temporary fix for the flesh worth losing your birthright? The devil will tell you that it is, but you know better. Don't yield to his temptations or take his detours. It's true that nothing can disqualify us eternally from the love of God if we acknowledge our wrongdoing and repent. God will pour out his mercy and pardon. But we waste our time when we dabble in disobedience and risk missing out on his favor and blessing. Why risk it?

VERSES TO DEEPEN YOUR JOY

1 Samuel 15:22; Galatians 5:13–26

Go share the joy today!

Don't Forfeit Your Anointing

Let no one deceive you with empty words, for because of these things the wrath of God comes upon the sons of disobedience.

EPHESIANS 5:6 ESV

We maintain the Lord's anointing when we are obedient to him. But disobedience may cost us our anointing, as it did for Saul in 1 Samuel 15. Remember how the prophet Samuel had anointed Saul king of Israel and commanded him, on God's behalf, to "totally destroy all" the belongings of the Amalekites, enemies of God (1 Samuel 15:3)? Did Saul listen? No, he and his army spared the best livestock and goods, keeping them for themselves (v. 9). God lamented ever having made Saul king: "I regret that I have made Saul king, because he has turned away from me and has not carried out my instruction" (v. 11).

Disobedience is a sin of rebellion, often resulting from a prideful attitude. When people think they know better than God, they will defy his instructions—to their own downfall. "Samuel said to [Saul], 'The LORD has torn the kingdom of Israel from you today and has given it to one of your neighbors—to one better than you'" (v. 28).

If we choose not to walk in obedience to the Lord, he always has someone else with a heart of obedience waiting in the wings to take our place. I don't want God to regret putting me where I am. I don't want to forfeit the anointing. As we stay close to him through prayer, the study of his Word, and worship, we can maintain fellowship with his Holy Spirit and enjoy his anointing for all our days.

VERSES TO DEEPEN YOUR JOY

PSALM 18:50; 1 JOHN 2:27

Go share the joy today!

Strength to Withstand Temptation

Each person is tempted when they are dragged away by their own evil desire and enticed. Then, after desire has conceived, it gives birth to sin; and sin, when it is full-grown, gives birth to death.

James 1:14–15

Every one of us must choose to stand against temptation. No one else can do it for us. That's right. Resisting temptation is an individual choice. If you're facing financial straits, for example, you must resist the temptation to take shortcuts, fudge your tax return, embezzle from your employer, and so forth. You don't have to rob a bank to steal; remember, it's "the little foxes that spoil the vines" (Song of Solomon 2:15 NKJV).

According to the Word, it's our own evil desires that tempt us—not God, not our friends, not our situations. Whenever we fall into temptation, we're following the lead of our own carnal flesh. Likewise, anytime we choose to resist temptation, it has to be our own decision. We must stand for ourselves.

Being tempted is not a sin, but yielding to temptation is. If you allow yourself to be dragged away and enticed by it, that's sin. The Word says that if you participate in that sin, don't repent, or don't stop the sinful behavior, the sin will grow. And if it's allowed to become full-grown, sin will produce death—spiritual, emotional, financial, and even physical death.

Don't be dragged away and enticed. Dig in your heels and cling to the Word of Truth. Hold fast to your faith, and the Lord will strengthen your ability to withstand temptation.

VERSES TO DEEPEN YOUR JOY

Psalm 119:11; Hebrews 2:18

Go share the joy today!

God Makes a Way

No temptation has overtaken you except what is common to mankind. And God is faithful; he will not let you be tempted beyond what you can bear. But when you are tempted, he will also provide a way out so that you can endure it.

1 CORINTHIANS 10:13

Praise God that he hasn't left us on our own to fight against temptation. He doesn't require us to go it alone. No, he provides a way out through the blood of his Son, Jesus.

It's so comforting to remember that whatever temptations we face, Jesus has faced them too. Being made a human like us, albeit still divine, Jesus experienced during his earthly life all the struggles and enticements we encounter. "Because he himself suffered when he was tempted, he is able to help those who are being tempted" (Hebrews 2:18). Hebrews 4:15 says, "We do not have a high priest who is unable to empathize with our weaknesses, but we have one who has been tempted in every way, just as we are—yet he did not sin."

Jesus knows what you're facing, and he gives you what you need to get through it. Just trust him! Commit not to quit. Choose to stand against the temptation to have a mental meltdown. As you keep deciding to stand, God stands with you. Yes, God will give you an out, but you have to be willing to take it. Then, when you call on the name of Jesus, he will show up with a host of angels to lead you out of those tempting moments. He always provides a way out, but you have to want to get out.

VERSES TO DEEPEN YOUR JOY

MATTHEW 26:41; JAMES 1:12

Go share the joy today!

Angelic Protection

If you say, "The LORD is my refuge," and you make the Most High your dwelling, no harm will overtake you, no disaster will come near your tent. For he will command his angels concerning you to guard you in all your ways; they will lift you up in their hands, so that you will not strike your foot against a stone.

PSALM 91:9–12

When we live under God's protective hand by submitting to his authority and following his law, he even commands his angels concerning us. God's will is for us to enjoy divine protection as we pursue his plans for our lives and for his kingdom—the promised land he has in store for us.

Seeing our promised land is one thing; taking possession of the land is entirely different. Yes, we have to see the land before we possess it, but seeing the land doesn't guarantee that we will possess it. When we have angelic forces working on our behalf against our foes, possessing the land becomes far more feasible.

Possess is another way of saying "to take ownership of." God wants us to take ownership of all the land he has reserved for us. He wants us to fulfill our purpose in its entirety. *Possession* also implies the acts of obtaining and maintaining. God wants us to obtain and maintain peace, joy, presence, love, health, financial blessings, and more.

What we possess, we own, no matter the time, season, or circumstance. But we can't possess the land without the help of God's angels, help that is ours when we walk in obedience to God's commands.

VERSES TO DEEPEN YOUR JOY

PSALM 89:1–8; DANIEL 6:22

Go share the joy today!

Live Victoriously

"The Lord your God is the one who goes with you to fight for you against your enemies to give you victory."

Deuteronomy 20:4

Angelic protection is just one way that God arms us against our enemies. With the Lord God on our side, we are sure winners, for "God…gives us the victory through our Lord Jesus Christ" (1 Corinthians 15:57). There's no need for us to wear ourselves out trying to fight our battles—be they financial, spiritual, emotional, mental, or relational—in our own strength. The battle belongs to the Lord, and he will give us the victory.

As we cooperate with the Lord and use the tools and traits he has given us to fight the Enemy, we will experience victory in every area of our lives. And this victory begins when we understand the true battleground of the fight. It also depends on our not getting preoccupied with minor skirmishes. The Enemy delights in distracting our focus with little fires that aren't important in the long run, but, if we let them, those fires will prove effective in wearing us out with stress and worry. If the devil can keep us busy putting out fires and fighting minor conflicts, he knows we won't have the time, energy, or attention to rise to the challenge of critical battles.

We need to let God fight our battles and keep our eyes on him through every struggle. Victory is ours if we'll only let the Lord do his thing.

VERSES TO DEEPEN YOUR JOY

2 Chronicles 20:15; Ephesians 6:12

Go share the joy today!

Pick Your Battles

*"Defend the oppressed.
Take up the cause of the fatherless;
plead the case of the widow."*

Isaiah 1:17

Like all parents, I've had to learn to pick my battles with my daughter and hone my focus on the big picture of what's best for her. For a while, fashion was the center of most of our disagreements, but as she grew, I learned to stop waging war over what she was wearing and started worrying more about what she was being exposed to on television and through other media, for example. I kept a tight rein on what she put into her spirit because I knew that was a fundamental area of susceptibility to the Enemy.

In the same way that parents must learn to pick their battles while raising their kids, believers need to focus on the most strategic spiritual battles that the Lord wants them to engage in (even as he fights on their behalf). One of those critical battles is the fight for our hearts and minds—ours and our children's. Unfortunately, many parents are so caught up in striving to provide worldly possessions for their kids that they fail to give them what they really need: time, love, attention, prayer, and godly guidance.

When it comes to parenting and mentoring those young people under your care, look to the Lord to establish your priorities and show you the areas where you need to stand firm.

VERSES TO DEEPEN YOUR JOY

Psalm 68:5; James 1:27

Go share the joy today!

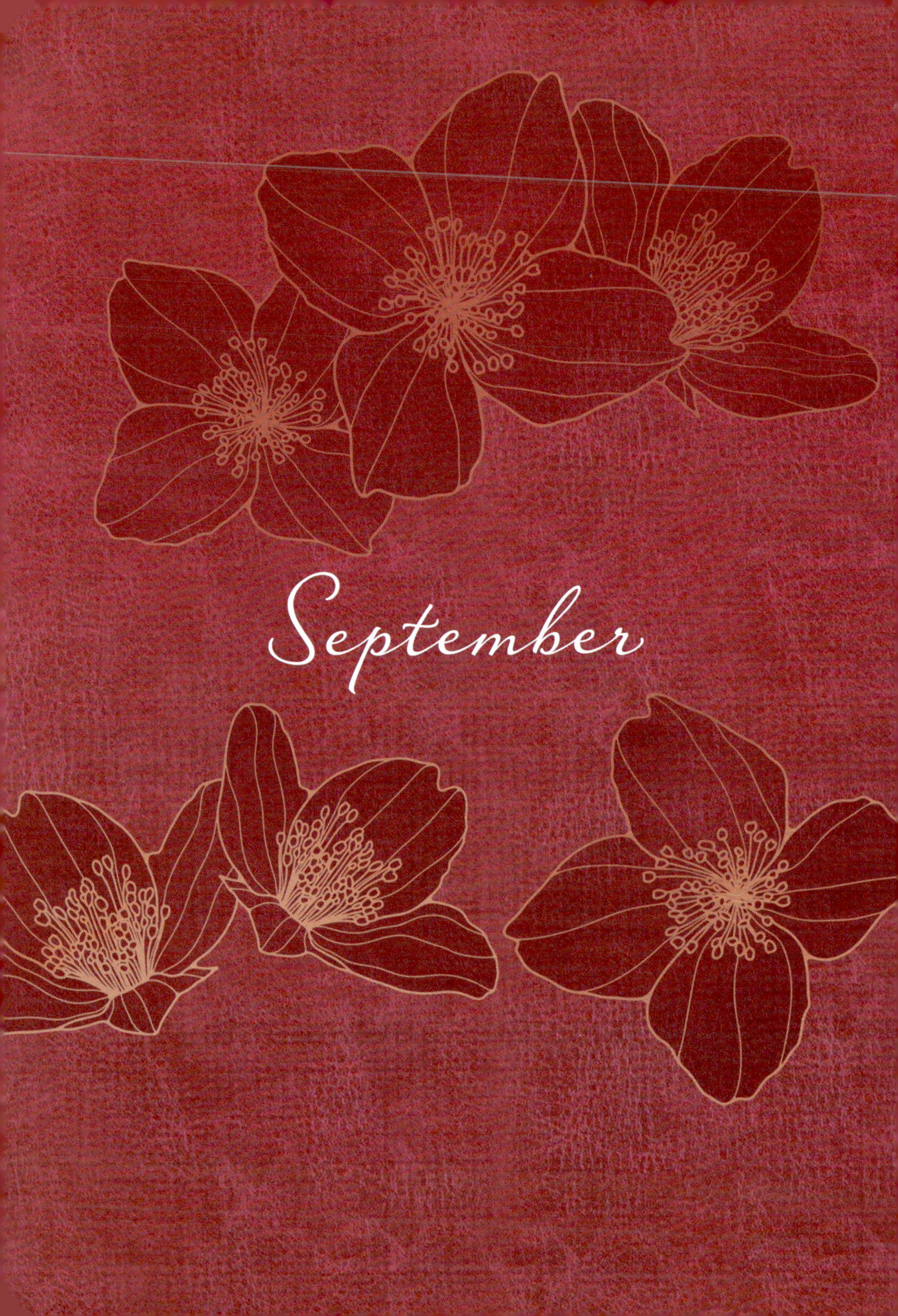
September

The Battle for Priority

"Seek first His kingdom and His righteousness, and all these things will be provided to you."

MATTHEW 6:33 NASB

The battle for our hearts and minds relates closely to the battle for priority—the war over where we'll spend our money and how we'll pass our time. I had to undergo a huge shift in priorities when my purse strings tightened after my husband walked out on me. The Lord showed me that if I were to continue living the same lifestyle, I would need to spend more time away from my newborn daughter to earn enough money to cover the bills. Not wanting to give up precious time with her, I learned to live more frugally than I ever imagined possible.

A nonnegotiable priority of believers should be to "defend the oppressed" (Isaiah 1:17), doing whatever we can to support single parents, widows, and orphans. The plight of such individuals should be something we care deeply about because we know the Lord cares deeply about them. Let's look to the Lord to pick our battles and trust him for the victory.

When we surrender our schedules to the Lord and prize his will over our own, all our priorities will align properly. He will order our priorities to match his heart if we'll only surrender to him and seek his ways. Prize his presence above all else, and you'll soon see what I mean.

VERSES TO DEEPEN YOUR JOY

EXODUS 20:3; MATTHEW 13:44–46

Go share the joy today!

The Battle for Peace of Mind

You will keep in perfect peace those whose minds are steadfast, because they trust in you.

ISAIAH 26:3

Looking to the Lord to fight our battles must include overcoming our fears because fear always tries to control. If we fear having inadequate funds, we will try to control our finances rather than entrusting our situation to God. If we fear rejection, we may resort to manipulation in our relationships to prevent ourselves from experiencing that particular pain. But when we face our fears with the power of the Holy Spirit, surrendering them to his control, we find ourselves enjoying the peace that comes from soundness of mind.

Philippians 4:7 assures us, "The peace of God, which transcends all understanding, will guard your hearts and your minds in Christ Jesus." It's the peace of God that guards our minds in every battle we face, but we first have to reach that place of peace by surrendering our minds to our heavenly Father.

God's Word instructs us, "Let the peace of Christ rule in your hearts" (Colossians 3:15). I have learned never to move forward with a decision until I have peace from the Lord. I don't need to understand why I have or don't have peace; I just have to let the peace of Christ rule over my decision-making. As we pursue the peace of Christ, trusting him to take the lead in all things, our hearts and minds will be guarded in his all-transcending tranquility.

VERSES TO DEEPEN YOUR JOY

ISAIAH 66:12; 1 PETER 3:11

Go share the joy today!

Heavenly Minded

Set your minds on things above,
not on earthly things.
COLOSSIANS 3:2

A sound mind that's protected by the peace of God is not plagued by thoughts of fear, rejection, or defeat, but instead it meditates on "things above." In other words, it dwells on the truth of God's Word, not on the Enemy's deceptions. The apostle Paul gave us the following instructions for maintaining a sound mind: "Whatever is true, whatever is noble, whatever is right, whatever is pure, whatever is lovely, whatever is admirable—if anything is excellent or praiseworthy—think about such things" (Philippians 4:8).

Our biggest battles always begin in our minds. Years ago, when the Lord started unpacking the emotional baggage I had been lugging around, he showed me just how closely my emotional wounds were connected to the thoughts from the Enemy that I had entertained for many years. He exposed those wounds for what they were and led me to release them, one by one, until I reached a point of wholeness and restored health.

If we can discern the tricks of the Enemy, such as the malicious lies he whispers in our ears, we can outwit him. By staying on guard through prayer and meditation on God's Word, we can renew our minds and expose Satan's schemes. God's Word is the weapon that will win every battle we wage against the Enemy of our souls.

VERSES TO DEEPEN YOUR JOY

2 CORINTHIANS 2:11; HEBREWS 4:12

Go share the joy today!

Withstand the Enemy's Schemes

"The thief comes only to steal and kill and destroy;
I have come that they may have life, and have it to the full."

JOHN 10:10

A mind that isn't sound is susceptible to believing the lies of the devil—including the notions of unworthiness, self-rejection, and even suicide that he drops into despairing minds. If you have been battling thoughts of self-hate or suicide—or if you know of someone else who has—the first thing you must understand is that suicide is a spirit that Satan sends from the pit of hell. When this spirit is trying to gain the upper hand, you must stand up and exercise the authority that is yours because of your status as a child of God. Don't let any demonic spirit push you around. You are the one with authority.

One of the devil's lies is that there isn't any other way out. The truth is that God's Word is your rope of hope, ready and able to lift you from any pit. As Paul explained, "We are destroying arguments and all arrogance raised against the knowledge of God, and we are taking every thought captive to the obedience of Christ" (2 Corinthians 10:5 NASB).

When we allow ourselves to dwell on the lies of the Enemy, we open the door for the devil to have his way in our hearts and lives. But when we keep thinking about things above and not below, we open the door for God's presence and power to fill us, leaving no room for the devil and his demonic lies to take up residence.

VERSES TO DEEPEN YOUR JOY

LUKE 10:19; JOHN 3:20–21

Go share the joy today!

Identify the Real Enemy

Our struggle is not against flesh and blood, but against the rulers, against the authorities, against the powers of this dark world and against the spiritual forces of evil in the heavenly realms.

EPHESIANS 6:12

As we encounter hardship and opposition in our daily lives, whether major or minor, we must remember where our battles are coming from. We must identify the real Enemy. Unless we recognize that our ultimate opponent is the devil himself, we will end up blaming other people, or even blaming God, and fighting against them rather than taking on our actual Enemy.

Our battle isn't against our family members, friends, coworkers, neighbors, or fellow church members. Although the Enemy tries to enlist other people to cause conflict with us, those people aren't our enemies—the devil is.

Remember that our fight isn't against "flesh and blood." The struggle we're engaged in is much greater than that. It has cosmic scope. It's against the rulers, authorities, and powers of this dark world and the spiritual forces of evil in the heavenly realms, whose king is Satan.

You don't have to be a decorated army general to know that if you're going to win a war, you have to know your Enemy. You have to realize whom you're fighting against. Otherwise, they'll outwit and defeat you. Your attention will be distracted while the actual Enemy sneaks up from behind and blows you away.

Recognize the source of your battles and be sure not to target "flesh and blood." You're on the same team after all.

VERSES TO DEEPEN YOUR JOY

EPHESIANS 6:11; 1 PETER 5:8–9

Go share the joy today!

Wield the Right Weapons

The weapons we fight with are not the weapons of the world. On the contrary, they have divine power to demolish strongholds.

2 CORINTHIANS 10:4

If we can recognize that Satan is the real Enemy and fight with the weapons Scripture has instructed us to wield, we'll be victorious every time. But what are our weapons, and what are the weapons of the world?

Let's start with the weapons of the world. They include anger, bitterness, hatred, jealousy, and backbiting. The world employs tactics of sin that stem from the arsenal of Satan himself. And these weapons, while they may exert temporary power, are essentially powerless in the face of the ultimate Victor—the Lord Jesus Christ.

Our weapons are altogether different, "for though we live in the world, we do not wage war as the world does" (v. 3). Our battle tactics "have divine power to demolish strongholds" (v. 4). When the Lord God has armed us, our weapons include love, joy, peace, patience, kindness, goodness, faithfulness, gentleness, and self-control (Galatians 5:22–23). They are the exact opposites of the world's weapons, and as a result, they have the strength of burning coals (Romans 12:20). Our weapons include the Word of God, the sharpest of swords (Hebrews 4:12). Let's make sure we're wielding the weapons that have been proven to work every time. Satan doesn't stand a chance against the arsenal of God's children.

VERSES TO DEEPEN YOUR JOY

PROVERBS 2:7–8; 1 CORINTHIANS 15:57

Go share the joy today!

Dress for Success

Be strong in the Lord and in his mighty power. Put on the full armor of God, so that you can take your stand against the devil's schemes.

EPHESIANS 6:10–11

In addition to our spiritual weapons, the Bible outlines certain character traits that are indispensable in our fight against the Enemy—qualities that we can "put on" and cultivate to thwart Satan's advances against us. The good news is that no matter what the Enemy tries to bring against us, it cannot prosper. God always wins.

Remember, "We know that God causes all things to work together for good to those who love God, to those who are called according to His purpose" (Romans 8:28 NASB). No matter what kind of battle you've been facing, no matter what kind of challenge has been set before you, it won't take you out. God can turn it around so that it works for your good. No, God is not the author of sickness, disease, struggles, or troubles, and what Satan means for evil, God will use for your good.

You will come out stronger in your character. You will come out stronger in your faith. And I believe you will even come out stronger in your health. Don't quit now, for victory is right around the corner. The Enemy's schemes against you will not succeed when you are clad in the right clothing and armed with the proper equipment.

VERSES TO DEEPEN YOUR JOY

PSALM 45:3; ROMANS 13:14

Go share the joy today!

Arm Yourself for Battle

Put on the full armor of God, so that when the day of evil comes, you may be able to stand your ground, and after you have done everything, to stand.

EPHESIANS 6:13

Standing our ground is a key to experiencing victory in any spiritual battle. We have to be determined not to back down. We cannot get weary in doing the good God has called us to do. Let's keep believing and keep standing for our miracle. In order to keep standing our ground, we must be disciplined not to entertain thoughts of defeat and discouragement that are contrary to the Word of God. Second Corinthians 10:5 says, "We take captive every thought to make it obedient to Christ." When the devil sets up pretensions and lies, we dismantle them with the Word of Truth, defend ourselves with the weapons of the Spirit, and rest in the confidence of salvation.

The first thing we should put on as we prepare to engage the Enemy is what Paul described in the book of Ephesians as the "armor of God." If we are to withstand the Enemy's schemes—such as worldly distractions, disease, mental distress, emotional imbalance, and greed—we need to dress for success in our full armor. Let's unpack each component over the coming days and find out what we need to "put on" to see the victory.

VERSES TO DEEPEN YOUR JOY

ISAIAH 59:17; 1 THESSALONIANS 5:8

Go share the joy today!

The Belt of Truth

Stand firm then, with the belt of truth buckled around your waist.

Ephesians 6:14

The truth is that you are engaged in spiritual warfare, and you must stand up, stay firm, and fight as the Lord empowers you. Don't give in to sickness and disease. Don't submit to the Enemy's schemes. Don't lie down in defeat but "stand firm." Even though the battle is not yours but the Lord's and even though he is fighting for you, there's still a part for you to play: you must renew your mind to the truth of God's Word daily. You must stand on the Word of Truth, which will nourish your faith and hope.

Many times, I felt sick and just wanted to go to bed and pull the covers over my head. There have been plenty of instances when I worried that my needs would go unmet. And each time I was about to give in, the Lord would say, *Stand up and fight. This is war.*

Occasionally, I lose sight of the fact that I'm engaged in a spiritual battle. While we shouldn't get so caught up in the warfare that we lose sight of the presence of God, we need to be attuned to the Enemy's schemes so that we may fend him off. And we need to have the Word within us to the extent that we can stand on it in faith, confident of God's promises to protect and deliver us.

VERSES TO DEEPEN YOUR JOY

John 8:32; John 17:17

Go share the joy today!

The Breastplate of Righteousness

Stand firm then,...with the breastplate of righteousness in place.

EPHESIANS 6:14

The Old Testament includes many examples of individuals whom God protected because of the righteousness God credited them for having. In the flood, only Noah and his family were spared because "Noah was a righteous man, blameless among the people of his time, and he walked faithfully with God" (Genesis 6:9). When God told Abram that he would bless him and increase Abram's offspring innumerably, "Abram believed the LORD, and he credited it to him as righteousness" (15:6). Abram was considered righteous for taking God at his word.

Yet it wasn't long before the Bible described fewer and fewer humans as "righteous." Job 15:14 says, "What are mortals, that they could be pure, or those born of woman, that they could be righteous?" While the possibility of a righteous person remained, everyone seemed to have reached the same conclusion: God alone is perfectly righteous. When it comes to humans, "all of us have become like one who is unclean, and all our righteous acts are like filthy rags" (Isaiah 64:6). The pursuit of righteousness is praised—for example, by Proverbs 21:21—but can anyone truly attain it on their own?

We would have been in a lot of trouble had God not sent his perfectly righteous Son, Jesus, to impart to us a "righteousness…given through faith in Jesus Christ to all who believe" (Romans 3:22). Because Jesus paid the price for our unrighteousness, we are credited with his righteousness, which we can wear as a "breastplate" that protects us from the snare of sin.

VERSES TO DEEPEN YOUR JOY

PROVERBS 21:21; 2 CORINTHIANS 5:21

Go share the joy today!

Shoes to Share the Gospel

Stand firm then,...with your feet fitted with the readiness that comes from the gospel of peace.

EPHESIANS 6:14–15

The wording that describes our proper footwear for battle is a little vague. To clear things up, let me share that many preachers and Bible commentators refer to these shoes as sandals of peace. In other words, we should be ready to move over any kind of terrain necessary to take the gospel, or the good news of Christ, to other people. The church is not meant to be immobile. Jesus told us to "*go* and make disciples of all nations" (Matthew 28:19). To obey this command of Jesus, we had better outfit our feet properly.

I realize it can be intimidating to share your faith with others. Sometimes we worry what they will think and how we will come across. We are anxious not to offend or upset them. But we have the greatest gift to give, and when we remember that Christ has defeated all our fears, we can be bold about sharing the good news.

Starting with someone you know well, such as a family member or friend, may help you to get more comfortable talking about what God has done for you. I challenge you to find one person this week with whom you can share the gospel. Start praying that God will open your eyes to see who needs to know him and his saving love.

VERSES TO DEEPEN YOUR JOY

MATTHEW 28:19–20; LUKE 19:37–40

Go share the joy today!

The Shield of Faith

In addition to all this, take up the shield of faith,
with which you can extinguish all the flaming arrows of the evil one.
Ephesians 6:16

Faith is really what the Christian journey is all about. We can't see God, but we trust he is there. We may not see his provision yet, but we believe he will meet and even exceed our needs.

For some believers, faith comes easily. They never really struggle to believe God for anything. For other believers, faith is something they need to grow. Like the man who needed a little help believing that Jesus could cure his son of demon possession, they may say, "I do believe; help me overcome my unbelief!" (Mark 9:24). Like the apostles in Luke 17:5, they may implore the Lord to "increase our faith!"

God will use different situations in our lives to build our faith. Revelation 12:11 says, "They overcame him because of the blood of the Lamb and because of the word of their testimony" (NASB). Our testimony builds our faith and reminds us that what God did before, he can do again. Once I needed mailing labels for my monthly newsletter. I was sitting in my home when the Lord said, *You have everything you need.*

I do? I thought. I looked in the shed at the back of my house, and behold, I found just enough labels for what I needed. Time and time again, I have thought about those mailing labels. My testimony builds my faith that where he provided before, he will provide again.

VERSES TO DEEPEN YOUR JOY

Psalm 7:10; Matthew 7:24–25

Go share the joy today!

The Helmet of Salvation

Take the helmet of salvation.

EPHESIANS 6:17

This particular piece of headgear is of primary importance because it assures us that we will spend eternity with the Lord. No matter the results of your life's race, no matter the victor of your daily battles, salvation is a gift that no one can take from you.

When you're wearing the helmet of salvation, you can proclaim with the psalmist, "The LORD is my light and my salvation—Whom shall I fear? The LORD is the refuge and fortress of my life—Whom shall I dread?" (Psalm 27:1 AMP). When your salvation is secure because of your right relationship with God, you can declare with David, "The LORD is my rock and my fortress [on the mountain] and my rescuer; my God, my rock, in whom I take refuge; my shield and the horn of my salvation" (2 Samuel 22:2–3 AMP).

I never want to miss an opportunity to lead someone to the Lord. If you haven't yet prayed to receive the gift of salvation by accepting Jesus Christ as your Lord and Savior, I invite you to do so right now. Pray with me: *Jesus, I believe that you are the Son of God and that you died on the cross for my sins and rose again so that I could be forgiven and have eternal life. I confess to you that I am a sinner. Please forgive me and come into my heart as my Lord and Savior. Amen.*

Salvation is a helmet no one can afford not to wear. Put it on and proceed confidently toward whatever challenges lie ahead, knowing that the most important part of your armor can never be taken off.

VERSES TO DEEPEN YOUR JOY

PSALM 51:12; ZECHARIAH 9:16

Go share the joy today!

The Sword of the Spirit

Take...the sword of the Spirit,
which is the word of God.

EPHESIANS 6:17

You should never engage with the Enemy without your "sword"—the Word of God. If you aren't properly armed with a heart knowledge of the Bible, you won't stand a chance against the Enemy. Keep your sword sharpened by reading the Word, thinking about the Word, and praying the Word daily.

As you meditate on the Word of Truth every day, your thoughts will align more and more closely with the mind of Christ. As you speak the Word regularly, you will build strength and courage to shore you up against fear and discouragement. So keep your sword sharp. Don't let it grow dull due to lack of use.

If the Enemy attempts to develop a stronghold of sickness and disease in your life, you must demolish it with the sword God has given you in his Word. Demolish devilish thoughts that set themselves up against what God's Word says about your situation. Don't allow yourself to meditate on anything that contradicts the Word of God and its promises. Don't give voice to thoughts of doubt and unbelief. Know that God is more than able to turn your situation around. Stand on his promises.

You don't have to strive to be healed. You don't need to bend over backward to receive provision. You just have to stand on the Word in faith.

VERSES TO DEEPEN YOUR JOY

JOSHUA 1:8–9; PSALM 19:14

Go share the joy today!

Clothed with the Right Traits

I delight greatly in the Lord…For he has clothed me with garments of salvation and arrayed me in a robe of his righteousness.

Isaiah 61:10

In addition to wielding the right weapons and getting dressed in the most effective armor, we need to clothe ourselves in the character traits that will give us victory over the Enemy. These traits are our "weapons" in the spiritual battle we're fighting for our very souls.

Remember, the Word says in 2 Corinthians 10:3–4 that we don't fight with the weapons of the world. Carnal "weapons" and "clothing items" of anger, bitterness, and unforgiveness can decrease our chances of experiencing victory over the Enemy in this lifetime. Instead, we must clothe ourselves with the kinds of "clothing" Paul describes in Colossians 3:12–14: "As God's chosen people, holy and dearly loved, clothe yourselves with compassion, kindness, humility, gentleness and patience. Bear with each other and forgive one another if any of you has a grievance against someone. Forgive as the Lord forgave you. And over all these virtues put on love, which binds them all together in perfect unity."

Over the past several days, we've talked about our spiritual armor. Now we're going to turn our attention to these aspects of clothing that will enable us to secure victory over sin and enjoy relationships of joy and peace with God and those around us.

VERSES TO DEEPEN YOUR JOY

Psalm 93:1; Ephesians 4:22–24

Go share the joy today!

Compassion and Kindness

As God's chosen people, holy and dearly loved,
clothe yourselves with compassion, kindness.
COLOSSIANS 3:12

Compassion softens our hearts and enables us to be kind toward others. We often develop this trait going through a particularly difficult time. Compassion helps us to be slow to judge and quick to help.

My daughter, Destiny, lost her father when she was only four years old. It was a devastating loss, especially on the heels of her losing him first, in a sense, to divorce. Yet the experience of losing her father created a deep compassion in her heart for hurting people. She has a special love for children who are growing up in broken homes and dealing with difficult domestic situations.

Ever since she was young, Destiny has felt compelled to minister to children in orphanages in the United States and overseas. Her heart goes out to children with just one parent or who are orphans. When she compares herself to children with no parents at all, she feels grateful to have a mom, but the comparison does not puff her up with prideful thinking; rather, it increases her passion for helping orphans and showing them God's love.

That's how compassion is meant to work in our hearts. Simply empathizing with others can ease their pain, but we can go a step further and actively help those who are hurting. We can extend kindness without expecting any reward besides the joy that comes from knowing that we're doing the Lord's work.

VERSES TO DEEPEN YOUR JOY

2 CHRONICLES 30:9; PSALM 112:4

Go share the joy today!

Humility

As God's chosen people, holy and dearly loved,
clothe yourselves with…humility.
COLOSSIANS 3:12

In God's kingdom, much of what the secular world espouses is reversed. To go up, we must go down: "Those who exalt themselves will be humbled, and those who humble themselves will be exalted" (Matthew 23:12). Our society exalts self-promotion and prideful striving, but those who follow God's way and dress themselves according to his specifications cultivate hearts of humility.

As we seek to develop humble hearts, we must make sure our humility is authentic. False humility doesn't fool God and doesn't get us anywhere with other people. If our humility isn't genuine, we may try hard to act humble, but our pride is written all over our faces. The kind of humility God rewards is marked by compassion, a teachable spirit, and a lack of self-serving agendas.

Humility is to be a hallmark of God's people in their relationships with one another and in their interactions with the world outside the church. Believe that false humility will be seen for what it is. Humility is hard to fake, and there is no substitute for it. Nothing short of true humility will promote godly relationships and the advancement of God's kingdom on earth.

Pray that God will show you any areas where you need to humble yourself and cast off the spirit of pride. You won't be sorry you did.

VERSES TO DEEPEN YOUR JOY

PSALM 25:9; JAMES 4:6

Go share the joy today!

Humble Like Esther

When the turn came for Esther...to go to the king, she asked for nothing other than what Hegai, the king's eunuch who was in charge of the harem, suggested. And Esther won the favor of everyone who saw her.

Esther 2:15

My favorite biblical example of a humble person is Esther. She was chosen by King Xerxes as his new queen not only because of her beauty but also because she won the favor of the king's courtiers through her obedience and her teachable spirit.

Esther also operated without a secret agenda of her own. When she was chosen as the new queen, it would have been easy to wallow in the riches of royalty with no regard for the fate of her people, whose destruction seemed imminent because of an edict the king had signed. But Esther wasn't above humbling herself to save her people. She didn't use her elevated status as a shield to protect herself while the rest of the Jews perished. With a heart of true humility, Esther adopted the Jews' agenda as her own and made it her mission to save their lives.

A humble heart is fully submitted to God, like Esther's was, and doesn't seek its own fame or fortune foremost. Let's learn from Esther's example and clothe ourselves in humility. Let's elevate others higher than ourselves and prize their well-being above our own.

VERSES TO DEEPEN YOUR JOY

Psalm 147:6; Isaiah 2:11

Go share the joy today!

Gentleness

As God's chosen people, holy and dearly loved,
clothe yourselves with…gentleness.

Colossians 3:12

The world tends to prize boldness and ambition over gentleness and meekness. People largely underestimate the power of a gentle word, a quiet spirit, and a softly spoken response. As the book of Proverbs points out, "Through patience a ruler can be persuaded, and a gentle tongue can break a bone" (25:15). There's power in gentleness.

Being loud and domineering usually has the opposite effect of what we intend: "A gentle answer turns away wrath, but a harsh word stirs up anger" (Proverbs 15:1). How many full-blown, knockdown arguments could have been defused and dismantled if one of the participants had walked away or responded with forgiveness rather than adding fuel to the fire?

Refraining from shouting can help us be more persuasive with the people we care about, such as our children. And gentleness was the essence of Jesus' character. We hear it in this invitation of his that hardly anyone could refuse: "Come to me, all you who are weary and burdened, and I will give you rest. Take my yoke upon you and learn from me, for I am gentle and humble in heart, and you will find rest for your souls" (Matthew 11:28–29).

Jesus gently urges us to let him share our burdens. Wouldn't it be great if the people around us received the same kind of loving acceptance and gentle treatment from us?

VERSES TO DEEPEN YOUR JOY

Matthew 21:5; Ephesians 4:2

Go share the joy today!

Patience

As God's chosen people, holy and dearly loved, clothe yourselves with…patience.

COLOSSIANS 3:12

Gentleness goes hand in hand with patience. Admittedly, patience is a virtue that doesn't come easily to us. Nobody likes having to wait patiently for something they want.

Proverbs 13:12 says, "Hope deferred makes the heart sick, but desire fulfilled is a tree of life" (NASB). What are some things you're longing for? Many of the good things we want will require a long wait. But when our ultimate hope is in the right place—not in an earthly desire but in the divine person of God himself—we can be content and practice patience even while we're waiting for his promises to be fulfilled.

Hope is a vital part of practicing patience. That's why we must put our hope in the proper place. Hope may be deferred in a certain area of your life, but that doesn't mean hope has been denied. Don't get stuck in the heartsick state if your desire has been deferred for now. Just keep your hope in the Lord, whom Romans 15:13 calls "the God of hope."

If our hope is in anything besides the Lord, our expectations are sure to go unfulfilled at some point. One sure way to be disappointed is to place unrealistic expectations on people or events to make us happy. Even the people who love us the most will let us down. But when our hope is in the Lord, we will overflow with joy, peace, and patience that can buoy the expectation level of those around us as well.

VERSES TO DEEPEN YOUR JOY

PSALM 37:7; ROMANS 8:25

Go share the joy today!

Forgiveness and Forbearance

Bear with each other and forgive one another if any of you has a grievance against someone. Forgive as the Lord forgave you.

COLOSSIANS 3:13

I can't emphasize it enough: we must forgive others as God has forgiven us. Jesus said, "If you forgive other people when they sin against you, your heavenly Father will also forgive you" (Matthew 6:14). Paul reinforced this statement when he instructed us to "bear with each other and forgive one another" (Colossians 3:13).

More often than not, instead of bearing with those who hurt us, we act like "bears" toward them, matching blow for blow. But there is nothing for which God won't forgive us, and there's nothing for which we aren't expected to forgive others. Whatever the grievance may be, we must forgive. Even if someone deeply wrongs us, when we hold on to the offense and refuse to forgive, we're only hurting ourselves.

The Enemy delights in convincing people that it's their right to stay bitter against those who hurt them. He wants us to stay mad until we hear a heartfelt apology. But that's not the way forgiveness is supposed to operate. We must uproot any bitterness (Hebrews 12:14–15) before it poisons our heart. Holding on to offense only weighs us down.

When someone wrongs you, remember this: don't nurse it; don't rehearse it; just curse it in the name of Jesus. Take it to the Lord and leave it at the foot of the cross, releasing those who hurt you. When you do this, you release yourself to walk free of the bondage of bitterness, able to surge forward in joy.

VERSES TO DEEPEN YOUR JOY

MATTHEW 18:21–35; LUKE 7:47

Go share the joy today!

Love

Over all these virtues put on love,
which binds them all together in perfect unity.
COLOSSIANS 3:14

We can't "put on love" without God in our lives because "God *is* love" (1 John 4:16). Some people may look like they're walking in love, but unless they know the Lord, their "love walk" is a charade. It's great to have faith and hope, but even those virtues are without value—and so are any acts of kindness and goodwill we might perform—unless we're acting from a heart of genuine love, as Paul made clear in 1 Corinthians 13:1–2.

Again, whoever doesn't love doesn't *really* know God: "Everyone who loves has been born of God and knows God. The one who does not love does not know God, because God is love" (1 John 4:7–8 NASB). We may claim to know God, but if we lack love—for our neighbors, for our family members, for our coworkers, for those we serve, and even for our enemies—we're living a lie.

By spending time in the Word and fellowshipping with the Lord, we can grow in genuine love. When we *really* know God, we take on his nature because we always become like the people we spend time with. Walking in love doesn't come automatically, however. We need the help of the Holy Spirit to develop the fruit of love in our hearts. And he is ready to do just that.

VERSES TO DEEPEN YOUR JOY

MARK 12:30–32; EPHESIANS 5:2

Go share the joy today!

Don't Get Worn Out

"The Lord will fight for you;
you need only to be still."
Exodus 14:14

The clothing of character traits and the spiritual weapons we've been talking about the past few weeks are critical in our fight against sin and Satan. But we have to be smart about the way we engage in warfare.

The Lord said to me one day, *Don't wear yourself out in the warfare.* He went on to give me a vivid picture of what I had been doing, basically trying to fight my way out of a paper bag. This picture was a message that I shouldn't wear myself out trying to escape the bag; I should rip it open and jump out, ending the struggle.

All believers are caught up in a spiritual battle. This battle is not against our family, friends, or coworkers but against the devil and his cohorts who seek to bring us down spiritually. Remember, Ephesians 6:12 says, "Our struggle is not against flesh and blood, but against the rulers, against the powers, against the world forces of this darkness, against the spiritual forces of wickedness in the heavenly places" (NASB).

The good news is that the battle is already won. Victory is ours! But we must live in such a way that shows we believe that to be true. We must live in a place of victory, not defeat, being confident that we will prevail over our enemies and enjoy the win that God has already secured for our sake. If we forget that the battle is already won, we're apt to get worn out in warfare, mistakenly believing that the outcome is up to us.

VERSES TO DEEPEN YOUR JOY

Deuteronomy 20:4; 1 Samuel 17:47

Go share the joy today!

Fight with the Right Mindset

Wait on the LORD, and keep His way,
and He shall exalt you to inherit the land.

PSALM 37:34 NKJV

While we wait for victory to manifest, we must keep doing what God has called us to do and maintain a proper mindset—one that hopes in the Lord and trusts him to come through for us. This is the place where many people grow discouraged and desire to quit. But God is looking for consistency and faithfulness. He is looking for us to have longevity as we stand in faith on his promises. He gives us perseverance and power in this long, drawn-out fight by the power of his Holy Spirit. Let's not forget that his help is only a prayer away.

Being dependent on the Lord is the best way to approach spiritual warfare. He wants us to draw ever closer to him as we depend on his power and his ability to equip us for every skirmish. In Joshua 1:13, God's message to the Israelites was this: "The LORD your God is giving you rest and is giving you this land" (NKJV). In other words, don't wear yourself out trying to fight your battle. Yes, you must face your enemy and stand your ground, but don't forget that God has already gone before you. He has secured your victory. He has already won the land for you, so go ahead and rest.

"Rest?" you may ask as the Israelites surely did. "In the midst of my biggest battle?"

Yes, rest! Don't wear yourself out and grow tired and weary. The battle is already won.

VERSES TO DEEPEN YOUR JOY

EXODUS 14:13–14; 2 CHRONICLES 20:15, 17

Go share the joy today!

Equipped for Battle

David triumphed over the Philistine with a sling and a stone, and he struck down the Philistine and killed him; but there was no sword in David's hand.

1 Samuel 17:50 AMP

Many people grow weary in warfare when they fixate on their limited abilities and resources. Let me encourage you today: whatever battle you're caught up in, God doesn't need your abilities or resources to win it. He has a long proven history of using small, weak, ill-equipped people to achieve powerful victories.

Take David, the little shepherd boy who slayed the giant Goliath after all Israel's brawniest soldiers had backed away from him in fear. David was the smallest of his brothers, with no training for warfare; his weapon was nothing more than a slingshot and some stones from the stream. But because of his assurance that God was with him and would give him the victory, David prevailed over the Philistines and their champion fighter.

We have a lot to learn from David and his demeanor as he faced off against his enemy. His level of faith can be ours when we trust in the Lord. Even if you think you're ill-equipped and poorly outfitted for battle, remember that as long as the Lord is with you, you have all you need. Never doubt his ability to provide above and beyond your requirements. Just look to the Lord and trust him to get you through.

VERSES TO DEEPEN YOUR JOY

Psalm 77:14; Acts 3:16

Go share the joy today!

Supernaturally Strengthened

I can do all this through him who gives me strength.

PHILIPPIANS 4:13

Do you need strength? I've got great news for you! God wants to give you strength to accomplish everything that you need to do today.

Not only does God want to give you strength, but he wants to give you supernatural strength. I am reminded of the supernatural strength that God gave Elijah in 1 Kings 18:44–46. "The hand of the LORD came upon Elijah [giving him supernatural strength]" (v. 46 AMP), and he was able to run ahead of King Ahab, who was riding on a chariot. It does not make sense that Elijah would be able to run ahead of a man who was being pulled by horses, but God's power was upon Elijah to do the supernatural.

Let God's supernatural power rest on you today so you can do what seems impossible for mere humans to do. When God calls you to act, don't say, *I can't*. Hear God's instruction for your day and walk boldly in the direction of obedience, knowing that with God, all things are possible. God had a destination for Elijah, and he has a destination for you. Don't let anything hinder you from running into the purposes of God for your life today.

VERSES TO DEEPEN YOUR JOY

ISAIAH 58:11; COLOSSIANS 1:11

Go share the joy today!

God Makes You Mighty

When the angel of the Lord appeared to Gideon, he said, "The Lord is with you, mighty warrior."

Judges 6:12

God used David despite his small size and seemingly weak weapons. He also used Gideon, a man ruled by sinful appetites, to deliver his people from the oppression of the Midianites. When the angel of the Lord called Gideon a "mighty warrior," Gideon couldn't take him seriously. His first objection was that God could not possibly be with his people, considering how badly they had been suffering lately (v. 13).

The angel's response simply affirmed Gideon's strength: "Go in the strength you have and save Israel out of Midian's hand. Am I not sending you?" (v. 14).

Once again, Gideon objected, this time pointing out his weakness (v. 15). But did that faze God? Not at all. God said, "I will be with you, and you will strike down all the Midianites, leaving none alive" (v. 16).

God told Gideon who he was, and more importantly, he told Gideon who was with him—the Lord Almighty! That assurance should have been the end of the conversation, but Gideon, in his weakness and insecurity, kept asking for confirmation that God was with him (vv. 17–40). What he needed was a change of mindset! And that's just what we need today: a change in mindset so that we see ourselves the way God sees us. When God is with us, we are mighty warriors, for God gives us everything we need to win whatever war we're waging.

VERSES TO DEEPEN YOUR JOY

Judges 7; 1 Corinthians 1:27

Go share the joy today!

Know Your True Identity

In all these things we are more than conquerors and gain an overwhelming victory through Him who loved us [so much that He died for us].

Romans 8:37 AMP

Instead of questioning whether God is with us and whether we have what it takes to win, as Gideon did, we should declare, like the prophet Jeremiah, "The Lord is with me as a dread champion [one to be greatly feared]; therefore my persecutors will stumble and not overcome [me]" (Jeremiah 20:11 AMP). When we continually acknowledge that God is with us, we stir up supernatural strength and courage from within. No longer weak, worrisome, battle-weary warriors, we turn into mighty conquerors full of faith who rise up in victory, enduring all kinds of trials and prevailing by the power of God within us. In fact, we are "more than conquerors," as Paul expressed in the book of Romans.

Talk about an empowering battle cry! We don't have to grow weary or discouraged in our warfare because our joy does not stem from how things look in the natural; it's built on the unshakable truth that God is for us, always and forever, and nothing can separate us from his love.

Instead of being intimidated by the battles before us and the giants we face, we can allow God to overcome our insecurities by reminding ourselves that we are mighty warriors equipped with all the power of the Holy Spirit. We can open our mouths wide and defeat our "giants" by the power of faith-filled declarations of who we are and whom we serve.

VERSES TO DEEPEN YOUR JOY

Romans 8:31–39; Revelation 12:11

Go share the joy today!

Faithful to Fight for You

Great is your love, higher than the heavens;
your faithfulness reaches to the skies.

PSALM 108:4

Your faith increases when you go through situations and circumstances that test your faith. It's not fun, but it does work. Your faith grows during those testing times. Your faith increases as you remember all that the Lord has done for you in the past. Remind yourself how God has been faithful to bring you through the hard times before and watch your faith rise as you look ahead to the future battles he will wage on your behalf.

I employ this faith-boosting technique all the time. When I receive ministry bills that are much bigger than our bank account can accommodate, I first tell God that he has mail, and then I remind myself of all the other times he has brought us through. God has never failed to take care of his mail, and he has never paid a bill late. He has always provided everything that my daughter and I have needed, from mortgage payments to meals, even when all the evidence pointed to empty pockets.

Every time it's looked like the end, God has come through, and I know he will do it again and again. But I couldn't feel so sure unless I had come through each of those close calls and uncomfortable realizations that we were out of money. God is faithful to fight for us; we just need to cling to our memory of his faithfulness.

VERSES TO DEEPEN YOUR JOY

2 CHRONICLES 20:5–12; 1 TIMOTHY 6:12

Go share the joy today!

Possess the Promises

The LORD gave Israel all the land which He had sworn to give to their fathers, and they took possession of it and lived in it.

JOSHUA 21:43 NASB

When God has made us a promise, that promise is as good as ours, but we have a part to play: we have to *possess* it. We can't just sit back and wait for it to fall into our lap. If we simply sit back and wait without taking proactive measures, the Enemy sneaks in with his distractions and discouragement, making us vulnerable to his efforts to derail our destiny. Claim your inheritance in God, and you will see his promises fulfilled in your life.

Joshua 21:45 says, "Not one of the good promises which the LORD had made to the house of Israel failed; everything came to pass" (NASB). And the same will be true for you if you will only seize the promises of God and not doubt.

The antidote to doubt is faith, which is belief in the truth—God's Word—which always trumps the "facts" in the natural realm. I love how the *Amplified Bible, Classic Edition* translates Hebrews 11:1: "Faith is the assurance (the confirmation, the title deed) of the things [we] hope for, being the proof of things [we] do not see and the conviction of their reality [faith perceiving as real fact what is not revealed to the senses]." Your faith truly is your "title deed" to all God's promises.

VERSES TO DEEPEN YOUR JOY

JOSHUA 23:14; 2 CORINTHIANS 1:20

Go share the joy today!

October

Keep Up the Work

God...will not forget your work and the love you have shown him as you have helped his people and continue to help them.

HEBREWS 6:10

As they push forward to possess God's promises, one particular area in which many Christians grow weary is their works—the good, well-intentioned things they do for others—sometimes to the point of becoming worn out, run-down, and even resentful of those they are serving. Have you been growing weary of doing good works? It's hard to serve others with joy when that very process is wearing you down.

God does honor our work and is pleased when we serve others in loving self-sacrifice. But what happens when we set out to do good because we want to earn spiritual brownie points or because we think that God will reward us in the here and now? We forget the purpose of good works, and we may fall into the trap of mistakenly believing that God will spare us from all hardships and injustice because we've been so faithfully serving him.

The truth is that he never promised an easy path, even for his faithful servants. Jesus told his disciples, "If the world hates you, keep in mind that it hated me first" (John 15:18). This reminder may not bring immediate comfort, but it can carry us through tough times when we remember that God is preparing us for better things to come.

VERSES TO DEEPEN YOUR JOY

ISAIAH 40:29; GALATIANS 6:9

Go share the joy today!

No Exemptions from Suffering

"Whoever wants to be my disciple must deny themselves and take up their cross and follow me."

MATTHEW 16:24

When my husband told me he was leaving me just days before our daughter was born, I remember saying to the Lord, *Why me? I've done all the right things!* I had a skewed understanding of the rewards of righteous living. Even if we think we've done all the right things, we are not exempt from suffering.

Consider Job, whom God called "blameless and upright, a man who fears God and shuns evil" (Job 1:8). Even with this glowing commendation, God allowed Satan to test Job. Satan sought only to steal Job's faith by sending him sorrow after sorrow. In the end, Job's children were dead, all his servants had been killed, his livestock had been stolen, his house was destroyed, and he was afflicted with painful sores (Job 1–2).

Despite so many struggles, "Job did not sin by charging God with wrongdoing" (1:22). In fact, Job *worshiped* God in the wake of these tragedies. If anybody should have been exempt from hardship because of good works, it was Job, yet he never complained about losing all the people and possessions he loved the most. This firm faith was possible for Job because he had an unshakable joy rooted in his relationship with the Lord, and the same is possible for us too.

VERSES TO DEEPEN YOUR JOY

JOB 1:21; JOHN 15:20

Go share the joy today!

Remember Whom You Serve

Whatever you do, work at it with all your heart, as working for the Lord, not for human masters, since you know that you will receive an inheritance from the Lord as a reward. It is the Lord Christ you are serving.

COLOSSIANS 3:23–24

We sometimes grow weary when we don't see the fruits of our labors right away. It can be downright discouraging to serve someone who never thanks us, to pray without seeing results, and to invest in a person's life without seeing much change to show for it. In these situations, I encourage myself with 1 Corinthians 15:58: "Be steadfast, immovable, always excelling in the work of the Lord [always doing your best and doing more than is needed], being continually aware that your labor [even to the point of exhaustion] in the Lord is not futile nor wasted [it is never without purpose]" (AMP). Any work we do for the Lord is never in vain, even when we can't see what that work is producing.

And whenever I grow weary of serving others, I find it helpful to remind myself of the ultimate person I am serving—God himself. This reminder always gives me an extra boost of energy. If you envision God in every face you see, hand you hold, and mouth you feed, I guarantee that you'll be strengthened and empowered for the job.

Always remember who it is you're ultimately serving. God will be sure to reward you even if you don't receive any accolades for your efforts on this side of heaven.

VERSES TO DEEPEN YOUR JOY

PROVERBS 14:23; ECCLESIASTES 9:10

Go share the joy today!

Choose Joy

This is the day the LORD has made;
we will rejoice and be glad in it.

PSALM 118:24 NKJV

There will be days when we experience hardship and suffering that seem as if they could never have any purpose behind them—that God could never turn them around for our good. We find ourselves weary and worn out by emotional stressors, relational problems, and health issues. What then? Well, no matter what our circumstances may be, each day is a gift. With the proper perspective, we can live with an attitude of gratitude and start each morning by choosing to be joyful.

We can rejoice despite our circumstances because the Lord has made each day and everything in it. He is still in control when every aspect of our lives seems out of control. God is still on the throne, and Jesus is seated at his Father's right hand, interceding for you and me.

The Bible makes it very clear when we are to rejoice. Is it just when things are going well? Is it only when we feel happy? No, it is *always.* "Rejoice in the Lord always. I will say it again: Rejoice!" (Philippians 4:4). We're meant to rejoice no matter what. Our circumstances may not give us reason to rejoice, but when God is the king of our lives, we can rejoice despite our situation. We can rejoice through anything life throws our way.

VERSES TO DEEPEN YOUR JOY

PSALM 51:12; 1 THESSALONIANS 5:16–18

Go share the joy today!

Rejoice in Righteousness

The hope of the [uncompromisingly] righteous (the upright, in right standing with God) is gladness.

PROVERBS 10:28 AMPC

The righteous—those who are "in right standing with God" because of salvation through Jesus Christ—can have joy in all circumstances. That's because our salvation can never be taken from us. No matter what else we may lose or what hardships we may endure, the Lord's presence is our precious, eternal treasure.

Doing what is right—something that the power of the Holy Spirit living within us enables us to do—brings us joy and causes our heavenly Father to rejoice. Doing what is wrong or sinful, while it may feel good in the moment, never brings lasting joy but results in guilt, remorse, and regret. But when we are purified through the blood of Christ and forgiven of our sins, we can rejoice because we know that our "prospect," or that which we hope for and expect, is joy.

Once we've chosen joy, we need to guard it. Plenty of people and scenarios can easily steal our joy if we allow them to. We need to hold on to our positive attitude and make sure to count our blessings more than we number our woes.

Don't buy the lie that sin will bring you lasting pleasure. The devil wants you to fall for his deceptions, but you're smarter than that. Rejoice as you pursue the righteousness of Christ.

VERSES TO DEEPEN YOUR JOY

ISAIAH 61:3; 1 JOHN 2:27

Go share the joy today!

Protect Your Peace

Do not be anxious about anything, but in every situation, by prayer and petition, with thanksgiving, present your requests to God. And the peace of God, which transcends all understanding, will guard your hearts and your minds in Christ Jesus.

PHILIPPIANS 4:6–7

Those who aren't at peace are likely to lose their joy. Personally, I find it hard to be at peace when I'm running late. If there's even a slight possibility that I will arrive somewhere behind schedule, it stresses me out. My shoulders tense up. The next thing you know, my peace is gone; pretty soon, so is my joy if I'm not careful to guard it.

Thankfully, after identifying the impact that running late was having on my peace and joy, I learned to catch myself before slipping too far into that cycle. Whenever I feel pressure building in my neck and shoulders, I say to myself, *You'd better reel it in, girl. It isn't worth losing your peace and your joy.*

In this scenario and others, I've learned to intentionally shift my focus to positive, praiseworthy things. I try to follow Paul's instructions in today's verses.

Identify those aspects of your life that most threaten to steal your peace and turn them over to God "by prayer and petition," not neglecting "thanksgiving," which brings to mind God's blessings and distracts our focus from hardship and sorrow. Counting our blessings is a great way to keep our joy tank full.

VERSES TO DEEPEN YOUR JOY

JOHN 14:27; ROMANS 15:13

Go share the joy today!

Refuel Your Joy Tank

Since, then, you have been raised with Christ, set your hearts on things above, where Christ is, seated at the right hand of God. Set your minds on things above, not on earthly things.

COLOSSIANS 3:1–2

Our joy tank goes from full to empty pretty fast when we allow ourselves to dwell on the wrong thing, whether sinful thoughts, despair and doubt, or negativity. In most cases, spiritual warfare starts in the mind, where the Enemy plants seeds of doubt, deception, and defeat.

It's the way we respond to these kinds of mental and emotional attacks that determines whether our joy tank remains full or gets depleted. We can't afford to let our minds be a launching pad for the Enemy's lying schemes. By replenishing our joy tank routinely, we can arm ourselves to withstand the devil's attacks.

What kinds of fuel should we use to fill our joy tank? We find some ideas in Romans 12:9–13: "Love must be free of hypocrisy. Detest what is evil; cling to what is good. Be devoted to one another in brotherly love; give preference to one another in honor, not lagging behind in diligence, fervent in spirit, serving the Lord; rejoicing in hope, persevering in tribulation, devoted to prayer, contributing to the needs of the saints, practicing hospitality" (NASB). God's Word is the perfect way to combat all the lies of the Enemy. The Bible has an answer for every trouble, and it is the absolute, indisputable truth. In it we find countless reasons to be joyful.

VERSES TO DEEPEN YOUR JOY

NEHEMIAH 8:10; ROMANS 11:29

Go share the joy today!

Dismiss Discouraging Thoughts

We demolish arguments and every pretension that sets itself up against the knowledge of God, and we take captive every thought to make it obedient to Christ.

2 CORINTHIANS 10:5

I can be having a great day with everything going right, only to feel, out of the blue, a mounting sense of discouragement and dread. When I take the time to trace this feeling back to its source, I often discover that I had been unconsciously dwelling on an unpleasant conversation I had with someone, on a larger-than-expected bill I received in the mail, on a situation that occurred at the office, or on another simple event. Shedding light on that fiery dart of discouragement by identifying what was bothering me, I can take that thought captive and start declaring the Word of Truth concerning the situation. When I do this, the meter on my joy tank immediately starts to rise.

If the source of discouragement was a negative comment someone made to me, I say to myself, *Don't let their issue be your issue*. I remind myself that my identity is in the Lord and not based on other people's opinions of me. If I'm panicked about a bill that's due, I affirm my confidence in God's ability to provide what I need. I may remind myself, for example, *God shall supply all my needs according to his riches in glory* (Philippians 4:19). God's Word is the antidote to every one of the devil's discouraging thoughts.

VERSES TO DEEPEN YOUR JOY

MARK 10:27; JOHN 8:44

Go share the joy today!

The Power of a Smile

A happy heart makes the face cheerful.

PROVERBS 15:13

I'll bet you didn't know just how powerful a smile can be. Today's verse from Proverbs indicates that we smile because we're happy, but it works both ways: a cheerful face can produce a happy heart. How? Studies have shown that the act of smiling releases powerful endorphins that boost your mood. Smiling has also been shown to calm heart rates and relieve pain. Isn't it amazing the way the physical and emotional aspects of our bodies are related?

I really can't overstate the power of smiling. Proverbs 15:15 says, "All the days of the afflicted are bad, but a glad heart has a continual feast [regardless of the circumstances]" (AMP). Your smile has medicinal powers—not only for yourself but also for those around you. When was the last time you indulged in a great big belly laugh? When was the last time you engaged in something that made you so joyful that you couldn't wipe the smile off your face?

Even if you can't think of anything to smile about, smile anyway. You'll experience a boost in your mood and maybe even generate a conversation with a stranger. When someone asks why you're so glad, you can say, "Just the knowledge that Jesus loves me," or something along those lines. You never know where the gladness of knowing God may lead you. So keep those pearly whites shining as you smile at those around you, brightening their days—and your own.

VERSES TO DEEPEN YOUR JOY

PSALM 100:2; ISAIAH 12:3

Go share the joy today!

Laughter as Medicine

A merry heart does good, like medicine.

PROVERBS 17:22 NKJV

I lost both my brothers at far younger ages than I should have, yet my grieving process with both looked radically different. My brother David died of cancer in January 2013. He had gone through so many treatments and hospitalizations that I had grieved along the way, in a process that was long and drawn out. We had time to spend with each other, time to say goodbye again and again, time to talk and pray together as we prepared for his transition to his heavenly home.

But with my brother Denny, there wasn't any preparatory grieving. His sudden death caught us all off guard. He passed in August 2021, and I spent the next nine months trying to catch my breath. The grieving process was shorter and more intense than with my other brother.

During this intense time of grieving for Denny, I was having lunch one day with a friend who said something that made me laugh. I don't remember exactly what she said, but I do remember my mouth stretching wider than it had in a long while and the way it made me feel. I had always been a joyful person prone to smiling and laughter, and that day I realized I had been so stuck in the grieving process that I had done neither of those things in the longest time. As I remembered what it felt like to laugh, an immense weight of grief dropped from me. I was amazed to realize the impact laughter had on my emotional state.

VERSES TO DEEPEN YOUR JOY

PSALM 126:2; PROVERBS 15:15

Go share the joy today!

Appreciate Simple Pleasures

Be joyful in hope, patient in affliction, faithful in prayer.

Romans 12:12

Everyday joys can carry us through times of drudgery and periods of pain. No matter what kind of season you're experiencing right now, if you keep your joy tank full (or at least more than half full), you'll have an easier time living out today's exhortation from the apostle Paul. You will overflow with joy to those around you as you celebrate the small things, rejoice in the big things, and praise God through thick and thin. The joy of the Lord is your strength, and it's always more than enough.

It's easy to forget to take time for yourself. Many people get so caught up in trying to please the Lord by serving others that they neglect their own comfort and joy altogether. Today think about one thing that brings you true joy and pursue it as soon as possible. It doesn't have to be something really big or expensive; for many people, it's the small, everyday joys that bring the most satisfaction.

For me, some favorite everyday pleasures are unsweetened iced tea, chocolate, and playing pickleball. What do you do that brings you joy? What are some favorite food items that put a smile on your face? It's good to relish those things, giving thanks to God for the pleasure they bring us.

VERSES TO DEEPEN YOUR JOY

Psalm 30:11; Ecclesiastes 8:15

Go share the joy today!

Embrace the New

Arise [from the depression and prostration in which circumstances have kept you—rise to a new life]! Shine (be radiant with the glory of the Lord), for your light has come, and the glory of the Lord has risen upon you!

Isaiah 60:1 AMPC

For the first year after my husband left me, I held out hope that we would be reconciled. I fasted often and prayed practically nonstop for the restoration of our marriage. Yet my husband slipped further and further away from God and our family.

One day during a conference, the Lord gave me this message: *You have to release the old so I can bring the new into your life*. In that moment, I knew he was telling me that a divorce was on the horizon. I hadn't entertained the possibility until that point, and I felt almost as shattered then as I had on the day my husband and I first separated.

My road to recovery wasn't easy or brief. Many days I was so emotionally devastated that I couldn't even hold my head up. But after about nine months of struggling to find energy and motivation for each new morning, I heard the Lord say, *Get up out of your mess and go do what I've called you to do*. In other words, it was time for me to release the old and embrace the new with his help.

VERSES TO DEEPEN YOUR JOY

Psalm 30:5; Isaiah 61:3

Go share the joy today!

Moving On

After the death of Moses the servant of the Lord, the Lord said to Joshua…, Moses My servant is dead. So now arise [take his place], go over this Jordan, you and all this people, into the land which I am giving to them.

Joshua 1:1–2 AMPC

The law of Moses allowed the Israelites thirty days to mourn the death of their leader. After those days of mourning were up, God told Joshua to arise and assume his position as the new leader. It was time to move on. Joshua had to release the old to embrace the new.

God's message to Joshua was another way of saying, "Release the old; now, arise! Don't stay stuck where you are now." When we face times of sorrow and disappointment, we need to release the old so we can step forward and embrace all the new things that our heavenly Father has in store for our future.

Joshua had to learn how to handle new responsibilities in his leadership role, and he may not have felt prepared for the position. That's where faith and total dependence on God come in. We don't have to feel ready or comfortable to obey the Lord. Most of the time, our flesh won't be comfortable as we step forward in faith. That's because we almost always have to move outside our comfort zones to reach our potential zones.

VERSES TO DEEPEN YOUR JOY

Numbers 27:18; Joshua 1:6

Go share the joy today!

Leave the Past Behind

"Forget the former things; do not dwell on the past. See, I am doing a new thing! Now it springs up; do you not perceive it? I am making a way in the wilderness and streams in the wasteland."

Isaiah 43:18–19

When the Lord challenged me to move on from my shattered marriage, I had to decide daily to release the old. Like Joshua, I was shouldering a mountain of new responsibilities I didn't necessarily feel like I could handle. I'd become a single mom to a newborn daughter almost overnight, and I had no income.

Many times we're tempted to remain in an old, familiar place even after the Lord has told us it's time to move on. Our inclination to cling to the old is usually rooted in our sense of security—a *false* sense of security, that is. Some people stay in harmful relationships and dangerous situations, meaning well but subjecting themselves and their children to untold misery.

As the Lord prompted me to release the old, I had to choose daily to embrace the new life I was building with my daughter. Father God assured me that his plan for me hadn't changed; I was to radiate his glory by fulfilling his call on my life. My call hadn't changed. God's love for me hadn't changed. And he reminded me over and over that, together, he and I were the majority. As I released the past and walked toward the future he had in store, I would experience the wonderful new things he would do in me and through me.

VERSES TO DEEPEN YOUR JOY

Romans 2:7; Philippians 3:13–14

Go share the joy today!

Transition Prompts Transformation

We all, with unveiled face, continually seeing as in a mirror the glory of the Lord, are progressively being transformed into His image from [one degree of] glory to [even more] glory, which comes from the Lord, [who is] the Spirit.

2 Corinthians 3:18 AMP

When our heavenly Father takes us through times of transition, leading us away from the old and into the new, it can be a painful process. But on the other side of a transition is a totally transformed person. When our transformation is finally complete, we will be glad that we went through the transition process, and we won't desire to return to our former state. We won't experience any regrets.

The caterpillar transitions from a hairy worm to a beautiful butterfly because it experiences a total transformation, which takes time. If the chrysalis is opened during the transition, the caterpillar will die without ever becoming what the Father intended it to be.

God the Father forms us, and it's the Holy Spirit who transforms us. If we will submit to the process and patiently follow his leading, we will complete the process and fully become the people he planned for us to be. But if we refuse to change or if we derail the process by taking shortcuts or trying to thwart the prescribed steps, we may get stuck. If you're going through a time of transition, hang in there. A beautiful transformation awaits you.

VERSES TO DEEPEN YOUR JOY

Psalm 51:10–12; Philippians 3:21

Go share the joy today!

Transformed to Teach and Reach

Praise be to the God and Father of our Lord Jesus Christ, the Father of compassion and the God of all comfort, who comforts us in all our troubles, so that we can comfort those in any trouble with the comfort we ourselves receive from God.

2 CORINTHIANS 1:3–4

As we release the old and embrace the new, we are to be Christ's ambassadors, continuing the work he did on earth, which he summarized as follows: "The Spirit of the Lord God is upon me, because the Lord has anointed and qualified me to preach the Gospel of good tidings to the meek, the poor, and afflicted; He has sent me to bind up and heal the brokenhearted, to proclaim liberty to the [physical and spiritual] captives and the opening of the prison and of the eyes to those who are bound" (Isaiah 61:1 AMPC).

When we've experienced a particular transition and transformation, we are supposed to look for ways to reach out a helping hand to others who are going through similar transitions. We're meant to teach others from our own experience, to empathize with them in their own suffering, and to pray them through their own process. As God's children, we are anointed and qualified to minister the gospel to others and act as a source of encouragement and strength.

VERSES TO DEEPEN YOUR JOY

2 CORINTHIANS 1:5–7; GALATIANS 6:10

Go share the joy today!

The New Has Begun

Anyone who belongs to Christ has become a new person.
The old life is gone; a new life has begun!
2 Corinthians 5:17 NLT

Once we've accepted Christ and have surrendered our lives to him, we're no longer the same carnal, worldly women we used to be. When Christ came to live in our hearts through his Holy Spirit, we died—died to sin, to self, and to our old ways of dealing with and responding to the people and experiences we encounter.

As Paul wrote in Colossians 3:3, "You died, and your life is now hidden with Christ in God." Technically speaking, dead people have no responses. They don't even notice when things don't go their way or when others speak negative words about them. We are to be dead to our old selves and to our former, strictly sinful ways. Now that we're new creations in Christ, we're told, "Do not lie to each other, since you have taken off your old self with its practices and have put on the new self, which is being renewed in knowledge in the image of its Creator" (vv. 9–10).

Now is the time to become what we *already are* in Christ. We must choose to take off the old self and put on the new. God's Word makes it very clear what to wear and what not to wear. We shouldn't spend more time and attention on how we're dressed in the natural than how we're clothed in the Spirit. The new life has begun. Let's dress like we believe that's true.

VERSES TO DEEPEN YOUR JOY

Romans 5:17; Colossians 3:12

Go share the joy today!

Act, Don't React

Jehoshaphat was afraid and turned his attention to seek the LORD.

2 CHRONICLES 20:3 NASB

When we've put on the new self that comes from surrendering to God, we become capable of acting rather than reacting to situations that normally would have sent us straight into panic mode. Reacting is a knee-jerk response to a stimulus while acting requires the presence of mind and self-command—neither of which is possible without the power of God's Spirit.

Today's verse refers to a time when King Jehoshaphat received some alarming news. A huge army was on its way to attack his people and destroy his city (2 Chronicles 20:1–2). He was afraid, yet he didn't react out of his flesh. Instead, he acted out of his spirit by going to God first and seeking the Lord's wisdom for the situation (vv. 3–12).

How do you respond when you get alarming news? All forms of freaking out are reactions of the flesh. Some people see a storm coming and run away from God at the very time they most need to run *to* him. But those who act like Jehoshaphat look to the Lord and seek his face.

Jehoshaphat proclaimed a fast, and "the people of Judah came together to seek help from the LORD" (v. 4). During his biggest battle, this wise king inquired of the Lord. He didn't scream, cry, flip out, or seek his friends' opinions. He went before the Lord in fasting and prayer, and the Lord honored his actions.

VERSES TO DEEPEN YOUR JOY

JUDGES 20:23; JEREMIAH 10:21

Go share the joy today!

Don't Panic in the Pit

"'Fear not, for I am with you;
be not dismayed, for I am your God.'"
Isaiah 41:10 NKJV

When we're stuck in a "pit" of life—a seemingly inescapable problem, an apparently hopeless situation—it's tempting to grab anything we can get our hands on to keep from going deeper. But if we panic, whatever we may grab becomes a shovel that only digs us deeper.

You may have witnessed this phenomenon when someone grabs a new relationship to escape the pit of a failed romance. What happens? Instead of escaping the prior relational pit, she ends up going deeper and getting into further trouble. Others grab a drug or alcohol, trying to numb the pain of their pit, only to dig their way deeper into other problems.

Although the news of an approaching army alarmed Jehoshaphat, he didn't panic or react based on his emotions; he acted by inquiring of the Lord. This type of response avoids the waste of time and energy that an emotional reaction expends. Jehoshaphat was a wise leader who knew that if he became unglued, his people would do the same. That's why he proclaimed a fast, uniting their response in a productive, God-honoring way. When we look to the Lord instead of pressing the panic button, we can climb out of every pit as winners.

VERSES TO DEEPEN YOUR JOY

1 Chronicles 29:12; Jeremiah 30:10

Go share the joy today!

Determine to Trust God

Cast your cares on the LORD and he will sustain you;
he will never let the righteous be shaken.

PSALM 55:22

We read a few days ago about how Jehoshaphat sought the Lord (2 Chronicles 20:3–4). Some translations say that he "resolved" to seek the Lord. *To resolve* means "to set oneself decidedly" or "to determine." This king *determined* to understand God's mind on the matter of the approaching army. He didn't consult his family, friends, or counselors; he went straight to God, being determined to trust him during oncoming troubles.

When the people of Judah gathered at the temple, Jehoshaphat led them, and he opened his prayer by acknowledging God for the all-powerful, all-knowing deity he is. He said, "Power and might are in Your hand, there is no one able to take a stand against You" (v. 6 AMP). If we fail to acknowledge God for who he is, we're apt to react out of our own strength (which is mostly weakness) and doubt what he will do for us. But acknowledging him and his might makes it easier for us to trust him with our situation.

Again, Jehoshaphat was determined to inquire of the Lord. Determination will get us just about anywhere we want to go. If we're determined to go in a direction that's not what God wants for our lives, we can. But it won't be pretty! Let's determine instead to trust him and follow his guidance no matter what.

VERSES TO DEEPEN YOUR JOY

PSALM 112:6–7; JOHN 10:14

Go share the joy today!

Calamity as Course Correction

*"I will offer sacrifices to you with songs of praise,
and I will fulfill all my vows.
For my salvation comes from the LORD alone."*

JONAH 2:9 NLT

Determination can definitely work to our disadvantage if the thing that we are determined to do is resist God's will—his perfect, preordained plans for our lives. Perhaps nobody in the Bible proved this point more strongly than Jonah. God had directed him to the city of Nineveh to convict the people there of their wickedness, but Jonah determined to go to Tarshish instead—anywhere but Nineveh (Jonah 1:1–3).

In God's great love for Jonah, he sent a series of apparent calamities designed to set Jonah on the right track once again. From a violent storm at sea—which Jonah recognized would stop only once the ship's crew tossed him overboard—to a giant fish that swallowed him up and kept him safe in its stomach for three days, these apparent setbacks caught Jonah's attention and corrected his course.

Not every setback is a scheme of Satan. It could be that God is using what appears to be an obstacle on your path to steer you back to him. Never determine to run away from God but determine to trust him every step of the way. Look for God's directions amid your apparent troubles and trust him to lead you in the way you should go.

VERSES TO DEEPEN YOUR JOY

PSALM 32:8; JEREMIAH 10:23

Go share the joy today!

Pray in the Pit

One day Jesus told his disciples a story to illustrate their need for constant prayer and to show them that they must keep praying until the answer comes.

LUKE 18:1 TLB

What was the first thing that Jonah did when he found himself in the belly of the giant fish? He prayed to God. Prayer should always be our first response when we find ourselves stuck and in need of help. Jonah's prayer acknowledged where he had messed up and declared how God had saved him. And immediately after praying, Jonah was delivered from his "pit": "The Lord ordered the fish to spit up Jonah on the beach, and it did" (Jonah 2:10 TLB). At this point, God again commissioned Jonah to go to Nineveh, as God had commanded before, and this time, Jonah obeyed (3:1–3).

There's nothing like a deep, dark, scary pit to get you to pray. Some of my best, most transformative prayer times have been while I was stuck in a pit. We shouldn't quit in the pit but should pray as never before.

The Lord delivered Jonah from the belly of the big fish, and he will deliver you too. It doesn't matter how or why you happened to get stuck in your pit. It's important to refuse to quit, turn to the Lord in prayer, and trust him to get you out.

VERSES TO DEEPEN YOUR JOY

PSALM 50:15; JONAH 2:1–9

Go share the joy today!

Don't Dwell On Your Circumstances

"When you go through deep waters, I will be with you. When you go through rivers of difficulty, you will not drown. When you walk through the fire of oppression, you will not be burned up; the flames will not consume you."

ISAIAH 43:2 NLT

No matter how high the waters rise, no matter how hot the fire burns, we have to determine to look up, get up, and never give up. When I say that we should look up, I'm talking about looking to the Lord. Don't look down in discouragement and don't look at the overwhelming circumstances around you; look only to the Lord, who gives you the strength to get up.

God sent the storm that shepherded wayward Jonah back on the right track into the bounds of God's will. Sometimes we may find ourselves in situations where our ship is on the brink of breaking into a million pieces because Father God is trying to get us back on track.

When the storm raging around Jonah was at its worst, he didn't dwell on the wind and waves but looked to God in repentance and hope. Rather than shifting blame or seeking a scapegoat, he took responsibility for the storm and looked to God to restore peace and calm (Jonah 1:12, 17). No matter what kind of a mess you're dealing with today, when you refuse to dwell on the circumstances and choose to get out of them, the Lord will hold your hand and gently lead you out, one step of obedience at a time.

VERSES TO DEEPEN YOUR JOY

PSALM 107:6; 2 PETER 2:9

Go share the joy today!

Focus on the Finish

"None of these things move me; nor do I count my life dear to myself, so that I may finish my race with joy, and the ministry which I received from the Lord Jesus, to testify to the gospel of the grace of God."

ACTS 20:24 NKJV

As we look to the Lord rather than at the troubles surrounding us, we can also focus ahead to the finish line. At the starting line, you have no idea what you'll face. You know only about the finish line—where the race ends and the journey is complete. When God is our Father, we can be certain of how this earthly race will end, and we can resist falling for the distractions and discouragements that we'll encounter along the way.

Our goal in life should be to do everything the Lord has called us to do and to complete the race he has laid out for us. He wants to show us the finish line, which is the fulfillment of our purpose. The sooner we get a glimpse of our own finish line, the better.

We may not know all the details, but we have a general framework that leads us in the right direction. We at least know that we are called to lead others to the Lord and love him with all our hearts. As we look forward to an eternity with him, we can stay encouraged on every leg of our earthly race.

VERSES TO DEEPEN YOUR JOY

PHILIPPIANS 3:14; 2 TIMOTHY 4:7

Go share the joy today!

Our Forerunner

[As a believer] you have been called for this purpose, since Christ suffered for you, leaving you an example, so that you may follow in His footsteps.

1 PETER 2:21 AMP

Having an advanced picture of the finish line can be helpful, but it doesn't guarantee an easy time as we forge ahead on our God-directed journey. Jesus knew before he was crucified what would happen to him. He was fully aware of the suffering that awaited him if he was to defeat sin and conquer death forever. He even talked about these eventualities with his disciples (for example, Luke 9:22; Matthew 26:2). It's hard to imagine living life knowing exactly how you're going to die, but that's just what Jesus did. He lived with a focus on the finish, reminding himself continually of the bigger purpose behind everything he did.

"Because of the *joy* awaiting him," said the writer of Hebrews about Jesus, "he endured the cross, disregarding its shame. Now he is seated in the place of honor beside God's throne" (12:2 NLT). Jesus kept his gaze fixed on what awaited him after his agonizing death: the honor and glory of sitting beside his Father forever. It was this promise—this picture, this prize—that kept him going and propelled him to persevere in carrying out the Father's plan in full obedience.

VERSES TO DEEPEN YOUR JOY

PSALM 110:1; HEBREWS 2:10

Go share the joy today!

The Ultimate Goal

Think of all the hostility [Jesus] endured from sinful people; then you won't become weary and give up.

HEBREWS 12:3 NLT

Thank goodness Jesus didn't lose heart and give up in his painful, agonizing quest for the cross. Thank goodness Jesus endured the hostility and humiliation he did by keeping the proper perspective.

Someone might say, "Danette, didn't Jesus ask his Father to take away the cup of suffering? Didn't Jesus request to get out of the cross, so to speak?" It is true that Jesus prayed in the garden of Gethsemane for a way out of his present pain and discomfort. Yet he made this request in conjunction with a verbal affirmation of his desire that his Father's will would be done.

Jesus prayed, "My Father, if it is possible, may this cup be taken from me. Yet not as I will, *but as you will*...My Father, if it is not possible for this cup to be taken away unless I drink it, *may your will be done*" (Matthew 26:39, 42). We read in Matthew's gospel a third record of his prayer (v. 44).

Jesus submitted to the will of the Father and chose God's plan above his personal desires and comforts. How did he do this? By keeping his sights set unswervingly on the joy set before him.

VERSES TO DEEPEN YOUR JOY

MATTHEW 10:22; 1 CORINTHIANS 9:24

Go share the joy today!

Persevere Past the Pain

[Jesus prayed,] "Father, if it is Your will, take this cup away from Me; nevertheless not My will, but Yours, be done." Then an angel appeared to Him from heaven, strengthening Him.

LUKE 22:42–43 NKJV

Trusting his Father to keep his promise, Jesus persevered past the pain and purchased our redemption. We are now inheritors of his glory because Jesus endured the cross with his eyes set on the prize. It's the reason we have received the Holy Spirit, "[whose] presence within us is God's guarantee that he really will give us all that he promised; and the Spirit's seal upon us means that God has already purchased us and that he guarantees to bring us to himself. This is just one more reason for us to praise our glorious God" (Ephesians 1:14 TLB).

The list of reasons for us to praise our glorious God goes on and on forever. Let's focus on that list, dwelling on God's precious, priceless blessings as we push negative circumstances and naysayers to the fringes of our minds. When we operate from the proper perspective, remembering our purpose and resting in the one whose ways we trust, we won't drop out of the race when the course gets hard. We won't lose our joy when the going gets tough. No, when we fix our eyes on God and trust him in all circumstances, we find a joy that outlasts all obstacles and will carry us through to victory.

VERSES TO DEEPEN YOUR JOY

GALATIANS 5:16; EPHESIANS 1:7

Go share the joy today!

Refreshing Your Soul

Even youths grow weary and tired, and vigorous young men stumble badly, but those who wait for the Lord [who expect, look for, and hope in Him] will gain new strength.

Isaiah 40:30–31 AMP

Are you growing weary of persevering? Has the struggle worn you down? Whenever weariness threatens—whether it's from waiting, warfare, or works—we must go to the one who never grows weak or weary: the Lord God, maker of heaven and earth. There is no other place to find the refreshment and reinvigoration we so desperately need.

> Do you not know? Have you not heard? The Lord is the everlasting God, the Creator of the ends of the earth. He will not grow tired or weary, and his understanding no one can fathom. He gives strength to the weary and increases the power of the weak. Even youths grow tired and weary, and young men stumble and fall; but those who hope in the Lord will renew their strength. They will soar on wings like eagles; they will run and not grow weary, they will walk and not be faint. (Isaiah 40:28–31)

What a powerful picture! When our natural strength fails and our resources wear out, there is one who is always ready to refresh our spirits, refuel our bodies, and reinforce our faith. If our hope is in the Lord, he will lift us above our troubles and empower us to prevail on every part of our journey. Look to him to increase your power and strengthen your energy for the hardships and hurdles ahead.

VERSES TO DEEPEN YOUR JOY

Psalm 73:26; 2 Corinthians 12:9

Go share the joy today!

The Eternal Prize

All athletes are disciplined in their training.
They do it to win a prize that will fade away,
but we do it for an eternal prize.
1 Corinthians 9:25 NLT

In the world, it seems that winning is everything. You'll hear parents tell their Little League baseballers and young competitive gymnasts, "Having fun is all that counts," yet how many of those adults really believe what they're saying? And how many of them adopt that attitude toward professional athletes—or even their own coworkers? Competition can be downright cutthroat in just about every realm of society. In the race of life, winning is everything too; it just doesn't mean what you think it does.

The world tells us that winning means earning the most money, driving the most expensive car, traveling to the most exotic destination, wearing the most fashionable clothes, and using the most advanced technologies. In God's economy, however, winning means securing the only prize that lasts forever, and that is salvation through a relationship with our heavenly Father. In the kingdom of God, the real winners get that "crown of life" (James 1:12). An eternal crown of glory is ours if we can run with the proper perspective, exercise godly endurance, and cultivate Christlike character all the way to the finish line. Are you ready to strive for the only prize that lasts?

VERSES TO DEEPEN YOUR JOY

Daniel 7:27; Revelation 5:10

Go share the joy today!

When Winning Looks like Losing

The foolishness of God is wiser than men,
and the weakness of God is stronger than men.

1 CORINTHIANS 1:25 NKJV

To illustrate just how opposed the Christian and worldly concepts of winning really are, let's look at the life of Jesus, the ultimate Victor. Most people would assume that dying a criminal's death on a cross would be a loss, not a win. The disciples sure couldn't figure out how Jesus was going to be a conqueror if he ended up dead, as he foretold time and again he would do. Let's consider just one example.

> From that time on Jesus began to explain to his disciples that he must go to Jerusalem and suffer many things at the hands of the elders, the chief priests and the teachers of the law, and that he must be killed and on the third day be raised to life.
>
> Peter took him aside and began to rebuke him. "Never, Lord!" he said. "This shall never happen to you!"
>
> Jesus turned and said to Peter, "Get behind me, Satan! You are a stumbling block to me; you do not have in mind the concerns of God, but merely human concerns." (Matthew 16:21–23)

This passage has always struck me as humorous. Peter had a lot of gall to basically tell Jesus, "You're missing it! How could dying possibly be the will of God for you?" As if it weren't unwise enough to advise the Son of God, Peter was dispensing advice from a human perspective—devoid of godly wisdom. But Jesus has all wisdom, and he knew what he was doing.

VERSES TO DEEPEN YOUR JOY

1 CORINTHIANS 1:30; COLOSSIANS 2:1–3

Go share the joy today!

Victory in Death

The word of the cross is foolishness to those who are perishing, but to us who are being saved it is the power of God.

1 CORINTHIANS 1:18 NASB

Human wisdom couldn't have understood how a death on a cross could save all humankind. The idea of letting oneself be caught, wrongly convicted, and killed to achive ultimate victory sounds preposterous.

By the death and resurrection of Jesus Christ, "death has been swallowed up in victory" (1 Corinthians 15:54 NASB). It is this declaration that precedes the apostle Paul's taunting of death in 1 Corinthians 15:55. And it was the resulting confidence of Paul that allowed him to say that he would actually prefer dying if it weren't for all the evangelizing he had left to do. Here is how he put it in 2 Corinthians:

> We know that if our earthly tent which is our house is torn down, we have a building from God, a house not made by hands, eternal in the heavens…Now He who prepared us for this very purpose is God, who gave us the Spirit as a pledge.
>
> Therefore, being always of good courage, and knowing that while we are at home in the body we are absent from the Lord—for we walk by faith, not by sight—but we are of good courage and prefer rather to be absent from the body and to be at home with the Lord. (5:1, 5–8 NASB)

What an amazing attitude, to prefer "to be at home with the Lord." Let's strive to live with that same perspective.

VERSES TO DEEPEN YOUR JOY

JOHN 10:28; 2 CORINTHIANS 5:1

Go share the joy today!

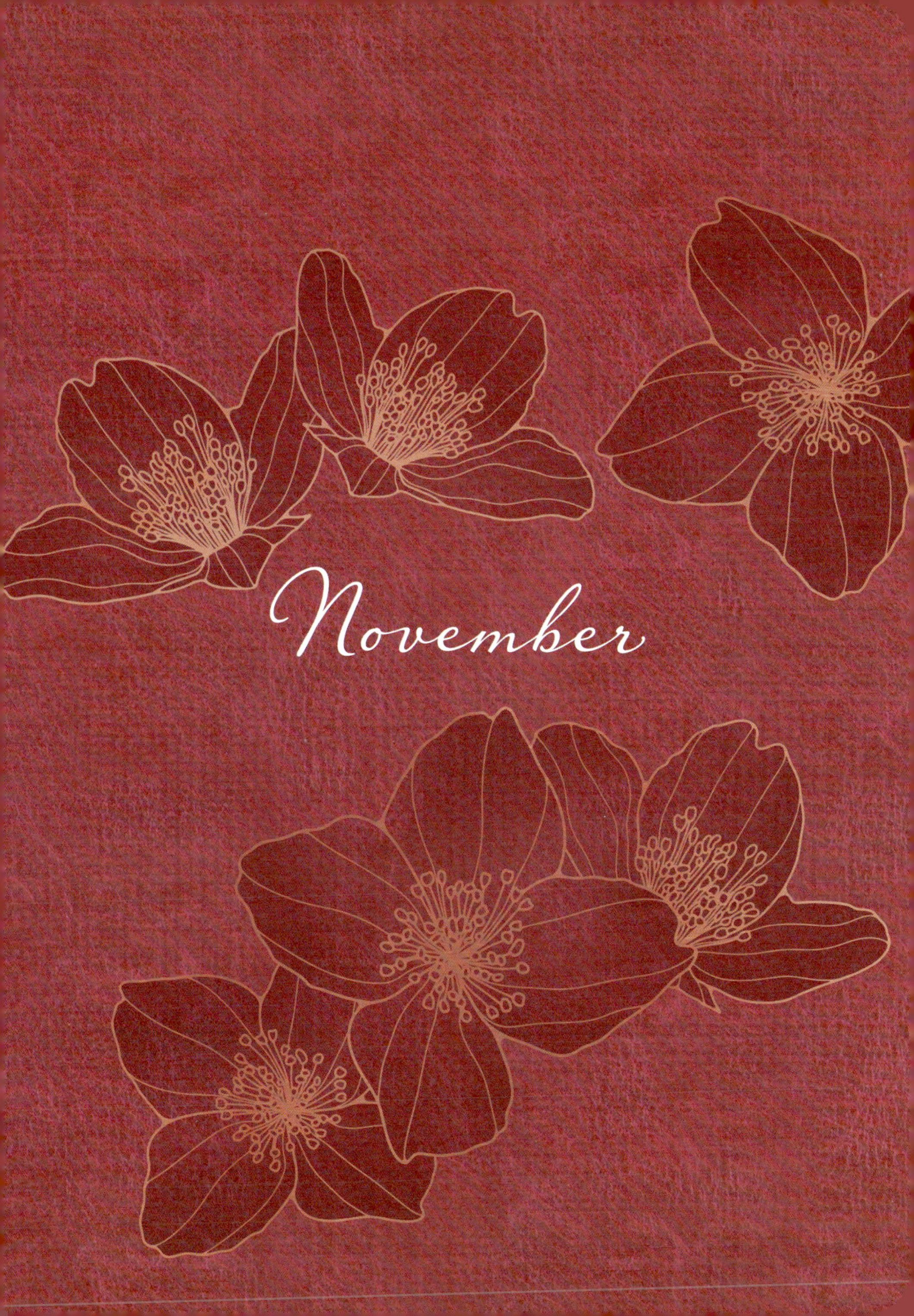
November

Longing for Heaven

I am hard-pressed between the two. I have the desire to leave [this world] and be with Christ, for that is far, far better; yet to remain in my body is more necessary and essential for your sake.

PHILIPPIANS 1:23–24 AMP

Can you imagine being in a position where you could say that you would rather leave this earthly life and be with the Lord? Many people talk wistfully about the joys that await us in heaven, but the way that they live day-to-day suggests they're still striving for an earthly prize.

When the dearest trophy we seek is eternal life in heaven, we know that we won't be disappointed. For believers, dying truly is gain, but living with that mindset doesn't come naturally. We need to live with a perspective that continually reminds us of our heavenly destiny. In the words of Jesus, "Where your treasure is, there your heart [your wishes, your desires; that on which your life centers] will be also" (Matthew 6:21 AMP).

I'm not talking about giving up all interest in the things of this world. After all, while we're not supposed to be *of* the world, we have to live in the world, stewarding its resources and shepherding its people into saving relationships with Christ.

When an eagerness to see Christ face-to-face is the foundation of our daily lives, it keeps our trials in perspective and encourages us to wait for our promised hope. The hope of heaven should be our daily joy.

VERSES TO DEEPEN YOUR JOY

1 CORINTHIANS 13:11–12; GALATIANS 2:20

Go share the joy today!

The First Will Be Last

"Everyone who exalts himself will be humbled [before others], and he who habitually humbles himself (keeps a realistic self-view) will be exalted."

LUKE 14:11 AMP

Literal death isn't the only way to victory in the Christian life. Dying to self by putting others first and serving with a heart of self-sacrifice is something Jesus talked about and modeled a lot, and it isn't hard to see why it's an unpopular approach to living in today's society. Social media and modern culture scream, "Go for it!" "Follow your dreams, whatever the cost!" "If you want something, take it!" Self-promotion and personal ambition are prized in every sphere, particularly among today's youth.

The look-at-me lifestyle that idolizes personal fulfillment and "success," as society defines it, conflicts starkly with the humble servanthood that Jesus emphasized in such statements as Matthew 23:11: "The greatest among you will be your servant" (AMP).

Sure, it feels good to win trophies and receive recognition for a job well done. But have you noticed that your mood is boosted even more when you lovingly serve other people? The Bible affirms, "It is more blessed [and brings greater joy] to give than to receive" (Acts 20:35 AMP). Giving is the ultimate show of love. Remember, "God so loved the world that he *gave* his one and only Son, that whoever believes in him shall not perish but have eternal life" (John 3:16).

VERSES TO DEEPEN YOUR JOY

PROVERBS 22:4; PHILIPPIANS 2:3–4

Go share the joy today!

A Prerequisite for Greatness

"Whoever wants to become great among you must be your servant, and whoever wants to be first must be slave of all. For even the Son of Man did not come to be served, but to serve, and to give his life as a ransom for many."

MARK 10:43–45

This quote of Jesus' has a significant context. Two of his disciples—brothers named James and John—were squabbling over which one of them should have a higher place in the kingdom of heaven. They had the nerve to request that Jesus position one of them at his right hand and the other at his left. Understandably, their fellow disciples were indignant when they heard about the request of these upstarts (v. 41). To restore peace among these friends, Jesus patiently explained that nobody who sought a high status would get very far in his kingdom.

Now don't misunderstand what I'm saying. If you're competing in an actual race or another sporting event, you shouldn't just stand back and let everybody speed past you. If you're a businessperson, you shouldn't perform poorly on purpose so that someone else gets promoted instead of you. That wouldn't be prudent, and it wouldn't highlight the gifts God has given you. However, your motives for excelling should be meaningful. We don't have to be doormats, but we do have to cultivate a spirit of selfless service and humble sacrifice if we expect to succeed according to Christ's standards and find joy while doing it. Serving is our prerequisite for greatness.

VERSES TO DEEPEN YOUR JOY

PSALM 149:4; MATTHEW 18:4

Go share the joy today!

Press On

Forgetting what is behind and straining toward what is ahead, I press on toward the goal to win the prize for which God has called me heavenward in Christ Jesus.

PHILIPPIANS 3:13–14

I don't know about you, but the promise of eternal life in heaven is enough of a trophy for me. We can enjoy eternal, abundant life, now and forevermore, when we follow Jesus all our days and seek to serve others as he did. Grasping at glory for ourselves will only end in disappointment. It is a "prize that will fade away," so let's not miss out on the "eternal prize" (1 Corinthians 9:25 NLT) that is ours to claim based on what Christ did for us.

The apostle Paul truly prized the Lord above everything else. "Whatever were gains to me," he wrote, "I now consider *loss* for the sake of Christ. What is more, I consider everything a loss because of the surpassing worth of knowing Christ Jesus my Lord, for whose sake I have lost all things. I consider them garbage, that I may gain Christ and be found in him" (Philippians 3:7–9). Anything less than Christ, no matter how good or how valuable, Paul considered as garbage compared to his Savior.

As we press on toward the same goal Paul pursued, there are some things we need to forget or stop focusing on—some distractions and deterrents that hold us back rather than push us ahead. We will discuss those in the coming days.

VERSES TO DEEPEN YOUR JOY

PHILIPPIANS 1:6; 2 PETER 1:1–11

Go share the joy today!

No Looking Back

"Is it because there were no graves in Egypt that you have taken us away to die in the wilderness?…It would have been better for us to serve the Egyptians than to die in the wilderness!"

Exodus 14:11–12 NASB

The Israelites had to learn not to look back as they journeyed out of bondage in Egypt to freedom. After being enslaved for more than four hundred years, crying out continually to God for deliverance, they finally received the go-ahead to leave. God had sent Moses to demand of Pharaoh, again and again, "Let my people go!" And after endless pleas and a long series of plagues, the Egyptian pharaoh had finally consented (Exodus 8–12).

As God's children fled Egypt, they went well-equipped. In Exodus 12:36, it's recorded that "the Lord had given the people favor in the sight of the Egyptians, so that they let them have their request. Therefore they plundered the Egyptians" (NASB). When you have the favor of God, you can't help but have the favor of other people.

But they couldn't cast off the nagging feeling that something would go wrong. Sure enough, it wasn't long before they saw Egyptian chariots chasing them down. Pharaoh had changed his mind—again—and wanted them back. Understandably, they started freaking out. But they went a step further and wished they'd never left the bondage of Egypt. They forgot that when God frees us from something, it's meant to be for good.

VERSES TO DEEPEN YOUR JOY

Proverbs 26:11; Hebrews 6:1–3

Go share the joy today!

When Breakthrough Looks Bleak

"Stand still, and see the salvation of the LORD, which He will accomplish for you today."

EXODUS 14:13 NKJV

Moses reassured the Israelites again and again that God was not going to let them down. He said to them, "Do not be afraid. Stand still, and see the salvation of the LORD, which He will accomplish for you today. For the Egyptians whom you see today, you shall see again no more forever. The LORD will fight for you, and you shall hold your peace" (vv. 13–14 NKJV).

The Israelites had reached their place of breakthrough and deliverance, yet their situation looked bleaker than ever before. That's because they were looking with their natural eyes rather than with eyes of faith. God was using the Egyptian army that was pursuing them so that he could get all the glory. He said so himself in Exodus 14:4: "I will harden Pharaoh's heart, and he will pursue [the Israelites]. But I will *gain glory for myself* through Pharaoh and all his army, and the Egyptians will know that I am the LORD."

We can't afford to rely on our natural eyes to inform our attitude and decisions. Even when our circumstances seem bleak and hopeless, let's resolve to rely on the Lord to deliver us. However unpromising our situation may seem, we can trust God to deliver us from our enemies and place our feet on solid ground.

VERSES TO DEEPEN YOUR JOY

PSALM 112:7; 1 PETER 5:7

Go share the joy today!

Don't Pine for the Past

"Do not call to mind the former things, or consider things of the past. Behold, I am going to do something new."

ISAIAH 43:18–19 NASB

The theme of "forgetting what's behind and focusing on what's ahead" came up again and again for the Israelites during their time of wandering in the wilderness. Once God had taken care of the threat of Pharaoh and the Egyptian army, the Israelites still had to deal with hunger and thirst and the tiresome nature of wandering. Within a very short time, they stopped rejoicing and started grumbling (Exodus 15:24; 16:2–3).

Talk about an ungrateful spirit! The Israelites had forgotten God's faithfulness and started remembering wistfully how "good" they'd had it back in Egypt—where they were enslaved! Instead of releasing those painful years and yearning for the next show of God's faithfulness, they regretted that they had left Egypt in the first place.

Despite the Israelites' awful attitudes and repeated instances of forgetting about God's faithfulness, God showed up and provided more water and food than they could handle. He was long-suffering in his patience with the Israelites, and he is the same with us today. But let's not deliberately test his patience. Let's focus forward and quit pining for the past. God holds our future in his hands, and we can trust him to get us there.

VERSES TO DEEPEN YOUR JOY

1 CORINTHIANS 2:9; PHILIPPIANS 3:13–14

Go share the joy today!

No Regrets

We do not look at the things which are seen, but at the things which are not seen. For the things which are seen are temporary, but the things which are not seen are eternal.

2 CORINTHIANS 4:18 NKJV

When I hear about someone longing for the past and glossing over its pains, I'm reminded of Lot's wife. Are you familiar with her story? Lot was the nephew of Abraham and had settled with his family in a wicked city called Sodom. When God prepared to destroy the city, he sent angels to warn Lot's family so that they could escape ahead of the destruction.

Once they were safely outside the city walls, one of the angels said to them, "Escape for your life! Do not look behind you nor stay anywhere in the plain. Escape to the mountains, lest you be destroyed" (Genesis 19:17 NKJV). Lot's wife looked back. She couldn't bear to leave behind the life she had come to love. So she turned into a pillar of salt (v. 26.)

If we are going to run our life's race with enough stamina to claim an eternal prize, we can't afford to indulge in wistful thoughts about yesteryear. We can't let sentimental memories from the past stall us. We need to keep our eyes on the prize and let Jesus guide us toward the finish line.

VERSES TO DEEPEN YOUR JOY

PROVERBS 28:26; 2 CORINTHIANS 4:16–17

Go share the joy today!

Things Worth Remembering

Do not be afraid of them; remember well what the LORD your God did to Pharaoh and to all Egypt.

DEUTERONOMY 7:18

At times, it's helpful for us to remember. If we feel faint and find ourselves wondering whether God is with us, we can boost our faith by recalling the times when God has shown up on our behalf and proven his faithfulness. The apostle Paul certainly would not fault us for that.

In his psalms, David engaged in this practice of bringing to mind past instances of God's goodness. He wrote, "Praise the LORD, my soul, and forget not all his benefits" (Psalm 103:2). Clearly, David was writing from experience as he reminded himself of times when God had healed him, satisfied him, and renewed him.

When David was setting up a tent as a temple to house the ark of the covenant, he appointed priests and urged them to remember God's great works (1 Chronicles 16:8–9, 12). And when Moses was exhorting the Israelites to face their enemies with confidence, he instructed them to remember God's power and abilities as witnessed in the past (Deuteronomy 8:11, 18).

Are you getting the picture? Remembering has an important place in the life of the believer but only when it comes to recalling the wonders and mighty acts of God. Dwelling on disaster and wallowing in self-pity only sets us back, but recalling God's faithfulness spurs us on to victory.

VERSES TO DEEPEN YOUR JOY

1 CHRONICLES 16:12; PSALM 77:11

Go share the joy today!

Read and Be Encouraged

Such things were written in the Scriptures long ago to teach us. And the Scriptures give us hope and encouragement as we wait patiently for God's promises to be fulfilled.

ROMANS 15:4 NLT

I love reading in the Bible about the men and women who experienced God's supernatural hand of help. It spurs my confidence and strengthens my faith that he will work in the same way on my behalf because he is the same God today that he was way back then.

One particular story that encourages me is the story of Nehemiah. He was the governor of Judah and had a heart for ministering to others. When he learned that the walls of Jerusalem had been torn down, fire had burned its gates, and the people were drowning in their distress, he felt called by the Lord to act.

In a long and heartfelt prayer, he asked God to give him favor with the king when he requested a leave of absence to go and rebuild the wall (Nehemiah 1:4–11). Nehemiah's heart was right, and his motives were pure. He knew that if he was going to pull off such a major feat for God as rebuilding the wall, he would need a huge dose of favor—with both God and people. And that's just what he got. Nehemiah received more than enough favor and blessing to carry out the plans God had put on his heart.

VERSES TO DEEPEN YOUR JOY

NEHEMIAH 2:2–6; PROVERBS 21:1

Go share the joy today!

Big Plans for You

"I know the plans I have for you," says the LORD. *"They are plans for good and not for disaster, to give you a future and a hope."*

JEREMIAH 29:11 NLT

God has big plans for the work he wants to do through you. But first, he has big plans to do a work *within* you. For most of us, the first big plan God has is to heal us. We live in a broken, sin-scarred world, so it makes sense that most of us have been through situations that have broken and scarred us. Thank God for the redeeming work of Jesus' blood and the power of the Holy Spirit to do big things in us.

Again, God has to do big things in us before he can do big things through us. I always tell people that the number one reason God led me to pursue a master's degree in counseling is because I needed counseling myself. I've had the call of God on my life since before my birth, but I needed to experience a great deal of healing before I was ready to answer that call.

If we try to do big things for God before he has helped us through our own issues, we won't produce an optimal harvest—not to mention, we're apt to make a big mess. And big messes can give God a bad name. Let's allow him to do his work of healing and sanctifying us from within, and then we'll be ready to follow his leading in the big plans he has for us.

VERSES TO DEEPEN YOUR JOY

PSALM 138:8; PHILIPPIANS 1:6

Go share the joy today!

Messes Become Messages

"In the end I will turn things around for the people."

ZEPHANIAH 3:9–13 MSG

In his unconditional love for us, God can turn our tests into testimonies and our messes into messages that will help advance his kingdom and minister to those around us. All we have to do is yield to his movement in our hearts and give him room to work. Sometimes his work may take years to complete. Be patient while God lovingly shapes and molds you, "being confident of this, that he who began a good work in you will carry it on to completion until the day of Christ Jesus" (Philippians 1:6).

In my case, God's work of healing and preparation took many years. But during that time, he didn't stick me on a shelf with a big label that read "Unusable." The degree to which I healed became the degree to which God used me in that season. The truth is that you can't take anyone to a place where you yourself have never been or do not currently find yourself. You can't take anyone to a higher place than you have reached.

God wants to bring you to a place of total healing—in body, soul, and spirit. Once you've allowed him to do big things in you, he will do big things *through* you. Ask God to take you to a place of total healing and submit to his timing. Remember that God's timing is perfect.

VERSES TO DEEPEN YOUR JOY

PSALM 126:1–3; ISAIAH 58:12

Go share the joy today!

Bold Intercession

Pray for each other so that you may be healed. The earnest prayer of a righteous person has great power and produces wonderful results.

James 5:16 NLT

Nehemiah had a heart for the people who were affected when their enemy tore down their city's walls. When you have a heart to help others to rebuild the fallen "walls" in their lives, it pleases your heavenly Father to send you to accomplish the necessary tasks and provide you with whatever you need. So be sure to pray boldly when you're asking on behalf of others.

When the Enemy tears down the literal or figurative walls in the lives of God's children, we must ask and expect the Lord to do a work of rebuilding and restoration. Nehemiah was the willing vessel God used to do supernatural things on behalf of the Israelites, all because Nehemiah didn't hesitate to ask God for big miracles so that he could bless others. Because Nehemiah had a big dose of God's favor, all the requests he made of the king for supplies and manpower were met and even exceeded. Never be afraid to intercede boldly on behalf of those you're seeking to serve.

Whom is God prompting you to serve today? What big requests can you make on behalf of that person or organization? Use your imagination and don't be afraid to think outside the box.

VERSES TO DEEPEN YOUR JOY

Nehemiah 2:7–9; Galatians 6:2

Go share the joy today!

Ask with Bold Faith

"Whatever things you ask for in prayer [in accordance with God's will], believe [with confident trust] that you have received them, and they will be given to you."

MARK 11:24 AMP

When you're asking God to do big things through you, it's crucial to ask in faith. As the Bible says in James 1:6, "When you ask, you must believe and not doubt." Too many people sit back and wait until they can see everything lined up. They wait until they have all the money they need in their bank account. They wait until they've assembled the team of people they think they will need to accomplish their vision. But part of asking big is asking with bold faith.

Nehemiah said to the officials in Jerusalem, "You see the trouble we are in: Jerusalem lies in ruins, and its gates have been burned with fire" (Nehemiah 2:17). Sounds pretty dire! But he simply went on to say, "Come, let us rebuild the wall of Jerusalem, and we will no longer be in disgrace" (v. 17). What else did he assure the people about? That the hand of God was on him and his work. Hearing this, the people said, "Let us start rebuilding" (v. 18). Nehemiah's bold faith proved contagious, pulling others into the effort.

Ask God to accomplish his will through you and take a bold leap of faith when he says it's time. You don't have to understand everything or have all your ducks in a row. When you sense in your spirit that God's will and timing have intersected, you need to start the work.

VERSES TO DEEPEN YOUR JOY

2 CORINTHIANS 3:12; EPHESIANS 3:11–12

Go share the joy today!

Blessings Enough to Share

"You shall generously give to [your poor brother], and your heart shall not be grudging when you give to him, because for this thing the Lord your God will bless you in all your work, and in all your undertakings."

DEUTERONOMY 15:10 NASB

God loves to do big things in us, through us, and for us if we will simply ask him with bold faith. He wants to bless us with big anointing, big favor, and big financial resources—not for the sake of our own selfish gain but for the benefit of his kingdom. When we ask for big blessings out of a pure heart, we will be rewarded. I have seen the promise of Proverbs 28:27 come to pass time and again in my own experience. As I've given generously to help those who are less fortunate or experiencing particular hardship, the Lord has brought me into a place of abundant blessing.

Don't forget to pray big prayers for your family, your neighbors, or yourself. Why don't more people pray boldly for themselves? Some are so hung up on past mistakes that they feel unworthy of blessing. Others can't conceive that God wants to bless them in a big way. More often than not, people who don't ask God for big things for themselves really don't believe it pleases him when they do.

But God delights in blessing his kids. He loves it when we acknowledge him as the source of all blessing. If you don't have a vision for big blessings in your life that spill over into the lives of others, you'll never ask God for big blessings. All that you see in the spirit, you can ask for with big faith.

VERSES TO DEEPEN YOUR JOY

1 CHRONICLES 4:9–10; PSALM 35:27

Go share the joy today!

Stand Firm for the Lord

My dear brothers and sisters, stand firm. Let nothing move you. Always give yourselves fully to the work of the Lord, because you know that your labor in the Lord is not in vain.

1 CORINTHIANS 15:58

When we are doing the work of the Lord, we can't allow anyone or anything to pull us away with detours and distractions. I want to encourage you to stand firm and let nothing move you, including your financial situation, your energy level, and your supply of resources. Stay where God has placed you and don't you dare move until you know without a shadow of a doubt that it's God who is moving you. The labor you are doing for his kingdom is not in vain, so stand firm. Never make a decision according to your bank accounts, especially if that decision is motivated by fear. You should always make your decisions according to the leading of the Holy Spirit.

God will often lead you to do things that seem out of the range of your resources and expertise because he is just waiting for your continual, faithful obedience. He's waiting for you to stand and keep standing, and then he will release that provision. If the children of Israel had never stepped into the Red Sea, the waters never would have parted for them to pass through.

VERSES TO DEEPEN YOUR JOY

1 CORINTHIANS 16:13; PHILIPPIANS 1:27

Go share the joy today!

Drown Out Distractions

Let us hold fast the confession of our hope without wavering, for He who promised is faithful.

HEBREWS 10:23 NKJV

I can hardly overemphasize the importance of being wary of the devil's cunning efforts to distract us from our purpose and discourage us from fulfilling God's call on our lives. The work of the Lord is never without such opposition, but with the help of the Holy Spirit, we can stand firm and drown out the devil's distractions.

Nehemiah encountered tough opposition as he led the work of rebuilding the wall of Jerusalem. For example, "When Sanballat the Horonite and Tobiah the Ammonite official heard of it, they were deeply disturbed that a man had come to seek the well-being of the children of Israel" (Nehemiah 2:10 NKJV). Nehemiah was doing the work of the Lord. He was helping the people rebuild their lives. And the Enemy didn't like it one bit.

Whether you are a pastor in the ministry, a professional in the secular realm trying to be a witness for Christ in your workplace, or a parent trying to raise godly children, the Enemy sees your efforts for the kingdom of God. He can tell when you're being effective in building God's kingdom, and he will do whatever he can to deter you. Don't fall for the tricks of the Enemy. Don't listen when he tries to distract and discourage you. Stand and keep on standing. The kingdom of God is counting on you.

VERSES TO DEEPEN YOUR JOY

1 CORINTHIANS 10:13; 2 TIMOTHY 2:15

Go share the joy today!

Stand in Prayer

Put on the full armor of God, so that you will be able to stand firm against the schemes of the devil.

EPHESIANS 6:11 NASB

When Nehemiah's enemies tried to hinder his work, he refused to talk to them. Nehemiah consulted God alone about what the Enemy was up to. He didn't get on the level of the Enemy. He didn't call all his friends to talk about it. And he didn't quake in fear. He talked only to God.

The Enemy tried to convince Nehemiah that the work he was doing was in vain, but that was just a big lie. The Enemy was attempting to discourage Nehemiah so that he would give up. But the proof was in the pudding. The wall was built in fifty-two days. So Nehemiah's work wasn't in vain after all!

Nehemiah 4:20 says, "At whatever place you hear the sound of the trumpet, assemble to us there. Our God will fight for us" (NASB). Nehemiah stood in prayer. Even as he worked, he prayed, knowing that as he did his part, God would do God's part by fighting for him.

We need to stand in prayer as we wage spiritual warfare against the Enemy. We need to stand in prayer against false accusations. As part of our full armor of protection against Satan's schemes, we need to pray and ask the Holy Spirit to give us discernment and power.

VERSES TO DEEPEN YOUR JOY

EPHESIANS 6:13–14; 2 THESSALONIANS 2:15–17

Go share the joy today!

Assume Your Position

"'You will not need to fight in this battle. Position yourselves, stand still and see the salvation of the LORD.'"

2 CHRONICLES 20:17 NKJV

Your position should always be the place where God instructs you to be, either directly in his Word—the Holy Bible—or a personal *rhema* (revealed) word from the Lord. If you haven't gotten a word from God regarding a particular situation, consider fasting and praying until he speaks to you. And then, when you get a word, stand on it and don't quit standing.

Today's verse comes from a speech that King Jehoshaphat gave to encourage his people when their enemies approached. He had just prayed to God and admitted that he didn't know what position to take: "O our God…we have no power against this great multitude that is coming against us; nor do we know what to do, but our eyes are upon You" (v. 12 NKJV). When all else fails, the best position to assume is to stand and wait for specific instructions from the Lord.

Just as Jehoshaphat encouraged the Israelites, I encourage you today: you will see the deliverance the Lord is about to give you. Don't be afraid! Don't succumb to a spirit of fear. You attack that spirit of fear with your faith, with God's Word, and with the word God gives to you. Go face-to-face with the Enemy. Don't run away in fear. Don't shrink back. God is going to fight your battle, so give a shout of victory as you take your position.

VERSES TO DEEPEN YOUR JOY

EXODUS 14:14; DEUTERONOMY 3:22

Go share the joy today!

Press into His Presence

In Your presence is fullness of joy;
at Your right hand are pleasures forevermore.

PSALM 16:11 NKJV

I am convinced that the Lord often requires us to wait on him—whether for our marching orders, for the manifestation of our miracle, or for the fulfillment of a promise—to develop us into the people he has called us to be. I also believe the Lord wants us to live a presence-driven life, continually pressing into God's presence and desiring it above all other things.

If we aren't careful, we can live life driven by any number of ideals and agendas that aren't of God. But when we live a presence-driven life, the Lord's presence remains our number one focus. As we wait, we can keep hope alive by hungering for and abiding in the Lord. With the psalmist, we can say to God, "In Your presence is fullness of joy; at Your right hand are pleasures forevermore."

As you assume your position in whatever battle you may be facing, the best place to be is in God's presence. There we gain refreshment for our souls, the refining of our character, and divine insights into how to wage war against the Enemy. Press into his presence today and stay there as long as it takes for you to be renewed and recharged.

VERSES TO DEEPEN YOUR JOY

PSALM 139:7–8; ZEPHANIAH 3:17

Go share the joy today!

Think Big in Battle

"This is what the Lord says: Do not be afraid! Don't be discouraged by this mighty army, for the battle is not yours, but God's."

2 Chronicles 20:15 NLT

If we set our gaze on whatever army is coming against us, fear can easily paralyze us. We're apt to think small as we compare our foe with the size of our own army and the strength of our own resources. Small thinking leads to discouragement, which tempts us to throw in the towel and stop trying altogether. But God commands us not to be afraid or discouraged because the battle isn't ours to fight. The battle belongs to him, and he is more than able to secure our victory.

Today's verse is from the Lord's instructions to King Jehoshaphat. God went on to tell the king, "Tomorrow, march out against them" (v. 16 NLT). In other words, "Don't delay! Face the enemy immediately, first thing in the morning. Don't put it off."

We shouldn't delay facing our foes or dealing with the storms that life sends our way. We must meet them head-on at the first chance we get. If we put off confronting our opponents, we give them an opportunity to mess with our minds and shrink our thinking. But if we're thinking big, we will respond immediately and trust God to fight for us.

"You will not even need to fight," the Lord told Jehoshaphat. "Take your positions; then stand still and watch the Lord's victory" (v. 17 NLT). There's no battle our God can't win. Let's sit back and watch him bring us victory.

VERSES TO DEEPEN YOUR JOY

Luke 10:19; Revelation 2:10

Go share the joy today!

Divine Insights

"I am God, and there is none like me. Only I can tell you the future before it even happens. Everything I plan will come to pass, for I do whatever I wish."

ISAIAH 46:9–10 NLT

God spoke to King Jehoshaphat through a priest named Jahaziel to reveal the Enemy's plans ahead of time (2 Chronicles 20:15–17). Knowing the Enemy's position and plan of attack in advance gives us a huge advantage. This type of divine insight is just one benefit of cultivating a powerful prayer life. If we continually abide in God's presence, communing with him through praise and prayer, he may reveal to us certain aspects of the Enemy's plan, giving us a better chance of outwitting him. We can think big, trusting God to tell us everything we need to know, right when we need to know it.

The Lord informed Jehoshaphat that he wouldn't even need to fight in the upcoming battle. All he had to do was take his position and stand firm, and he would see the deliverance of the Lord.

What's your position? It should be one of standing on God's Word, being faithful in prayer and fervent in worship. We were created to worship God in all that we think, say, and do and in the way we live our lives. When we think big, it's easy to let go and let God be God. Go ahead and get your praise on, even during battle. God will give you the insights you need to emerge victorious.

VERSES TO DEEPEN YOUR JOY

ISAIAH 7:14; DANIEL 2:28

Go share the joy today!

Speak the Truth in Love

We will speak the truth in love, growing in every way more and more like Christ, who is the head of his body, the church.

EPHESIANS 4:15 NLT

In addition to being bold in our faith, we need to boldly speak the truth into the lives of those around us. True friends don't attend each other's pity parties; they speak the truth to one another in love.

The entire third chapter of Ezekiel talks about this very subject. The bottom line is that we are responsible for speaking the truth to people. It's our responsibility to give them the word of the Lord. If they refuse to listen, we shouldn't be shaken or surprised. God basically said to Ezekiel, "If they aren't willing to listen to you, don't worry because they aren't even willing to listen to me!" Nevertheless, we must do our part, boldly speaking the truth in a loving way and giving others an opportunity to respond. Their reaction is not our responsibility, but we must obey God in speaking the truth, "whether they listen or fail to listen" (Ezekiel 3:11).

Later in Ezekiel, it says that if we don't speak up and convict people when God tells us to, he will hold us accountable for their very lives (v. 18). God wants you and me to be his watchmen on the wall like never before. If we are too focused on our own problems or get too caught up looking for our own turnaround, we'll miss the everyday opportunities God sends for us to speak his truth into others' lives. Let's not be silenced by fear, busyness, or any other excuse.

VERSES TO DEEPEN YOUR JOY

MATTHEW 7:1–5; COLOSSIANS 3:16

Go share the joy today!

Speak Up

"Listen carefully and take to heart all the words I speak to you. Go now to your people in exile and speak to them. Say to them, 'This is what the Sovereign LORD says,' whether they listen or fail to listen."

EZEKIEL 3:10–11

When the Lord took me to Ezekiel 3 and showed me some people who needed to hear a word from him, I feared their response. Yet I knew that I needed to take captive all the feelings and thoughts that threatened to prevent me from obeying the Lord. After God showed me whom I was supposed to talk to and what I was supposed to tell them, I asked him to show me his perfect timing and to prepare these individuals' hearts. As I made my first phone call, I felt nervous and sort of sick to my stomach—not unlike the feeling of looking down at the water from a high dive. Yet I learned long ago that the best thing to do is to go ahead and jump: just start preaching, speaking, and doing whatever God is directing you to do.

So that's what I did that day on the phone. I jumped, opened my mouth, and spoke my piece. To my surprise, the person thanked me for telling them the truth.

God didn't hold me personally responsible for the choices made by those people I held accountable, but he did expect me to walk in obedience to him by delivering his message in a loving, tender way. God has called you, also, to take his message to those all around you. When you do, lives will be saved, and the Lord will be glorified.

VERSES TO DEEPEN YOUR JOY

EPHESIANS 4:29; 1 JOHN 3:18

Go share the joy today!

Saving by Speaking

"If you do warn the righteous person not to sin and they do not sin, they will surely live because they took warning, and you will have saved yourself."

EZEKIEL 3:21

Our greatest purpose in this earthly existence is to fellowship with the Lord and bring him glory with our lives. Speaking the truth in love to those around us fulfills that purpose perfectly, for we both glorify God and populate heaven with souls when we deliver life-saving messages to others. As we faithfully speak the truth to those around us, we point out the places where they need turnaround, and we pave the way for that turnaround to occur.

Just because someone we know has entered a saving relationship with Jesus Christ does not exempt us from the responsibility for speaking into that person's life if the Lord impresses on our heart to do so. We will be held accountable when we fail to deliver the Lord's messages faithfully. The fruit of faith in our lives shows where our heart lies with the Lord.

If a righteous person who knows the Lord as their Savior turns from righteousness and does evil, that person should repent and get back on the right track with the Lord. Often, it's the word of the Lord spoken by you or me that will draw people back into a restored relationship with the Lord when they have drifted away from him. And nothing is more rewarding than growing the population of heaven by winning souls.

Keep an open ear to the directives of God. He will use you to speak life-saving truth and instruction to those he puts on your path.

VERSES TO DEEPEN YOUR JOY

JONAH 1:1; GALATIANS 6:1–2

Go share the joy today!

Ask Big in Prayer

[Jabez] prayed to the God of Israel, "Oh, that you would bless me and expand my territory! Please be with me in all that I do, and keep me from all trouble and pain!" And God granted him his request.

1 CHRONICLES 4:10 NLT

God wants us to ask him for big things because he desires to do big things in us, through us, and for us. I don't want to get to heaven and hear the Lord say, "Why didn't you ask me for more? Why did you ask for so little? Why were your expectations so small?"

Asking for and expecting big things from God are essential for you to see major quantities of fruit manifest in your life. And these are practices that we see modeled in the life of Jabez. Because he boldly asked God for blessings, Jabez was richly rewarded, and his life produced a great harvest of fruit for the kingdom of God.

Jabez was an honorable man (1 Chronicles 4:9). He was willing to pay the price of living a life dedicated and consecrated to the Lord. It's from this kind of position that we can ask big things of the Lord. When we have a powerful prayer life and commit to following God in all we do, we can be confident that our requests are made in the right spirit and from a pure heart of proper motives.

Jabez wanted to be more and to do more for God, and God granted his request. God wants to do the same for you today. Align your heart with his and start asking big in prayer. He's just waiting to grant your request.

VERSES TO DEEPEN YOUR JOY

PSALM 23:6; EPHESIANS 3:20

Go share the joy today!

Asking, Seeking, and Knocking

"Keep on asking, and you will receive what you ask for. Keep on seeking, and you will find. Keep on knocking, and the door will be opened to you."

MATTHEW 7:7 NLT

Jesus had a lot to say about how to make requests in prayer. He confirmed the instructions in today's verse by adding, "For everyone who asks, receives. Everyone who seeks, finds. And to everyone who knocks, the door will be opened" (v. 8 NLT).

"Keep on asking, and you will receive what you ask for"—not "Keep on asking, and you *might* receive what you ask for." The key is having faith as we make our requests. Each of us has been given a "measure of faith" (Romans 12:3 KJV), and even if your particular measure of faith is no bigger than a mustard seed, that's all the faith you need.

Your measure of faith may be teeny tiny, but that isn't what counts. The key is allowing the Holy Spirit to work with your unique measure of faith no matter how small it may be. If you entrust it to the Lord and keep asking, seeking, and knocking, your faith can grow like crazy and produce great fruit.

Have you been asking? Seeking? Knocking? Don't give up! Keep on doing what you're doing. You will receive what you're asking for, find what you're seeking, and see doors opening left and right.

VERSES TO DEEPEN YOUR JOY

MATTHEW 17:20; LUKE 18:1–8

Go share the joy today!

Right Desires Produce Delight

Delight yourself in the LORD;
and He will give you the desires of your heart.

PSALM 37:4 NASB

What a beautiful truth Psalm 37:4 expresses! When we are delighting ourselves in the Lord—loving God with our whole heart and abiding continually in his glorious presence—our wills become pliable so that he may mold, shape, and direct us to desire those things that he desires for us.

When we delight ourselves in the Lord and saturate ourselves with his presence through prayer, then the requests that we make of him are proceeding directly from the heart of God. And when we ask according to the will of God, as the Holy Spirit leads us, we can be confident that we will receive what we've asked for.

God always has our best interests in mind. He will always lead us to whatever is best for us, and he often does this by placing specific desires in our hearts. It stands to reason that when we're abiding in his presence and we find that we've lost a desire for something or someone, it's usually because the Holy Spirit is leading us away from that place, person, or pastime.

Likewise, when we begin to desire something godly that we had never found appealing before, we can trust that the Lord is shaping our desires. This is one way that the Holy Spirit guides us to do the Father's will.

VERSES TO DEEPEN YOUR JOY

PSALM 37:23–24; 1 JOHN 5:14–15

Go share the joy today!

Don't Miss Out

I pray that the eyes of your heart may be enlightened in order that you may know the hope to which [God] has called you, the riches of his glorious inheritance in his holy people.

EPHESIANS 1:18

Whenever God is about to do something big in our lives, there is always a chance we will miss it. Such was the case for the prophet Elisha, the protégé of Elijah, who ultimately received that man's prophetic mantle.

When God was getting ready to take Elijah home to heaven, it would have been easy for Elisha to miss the event altogether and fail to receive Elijah's mantle. After all, Elijah told Elisha to stay put three times while he went on to a different place, yet at every instance, Elisha committed to remaining with his mentor and following him. He wasn't about to miss out on the impartation of Elijah's prophetic role (2 Kings 2:1–14).

Don't miss what God is about to do in you and through you by failing to qualify. Elisha qualified for his mentor's mantle because he was a faithful student and a wise steward of what God had given him. Elisha paid the price by inconveniencing himself to serve Elijah until the end of Elijah's earthly appointment.

Now is not the time to tarry or take a pit stop on the road to your divine destiny. Follow your leader all the way to the place God is leading you. Don't give up until you get there.

VERSES TO DEEPEN YOUR JOY

GALATIANS 5:25; 1 PETER 2:21

Go share the joy today!

A Double-Portion Blessing

Elijah said to Elisha, "Ask me what I should do for you before I am taken from you." And Elisha said, "Please let a double portion of your spirit be upon me."

2 KINGS 2:9 NASB

After Elisha had gone the distance and crossed the Jordan River with his mentor, Elijah, he asked for a double portion of the prophet's anointing. When we cross over with God to the place he has called us, we can ask for and expect a double-portion blessing. Let's not be hesitant or timid about making this kind of request. Elijah conceded that what Elisha was asking for was "a hard thing" (v. 10 NASB), but he never called it impossible. With God, nothing is impossible.

Elijah told Elisha that if he witnessed God take Elijah up to heaven, God would grant Elisha the double portion of his anointing. Sure enough, "As they were walking along and talking, behold, a chariot of fire appeared with horses of fire, and they separated the two of them. Then Elijah went up by a whirlwind to heaven. And Elisha was watching it" (vv. 11–12 NASB). With his own eyes, Elisha saw his mentor being spirited away from this earth. Immediately he began operating with the anointing of Elijah, proving that he had indeed received a double portion of his anointing (v. 14).

We must determine to go all the way, as Elisha did. Too often, we get out of alignment with God's will by stopping short rather than going the distance. Be determined to get out of the way and to move forward in God's will as you expect a double-portion blessing from him.

VERSES TO DEEPEN YOUR JOY

ISAIAH 44:3; JOEL 2:28

Go share the joy today!

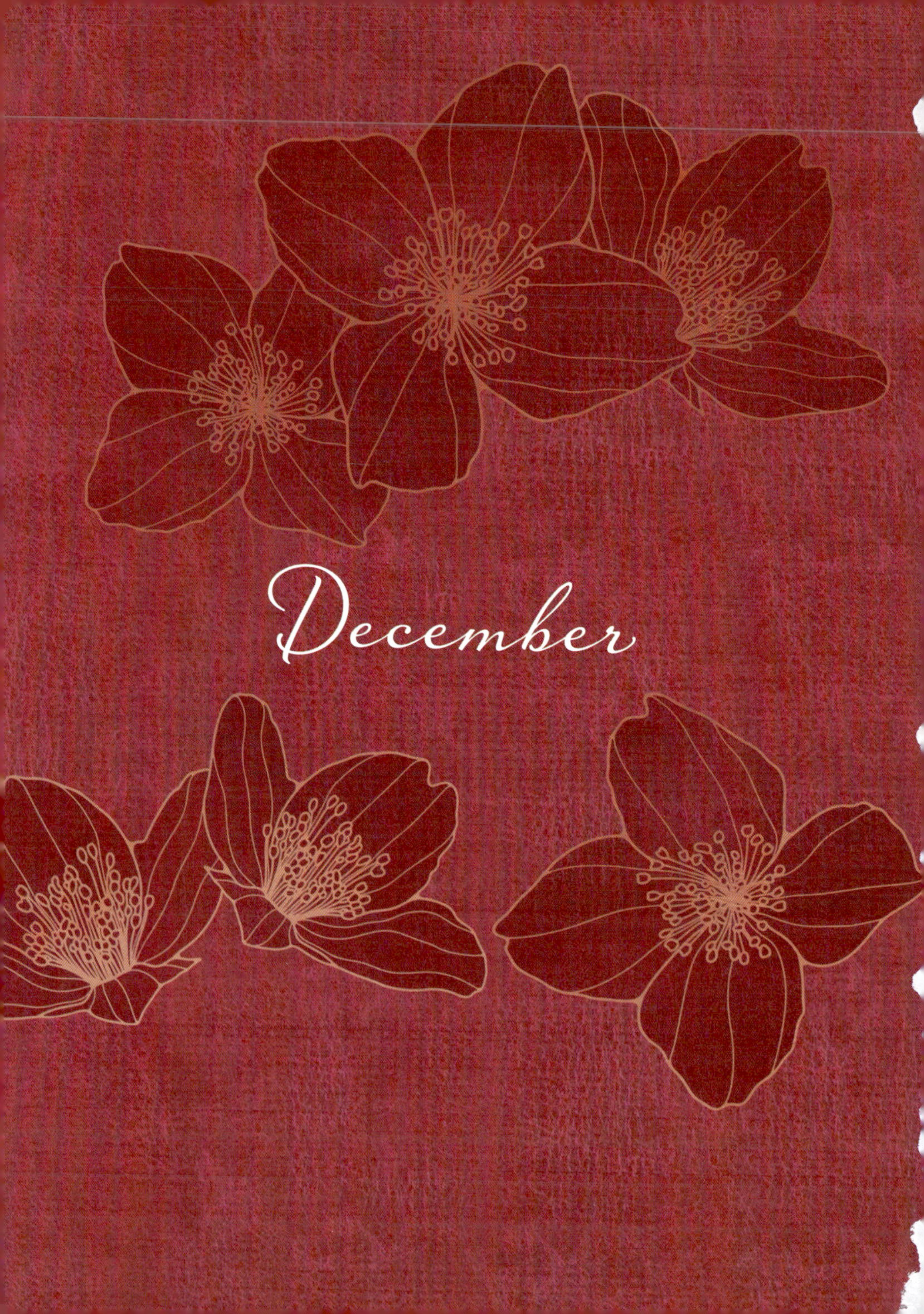

December

Receive His Peace

Peace I leave with you; My [own] peace I now give and bequeath to you. Not as the world gives do I give to you. Do not let your hearts be troubled, neither let them be afraid. [Stop allowing yourselves to be agitated and disturbed; and do not permit yourselves to be fearful and intimidated and cowardly and unsettled.]

JOHN 14:27 AMPC

Father God wants to give us his peace in every area of our lives, but most people struggle to receive his peace, especially regarding their finances.

Notice that in today's verse, Jesus put the responsibility for our state of mind on our own shoulders: "Stop allowing yourselves to be agitated and disturbed; and do not permit yourselves to be fearful." That's a lot easier said than done. The only way to stop feeling agitated is to shift our focus from the source of our agitation to something that brings the opposite feeling.

It isn't enough to look at our latest bank account statement and say, "This doesn't bother me." We need to look to the Father and acknowledge that he is in control. Only then will we experience a sense of peaceful confidence that our needs will be met, regardless of how much money we have.

Maybe you are in a financial storm. Stop quaking and start calming the storm, just as Jesus did (literally speaking) in Luke 8. Jesus is in your boat, so calm down. With Jesus in your boat, you don't need to worry about anything. The key is to focus on Jesus and his promises.

VERSES TO DEEPEN YOUR JOY

LUKE 8:22–25; 2 PETER 1:2

Go share the joy today!

Safe in the Secret Place

In the secret place of Your presence You hide them from the plots and conspiracies of man; you keep them secretly in a shelter (pavilion) from the strife of tongues.

Psalm 31:20 AMP

Peace and fear can't coexist in our hearts or in our minds. If we allow the spirit of fear to invade any area of our lives, we will not have peace until we dispel that fearful spirit. We must actively pursue peace as a powerful defense system against fear. And one way to do this is to dwell in God's secret place.

Stop and ask yourself these questions: *What have I been dwelling on? Where has my mind been hanging out?* When we dwell in the presence of the Lord, we receive a constant supply of his peace, which equips us to defeat every fearful thought.

Another result of dwelling in the presence of God is remaining stable. Some people are stable one day but become quickly unglued by an identical situation the next day. Why? Because they start dwelling on the natural facts and stop residing in the presence of their supernatural God.

When we put more stock in the opinion of people—the predictions of the newscasters, the positions of naysayers—we move out from the secret place of God and away from his all-surpassing peace. Never forget that the "facts" are no match for the truth—God's Word! The facts, whether in the form of a bank statement, a medical diagnosis, or some other "official" documentation, may be unsettling, unnerving, and downright scary. But one look at the truth and we're on our way back to peace and stability.

VERSES TO DEEPEN YOUR JOY

Psalm 119:165; Philippians 4:7

Go share the joy today!

Cast Off the Mindset of Lack

There is the one who [generously] scatters [abroad], and yet increases all the more; and there is the one who withholds what is justly due, but it results only in want and poverty.

Proverbs 11:24 amp

Some people don't have peace even in seasons of abundance because their minds are stuck in the memory of an earlier season of lack. Often, this occurs to those who lived during the Great Depression or were raised by parents who remember that period in history. Someone with a depression mindset uses the same piece of aluminum foil fifteen times because she doesn't want to be wasteful. No, we don't want to be wasteful, yet God wants us to enjoy our season of blessings.

When we are in a season of lack, sowing is another key to seeing the season of blessing approach. We can actually sow our way out of the season of lack. That's what God did for me, and he can do it for you too. It was during a season of extreme scarcity that the Lord taught me to be very frugal in my spending and very generous in my giving. He rewards those who give faithfully to the work of his kingdom.

Even if we are in a season of abundance, it doesn't mean that we spend excessively; that would not be wise. The key is to balance our spending, our saving, and our sowing—our faithful giving to the kingdom of God through tithes and offerings. It's the financial seed sown into good ground for the work of the Lord that really assures a future in eternity. And, when we know where we're ultimately headed, we can have true, lasting peace.

VERSES TO DEEPEN YOUR JOY

Psalm 84:11; Malachi 3:10

Go share the joy today!

Thrive in Shifting Seasons

I know how to get along with little, and I also know how to live in prosperity; in any and every circumstance I have learned the secret of being filled and going hungry, both of having abundance and suffering need. I can do all things through Him who strengthens me.

PHILIPPIANS 4:12–13 NASB

The apostle Paul's secret to contentment in every season was relying on God for strength. He didn't say he could weather the financial seasons of life on his own; he said that he could "do all things," including thrive in times of plenty and want, because he leaned on the Lord for strength. We have the same option today. God will give us the strength and the grace we need to endure every financial season if only we'll lean on him.

When we are faced with challenging circumstances, we need to remember that they are temporary. One night years ago, as I sat on the floor crying because I was so overwhelmed with the financial responsibilities of being a single mom coupled with the stress of providing constant care to a newborn, God reminded me, *This is temporary. Temporary, not permanent*. Basically, he was saying, *This is only a season—a temporary season*. What a helpful reminder that was!

The experiences and circumstances we encounter are often painful and too perplexing to understand. If nothing else, we know at least this much: those circumstances are temporary. Just as winter is always followed by spring, "weeping may endure for a night, but joy comes in the morning" (Psalm 30:5 NKJV).

VERSES TO DEEPEN YOUR JOY

ECCLESIASTES 3:1–7; ISAIAH 61:3

Go share the joy today!

Reasons to Rejoice

We are hard pressed on every side, but not crushed; perplexed, but not in despair; persecuted, but not abandoned; struck down, but not destroyed.

2 CORINTHIANS 4:8–9

My translation of today's passage is this: "Things are hard, but they could be a whole lot worse." Yes, we are hard-pressed, but we aren't crushed. We may be persecuted, but we aren't abandoned. We are struck down, but—hallelujah!—we aren't destroyed. Life is hard, but God is good. The hard times we face can always be worse, but they're only temporary.

Yes, the seasons of life are always changing. And so, even in the cold, blinding blizzards of life, we can take courage and follow Paul's instructions in 2 Corinthians 4:18: "We fix our eyes not on what is seen, but on what is unseen, since what is seen is temporary, but what is unseen is eternal." When we fix our eyes on the unseen, we rise above our current, temporary circumstances. And doing so is a step of faith, which the writer of Hebrews defined as "the certainty of things hoped for, a proof of things not seen" (11:1 NASB).

My financial situation has improved significantly since that night years ago when God gently reminded me of the temporal nature of my circumstances. The overwhelming financial straits we were experiencing were indeed temporary, just as God had told me, and what I learned during that season of life I now apply to every other area in which I'm facing a challenge. I've learned to put up my hand and say, "Temporary!" Yes, life can be hard, but God is always good.

VERSES TO DEEPEN YOUR JOY

PSALM 46:1; 1 JOHN 5:5

Go share the joy today!

An Attitude of Gratitude

*Give thanks in all circumstances;
for this is God's will for you in Christ Jesus.*
1 THESSALONIANS 5:18

Storms expose what's in our hearts more effectively than seasons of peace do. This is because times of stress and struggle bring out the attitudes that reside in our hearts. Sometimes what we find out about ourselves is scary. God wants us to have an attitude of gratitude, storm or no storm, as we cross over from the land of "not enough" to the land of "more than enough."

The children of Israel who wandered in the wilderness for forty years failed to realize that their time in the desert was temporary. One little trial caused them to lose their vision of the promised land. After some minor discomfort to their flesh, they lost sight of the fact that their temporary circumstances were leading them to the next season of life.

Our attitude in the wilderness will determine how long we stay there. The children of Israel could have made the trip into the promised land in just eleven days, but because of their lousy attitude, it took them forty years to get there. We must avoid an ungrateful attitude that ends up prolonging our seasons in the desert.

All of us will experience desert seasons. Some of us will make the trip in eleven days, others will take forty years, and still others will "die" in the desert, never reaching the promised land. Make the most of your current season by maintaining a grateful attitude. You can even enjoy the wilderness when you realize it's temporary.

VERSES TO DEEPEN YOUR JOY

1 CHRONICLES 16:34; PSALM 100:4

Go share the joy today!

Cultivate a Grateful Heart

Let the word of Christ richly dwell within you, with all wisdom teaching and admonishing one another with psalms, hymns, and spiritual songs, singing with thankfulness in your hearts to God.

COLOSSIANS 3:16 NASB

One of the best methods for maintaining a godly attitude of gratitude is to study the Word of God daily. Reading the Word will reveal to us any impure heart attitudes. As the writer of Hebrews said, "The word of God is living and active, and sharper than any two-edged sword, even penetrating as far as the division of soul and spirit, of both joints and marrow, and able to judge the thoughts and intentions of the heart" (4:12 NASB).

If we discover an attitude that doesn't belong in our hearts, our response should involve humble repentance, which the Lord will reward. A bad attitude can cost us a lot, as it did for Solomon. First Kings 11:11 says, "The LORD said to Solomon, 'Since you have done this, and you have not kept My covenant and My statutes, which I have commanded you, I will certainly tear the kingdom away from you, and will give it to your servant'" (NASB). Attitude is everything!

When we sing to and worship God, we cultivate a grateful attitude toward him in our hearts. During the storms of life, if we just keep worshiping and praising God for all that we do have, we take our focus off what we are lacking and put it on what he has already given us.

VERSES TO DEEPEN YOUR JOY

PHILIPPIANS 4:4; 1 TIMOTHY 4:4–5

Go share the joy today!

Peace for Every Season

Make every effort to live in peace with everyone and to be holy.

HEBREWS 12:14

God wants us to experience peace in every area of our lives. One of those areas is in our relationships. A key to experiencing peace in our relationships is knowing that our job is not to change people but just to love them.

The Word tells us to make every effort to live in peace. In addition to practicing the fruit of the Spirit in our relationships, we must learn not to let other people's issues become our issues. Sometimes our desire to fix people's problems can worsen the problem while harming the relationship. We must maintain strong boundaries and try not to do for others what God wants them to do for themselves.

When we don't have healthy boundaries or when we fail to communicate in our relationships, we open the door for strife and frustration. There are times when we are to speak the truth in love and other times when we need to keep our opinions to ourselves. The key is to listen to the leading of the Holy Spirit and to make sure that we keep our hearts pure before the Lord. When we keep our hearts right and walk in obedience to the Lord, we are doing our part to be peacemakers in the relationships that God gives us.

VERSES TO DEEPEN YOUR JOY

PROVERBS 10:2; MARK 10:21

Go share the joy today!

Where Is Your Treasure?

"Do not store up for yourselves treasures on earth, where moths and vermin destroy, and where thieves break in and steal. But store up for yourselves treasures in heaven…For where your treasure is, there your heart will be also."

MATTHEW 6:19–21

When my brother David was nearing the end of his earthly life after a long battle with bone cancer, he confided in me that he was somewhat fearful of death. Having rededicated his life to the Lord months earlier, he knew he would soon be with his Father in heaven, but he still wondered what he was going to experience when he died.

As we discussed heaven, I could tell that he felt comforted, but then he confided in me another fear: "I'm afraid I haven't done enough for the Lord in this life." As a pastor, I regularly deal with birth, death, and everything in between. And I have yet to hear someone on their deathbed say, "I wish I would have put in just a little bit more time at the office," or "I wish I would have made just a little bit more money."

Ever since that conversation with my brother, my approach to this earthly life has been vastly different. Sometimes we can get so busy working for the Lord that we forget about what we are working toward—heaven! The truth is, like my brother stated, the only thing that counts in this life is what we have done for the Lord. If you tend to focus more on the world at hand than on eternity, it's time for a turnaround in your perspective.

VERSES TO DEEPEN YOUR JOY

PHILIPPIANS 3:20; REVELATION 21:4

Go share the joy today!

A Heavenly Perspective

Command those who are rich in this present world not…to put their hope in wealth, which is so uncertain, but to put their hope in God, who richly provides us with everything for our enjoyment. Command them to do good, to be rich in good deeds, and to be generous and willing to share. In this way they will lay up treasure for themselves as a firm foundation for the coming age.

1 Timothy 6:17–19

You don't need to travel the globe as an evangelist to make a difference in the kingdom or to store up treasure in heaven. Your hope should never be in your wealth, possessions, or status. Putting your hope in anything uncertain can open the door to the spirit of fear, which is often born out of instability. But when your hope is in God, its foundation will never be shaken.

First Timothy 6:17 says that God blesses us with good things for our enjoyment. We shouldn't be afraid to enjoy the blessings of the Lord. But we also shouldn't be content to please just ourselves. Otherwise, our lives become all about us. But we are blessed to be a blessing to others. When we are rich in good deeds and liberal in sharing our blessings with others, we lay up treasures for ourselves in heaven. And as we keep a heavenly perspective on our treasure, we have no need to fear what awaits us when this earthly life is over.

VERSES TO DEEPEN YOUR JOY

2 Corinthians 5:1; Colossians 3:2

Go share the joy today!

The Test of Time

See then that you walk circumspectly, not as fools but as wise, redeeming the time, because the days are evil. Therefore do not be unwise, but understand what the will of the Lord is.

EPHESIANS 5:15–17 NKJV

No matter how much money you have, it will never be your greatest asset. God owns it all, and he could just drop a couple million your way at any time (get in agreement and start declaring that, right?). Money is nothing to God, and it's never a problem for the Lord, so it should never be a problem for you. If you keep your part of the covenant—if you tithe and give when God says give, if you walk in obedience with every dollar he puts in your hand—abundant provision will always be there for you.

So if not your money, what is your greatest asset? It's your time. Time is limited, which makes it a precious resource indeed. No one has more than twenty-four hours in a day. No one has more than seven days in a week. So we must invest our greatest resource very wisely! Time will tell whether we've spent our time wisely.

First Corinthians 3:13–14 says, "On the judgment day, fire will reveal what kind of work each builder has done. The fire will show if a person's work has any value. If the work survives, that builder will receive a reward" (NLT). How you spend your time reveals what you truly treasure. What have you been investing your precious hours in lately? Does it reflect a heavenly perspective on what's really important? Will it pass the test?

VERSES TO DEEPEN YOUR JOY

PSALM 90:12; COLOSSIANS 4:5

Go share the joy today!

Check Your Motives

"Be careful not to practice your righteousness in front of others to be seen by them. If you do, you will have no reward from your Father in heaven...But when you give to the needy, do not let your left hand know what your right hand is doing, so that your giving may be in secret. Then your Father, who sees what is done in secret, will reward you."

Matthew 6:1, 3–4

Giving our time to others is a wonderful investment in the kingdom of God, as long as what we do for the Lord comes from a pure heart and upright motives. If we perform an act of service to be seen, we have already received our reward—recognition from people, the approval of our peers. But if we serve others from a heart of obedience to God and with a desire to build up his kingdom, our works will receive great reward in heaven.

By keeping our eyes on the Lord and others rather than on ourselves, we can act with pure motivation that prioritizes the glory of God and the good of others. We can't afford to give in to fear and self-consciousness, for they will only paralyze us from launching forward in all that God has for us in his kingdom. The Enemy tries to keep our focus on ourselves and our own goals. He works to distract us from maintaining an eternal perspective that prizes the things of God's kingdom. But if we remain in the Word and stay focused on the Lord, we can store up treasures in heaven and reap an eternal reward.

VERSES TO DEEPEN YOUR JOY

Proverbs 16:2; Galatians 1:10

Go share the joy today!

Complete Confidence

David said to the Philistine, "You come to me with a sword, a spear, and a saber, but I come to you in the name of the LORD of armies, the God of the armies of Israel, whom you have defied. This day the LORD will hand you over to me, and I will strike you and remove your head from you."

1 SAMUEL 17:45–46 NASB

David was someone who reached out with the right motives—in this case, to slay the enemy of God's people and give glory to God. I always come back to his story because it's the perfect example of placing one's confidence in the right person—the Lord Almighty—and acting boldly based on that confidence. Because he was certain that God would go with him and equip him to fight the giant, David was fearless, not fearful. Again, he knew that since he was fighting to display the glory of God, he would get the victory.

We have to be fearless and courageous like David. We must be ready and willing to lay down our lives for the purposes of the Lord. As we do, God will use us greatly, just as he used David. David grew up to be the greatest king Israel ever had. Just because someone starts out as the least likely candidate for a major undertaking doesn't mean God hasn't appointed him or her for the task.

Are you the least likely? If you have the favor of God, get ready. Today is your day for a total turnaround. God has great feats for you to accomplish for the sake of his kingdom. Place your total confidence in him, and he will see you through.

VERSES TO DEEPEN YOUR JOY

PROVERBS 3:26; HEBREWS 13:6

Go share the joy today!

It's What's Inside That Counts

"God does not see as man sees, since man looks at the outward appearance, but the LORD looks at the heart."

1 SAMUEL 16:7 NASB

Even before David fought Goliath, God had anointed him as the future king of Israel. And everyone was surprised at God's choice. David was just a shepherd boy, the youngest of Jesse's sons, completely inexperienced in matters of state and warfare. Yet God saw his heart, and that was the basis of his promotion.

God uses people whom others don't even consider. After seven strong, formidable sons of Jesse paraded passed Samuel as candidates to be the next king, I can imagine that both Jesse and the prophet were wondering what was going on. You see, little David wasn't even considered to be in the running. His father had dismissed him as a potential candidate. Finally, Samuel asked him, "Are these *all* the boys?" (v. 11 NASB). Samuel may have begun to doubt if he was correctly hearing the Lord.

When David was summoned, God said, "Arise, anoint him; for this is he" (v. 12 NASB). And he is saying the same thing to you today. You may be the least likely, but so was David. Little David had been trained and equipped. Little David had been prepared right where he was—being faithful over a flock of sheep. But in God's perfect timing, he anointed David and used him for an important job that only little David could do. It isn't the outward appearance that counts. It's what's inside that qualifies you to be used by God.

VERSES TO DEEPEN YOUR JOY

PROVERBS 31:30; HEBREWS 4:12–13

Go share the joy today!

Get in Agreement with God

David said,... "Your servant has killed both the lion and the bear; this uncircumcised Philistine will be like one of them, because he has defied the armies of the living God. The LORD who rescued me from the paw of the lion and the paw of the bear will rescue me from the hand of this Philistine."

1 SAMUEL 17:34, 36–37

David was confident that God would give him victory over Goliath, and what he said aligned with his mindset. He refused to speak forth fear but declared only victory and assurance.

We need to do the same thing. Too often, our own words start a cycle of fear in our hearts. What are you declaring over yourself? The Enemy works hard to get us to buy the lies he tries to sell. If we buy the lie, we may declare the words of the Enemy over ourselves and our situations. We should be declaring what God says in his Word.

The Enemy whispers such lies as the following: *You aren't going to make it. You'll probably die of this sickness. You won't be able to make it financially. Why not just quit right now, before you look foolish for failing?* If we aren't careful, we will internalize those lies in our thoughts, voice them with our mouths, and live them out with our actions.

God always declares victory, health, and blessings over his children, and we need to stay in agreement with him. When we are in agreement with the Lord, we declare his truth. When we are in agreement with the devil, we declare his lies. With whom are you in agreement today?

VERSES TO DEEPEN YOUR JOY

ZEPHANIAH 3:17; 1 JOHN 5:4

Go share the joy today!

Consult the Only Infallible Guide

*Don't worry about anything; instead, pray about everything.
Tell God what you need, and thank him for all he has done.*

PHILIPPIANS 4:6 NLT

The devil can't create anything. All he can do is destroy, and the closest he can come to creating is to pull off cheap imitations of what God has created. The devil's imitations are designed to bait people into buying his lies and get them to fall for his false knockoffs that cause only death and destruction.

Everything that God has created is good and intended to bring life, hence the guidelines he provides to show us how to pursue righteous living. When we fail to seek the Lord—when we rush ahead and make decisions based on our natural minds and desires rather than consulting his infinite wisdom—we can find ourselves in a real mess, just as Abraham's nephew Lot did when he chose to settle near ungodly people.

While Abraham (who originally went by the name Abram) sought the Lord for his every move, Lot looked in the natural, saw what he thought looked good, and made his choice. Not everything that looks good is good. Not everything that looks like a God thing is. That's why we need to rely on the guidance of the Holy Spirit, not the inclinations of our unholy flesh.

When facing a decision, no matter how significant or trivial, you should consult the only infallible guide there is: the Lord Almighty. Don't listen to the so-called experts and don't rely on your own sense but trust only the Lord to show you what's right.

VERSES TO DEEPEN YOUR JOY

PSALM 37:5; ISAIAH 30:21

Go share the joy today!

Guided to Holy Ground

The LORD said to Abram, after Lot had left him,
"Now lift up your eyes and look from the place where you are standing,
northward and southward and eastward and westward;
for all the land which you see I will give to you
and to your descendants forever."

GENESIS 13:14–15 AMP

God showed Abram all that he had for him after Abram separated from his nephew Lot. God told Abram that all that Abram could see would be his. If God spiritually shows you something, it can manifest in the natural for you. Because Abram remained obedient to God's commands, he could move toward the holy ground God had prepared for him.

However, when those who are living apart from God's truth influence us, our vision blurs, and we cannot clearly see all that God has for us. The key is to avoid places where sin is widely accepted, which opens the door to deception. When unbiblical practices surround us, we're more easily deceived into thinking we are doing the right thing or that we're hearing from God correctly when we really aren't. Even when our actions violate God's Word, we don't think there is anything wrong with what we are doing.

Sometimes we are tempted to make decisions based on our emotions, our fears, our lust for the things of this world, our anger, and other things that are subject to the influence of others. When we seek instructions for how to live from the Bible rather than from the world, we can hear God clearly and know which course to take. Let the Lord guide you to holy ground where sinfulness cannot dwell.

VERSES TO DEEPEN YOUR JOY

EXODUS 3:5; LEVITICUS 11:44

Go share the joy today!

Where You Pitch Your Tent

Abram dwelt in the land of Canaan, and Lot dwelt in the cities of the plain and pitched his tent even as far as Sodom. But the men of Sodom were exceedingly wicked and sinful against the LORD.

GENESIS 13:12–13 NKJV

We read in Genesis 13:12 that Lot pitched his tent near Sodom, a wicked city filled with sinful people and compromising practices. We have to be careful where we "pitch our tents"—where we choose to live, raise our families, and spend our time. Lot pitched his tent and took up residence in a place that was riddled with practices that pained the heart of God, and Lot was completely oblivious.

I can imagine that Lot thought, *I'm not going to live* in *Sodom. I'm just going to live on the outskirts of town.* Only guess what? The next chapter tells us that Lot was indeed living in Sodom. Some evil men "carried off Abram's nephew Lot and his possessions, since he was living *in* Sodom" (Genesis 14:12).

You can never pitch your tent near sin and think it won't affect you. If you hang out in a place where sin runs wild, it won't be long before you, too, are living in sin and engaging in unholy practices. When you expose yourself to sin, you quickly become inoculated and are prone to being deceived.

God wants to give you a Holy Spirit GPS to recalculate your route right out of the pit of sin. Your willingness to compromise may have put you in the pit, but the power and direction of God will get you out if you'll look to him and surrender your sinful ways.

VERSES TO DEEPEN YOUR JOY

JEREMIAH 15:21; MATTHEW 6:13

Go share the joy today!

Destination: Mercy

People who conceal their sins will not prosper,
but if they confess and turn from them, they will receive mercy.

PROVERBS 28:13 NLT

Jesus said that the devil comes only to steal, kill, and destroy (John 10:10). Satan has a dirty game going on, and he plays for keeps. Don't ever buy his lie when he whispers, *This little bit won't hurt. You can do it just this once. No one will ever know.*

The Holy Spirit speaks clearly to our hearts with a voice that leads us in paths of righteousness. We should never flirt with the devil's detours by entertaining evil thoughts or pursuing destinations we know God wouldn't want for us. Sometimes we're tempted to try to talk ourselves into the "rightness" of a decision. We think, *Maybe that wasn't God telling me not to do that.* Never flirt with a detour from God's ordained path for your life. Detours can be very destructive, and they may take you so far off track that it will be difficult to regain your focus on God's will for your life.

If you are concealing a sin that you think no one knows about, don't kid yourself. God knows everything, and he's the one who really counts. Confess your sin, repent of it, and ask the Holy Spirit to give you the power to stay on God's course for your life. Then ask God to give you some Christian friends who are on fire for God, are filled with the Holy Spirit, and will encourage you and hold you accountable as you pursue holiness, righteousness, and uncompromising faith. Your next stop is a filling station to refuel with God's mercy.

VERSES TO DEEPEN YOUR JOY

PSALM 23:3; 1 JOHN 1:9

Go share the joy today!

Fertile Soil for Spiritual Growth

Oh, the joys of those who…delight in the law of the Lord, meditating on it day and night. They are like trees planted along the riverbank, bearing fruit each season. Their leaves never wither, and they prosper in all they do.

Psalm 1:1–3 NLT

When you live according to God's Word, you will prosper in everything you do. A life of holiness and righteousness causes you to be firmly planted in the fertile, well-watered soil of the favor of God.

When Jesus related the parable of the sower, he emphasized the importance of strengthening your roots as you abide in his Word. Comparing Scripture to seeds, he explained that those who don't allow the seed to penetrate deep within the soil of their heart will "fall away" in times of testing (Luke 8:13). Others absorb God's Word but fail to weed their gardens effectively so that temptations, toils, sins, and struggles all choke out the seedlings before they can bear fruit (v. 14). Only those who had maintained "fertile soil" (v. 8 NLT) in the gardens of their hearts managed to produce an abundant harvest from the seeds that were planted and cultivated within them.

You should endeavor to grow every day in righteousness by steeping your spirit in the Word of God. When you have righteousness strengthening your root system, you won't fall over and flow away when the storms of life threaten you. Be sure to fertilize the soil of your heart's garden by staying in the Word and communing with the Lord throughout each day.

VERSES TO DEEPEN YOUR JOY

Isaiah 55:10–11; John 4:14

Go share the joy today!

Shine Your Light

Have no fellowship with the unfruitful works of darkness, but rather expose them. For it is shameful even to speak of those things which are done by them in secret. But all things that are exposed are made manifest by the light, for whatever makes manifest is light.

EPHESIANS 5:11–13 NKJV

Righteousness comes from doing the right thing as the Holy Spirit empowers us in our relationships with other people and with the Lord. As we pursue righteous living, our example can convict those around us who have been living in sin and compromise. Our lives should be beacons of hope to those trapped in bondage to darkness and sin.

You may find that the people close to you whom you've convicted by your righteous living will avoid you. They'll go out of their way not to cross paths with you because they fear judgment and condemnation. We should be loving and gentle in the way that we live out our faith, never calling people out in a spirit of superiority or with a holier-than-thou attitude.

Those who aren't living righteously may attack you verbally and accuse you of judging them or say that your idea of holiness is bondage. Holy, righteous living is hardly the same thing as bondage. It's actually true freedom. And only those who have been freed from bondage to sin are able to enjoy true freedom.

God wants your lifestyle to expose the evil deeds of darkness. Sometimes you don't even have to say a word. Your lifestyle and the presence of the Lord in you do all the talking. Shine your light of God's love today.

VERSES TO DEEPEN YOUR JOY

JOHN 16:8; 2 CORINTHIANS 7:9–10

Go share the joy today!

Uprooting Sin from Our Midst

"Nothing is hidden that will not be revealed [at the judgment], or kept secret that will not be made known [at the judgment]."

MATTHEW 10:26 AMP

God is asking us to expose sinfulness today as part of his plan to bring total turnaround to his body, the church. Once you have experienced a turnaround in your own life and are walking in the righteousness of God, he can use you to usher turnaround into the lives of others.

Many churches and ministries today are divided, putting up with unbiblical lifestyles among their parishioners and even their leadership. Often, ministry leaders are oblivious to the sinful habits in the ranks of the leaders working alongside them. Such was the case for King Xerxes when Esther became his wife. His kingdom was divided, and he didn't even know it (Esther 2:17–3:1).

Esther, representing righteousness, rose to power as the new queen. Only a few verses later, we read of the promotion of Haman, an adviser who brought wickedness and sin into the government. Even though Haman tried to have all the Jewish people killed because of his pride, righteousness through Esther's brave actions and spotless character prevailed over him. Esther had been called to expose evil deeds in the kingdom and be a voice of righteousness.

The same is true of you today. You are called for such a time as this, to be a voice of righteousness for the kingdom of God, expose sin for what it is, and be a catalyst of the turnaround in the lives of those around you.

VERSES TO DEEPEN YOUR JOY

PROVERBS 14:34; JAMES 3:16

Go share the joy today!

Fully Persuaded

Against all hope, Abraham in hope believed and…did not waver through unbelief regarding the promise of God, but was strengthened in his faith and gave glory to God, being fully persuaded that God had power to do what he had promised.

Romans 4:18, 20–21

Abraham refused to dwell near people who lived unrighteously. We discussed earlier in December how, when his nephew Lot went one way and "chose for himself" (Genesis 13:11) the best of the land—becoming neighbors with some extremely wicked people—Abram moved in the opposite direction, affirming his commitment to follow God (v. 18).

Abram wasn't perfect, but he pursued the ways of God with his whole heart, and the Lord considered him righteous—but not because of his good works or flawless character. Genesis 15:6 says that "Abram believed the Lord, and the Lord counted him as righteous *because of his faith*" (NLT).

What is faith? It's being "fully persuaded," as Abram was, that God has the power to do whatever he has said he's going to do. Faith is being sure of what you hope for and 100 percent certain that it will come to pass no matter what happens in the natural realm. Faith knows that God has all the power to do whatever he wants to do however and whenever he wants to do it.

Are you fully persuaded that God can do and will do what he has promised? Or are you partially persuaded sometimes and not persuaded at all other times? Pray that God will give you a faith that remains fully persuaded at all times, that is never daunted by circumstances or the way things look.

VERSES TO DEEPEN YOUR JOY

Genesis 15:1–4; Hebrews 11:1

Go share the joy today!

Faith Fuels Bold Belief

The centurion answered [Jesus] and said, "…But only speak a word, and my servant will be healed."…When Jesus heard it, He marveled, and said to those who followed, "Assuredly, I say to you, I have not found such great faith, not even in Israel!"

MATTHEW 8:8, 10 NKJV

The Roman centurion in this story from Matthew 8 sure had what I would call feisty faith—the feistiest, in fact, that Jesus had ever witnessed. He asked Jesus to heal his servant from a remote location, making his request with full confidence in Jesus' ability to perform such a miracle. Jesus told the man, "As you have believed, so let it be done for you" (v. 13 NKJV), and his servant was healed that very hour.

How feisty is your faith? How bold is your belief? Do you believe enough to ask and expect the miraculous? Are you so determined to receive what you're believing for that you would dig through a thatch roof to receive it? That was what four men did for their friend in Mark 2:4. Talk about bold determination! The desperation of these men who acted on their strong faith moved Jesus. And he responded by healing the friend and, even better and of eternal significance, forgiving his sins (v. 9).

When Jesus sees our faith, he responds. When God hears our bold requests that are fueled by firm belief, he is moved. What will you boldly ask of him today?

VERSES TO DEEPEN YOUR JOY

PSALM 119:30; MATTHEW 15:28

Go share the joy today!

The God of Restoration

"The thief does not come except to steal, and to kill, and to destroy. I have come that they may have life, and that they may have it more abundantly."

JOHN 10:10 NKJV

As we celebrate the birth of our Savior, we remember that God not only restores our health, but he also restores everything in our lives. And we need to think, speak, and live in light of that truth.

Make sure these declared words are on the right side of the fight. Yes, it's a fight. It's a spiritual battle. But if you stand up and fight, everything will be all right. Stand and fight with a declaration of victory over every one of your situations, as promised in God's Word.

We should always be declaring God's Word, works, and illustrious acts. The way we live each day should announce God's goodness and great power. We declare God's works and power with our words and our very lives, which is how we cast out the spirit of fear and defeat the devil.

"There is therefore now no condemnation to those who are in Christ Jesus" (Romans 8:1 NKJV). If you are in Christ, you can be confident that there is no condemnation. Jesus was born and lived a life among us before dying on the cross to pay the price for every sin we have ever committed—and those we will commit in the future. If the Lord is your Savior, rest assured that God has secured a place for you in heaven with him. It's yours for the taking. Final, eternal restoration is yours when your name is in the Lamb's Book of Life.

VERSES TO DEEPEN YOUR JOY

ROMANS 8:35–39; REVELATION 21:6–7, 27

Go share the joy today!

Mountain-Moving Faith

"Truly I tell you, if you have faith as small as a mustard seed, you can say to this mountain, 'Move from here to there,' and it will move."

MATTHEW 17:20

Many years ago, I was lying in bed crying as I poured out my heart to God, pleading with him to act on my behalf—and to be quick about it! My argument was highly emotional and punctuated with plenty of tears and wailing. The answer he gave my spirit was very clear: *I'm not moved by your emotions; I'm moved by your faith.*

When he told me he was moved by my faith alone, I snapped out of it. I stopped praying prayers of self-pity and sorrow, and I started praying bold prayers and daring declarations of faith. I would proclaim out loud, "God, I thank you that you are going to meet all my needs. I thank you that you have always come through for me. Thank you that I'm standing on your Word and on your promises."

As I prayed firmly, with boldness, rather than in a sniveling voice overwrought with emotion, faith rose up within me, and I immediately felt stronger and more settled. Pretty soon, I was no longer overtaken by my own emotions, and I experienced a sense of peace.

Doubt says, "Maybe God will bring me through," but faith says, "Of course God is going to do it. Of course God is going to hear my prayers and answer them. Of course!" Pray the prayers that move mountains. Those are the prayers that move God.

VERSES TO DEEPEN YOUR JOY

ACTS 4:29; 2 CORINTHIANS 3:12

Go share the joy today!

Belief to Build a Boat

[Prompted] by faith Noah, being forewarned by God concerning events of which as yet there was no visible sign, took heed and diligently and reverently constructed and prepared an ark for the deliverance of his own family.

HEBREWS 11:7 AMPC

When we have faith, we do great things for God as we follow his leading, just like Noah did. God told Noah to build an ark, and he gave Noah some seriously specific details that sounded illogical to most everyone Noah knew (Genesis 6). Yet "Noah did everything just as God commanded him" (v. 22). The author of Hebrews recognized Noah's faith—and faithfulness—in the Faith Hall of Fame (Hebrews 11).

Faith will prompt you to pursue plans and purposes that are way outside your comfort zone. Consider Noah. His neighbors probably thought he was crazy. There were probably days when even he questioned his own sanity. Remember, he lived in a desert and had probably rarely seen drizzle, let alone enough rain to cause a flood. Yet he knew what God had told him. He'd received some very specific instructions.

Faith will prompt you to do great things for God as long as you yield to the prompting of the Holy Spirit. Don't stop at your current faith level but keep going forward, always pressing to the next level of faith and resulting works, whether building a boat in the middle of a desert or some other seemingly illogical yet God-ordained activity.

VERSES TO DEEPEN YOUR JOY

LUKE 1:37; HEBREWS 13:7

Go share the joy today!

Put Your Faith to Work

Just as the body is dead without breath,
so also faith is dead without good works.

JAMES 2:26 NLT

Having faith is great, but it won't do much good until we put it to work. That's because works are the evidence of our faith in action. You can have all the faith in the world, but if you don't step out of the boat, you'll never walk on the water.

A prophet spoke over me years ago with a word that God would open my womb and that I would conceive a baby girl. When I heard this, I was so excited, and faith in this particular event really rose up in me. But I needed to add some works to my faith, if you know what I mean. There wasn't going to be another virgin birth after all. My faith in the fulfillment of this wonderful prophecy would have been "dead" and useless if I hadn't added some action.

We don't work to earn our salvation or to secure some special status in the eyes of God. Rather, we work because we've been saved and want to show the world what our God can do. Acting in faith is a sign of gratitude, an overflow of the love we've received. As James put it, "Someone may argue, 'Some people have faith; others have good deeds.' But I say, 'How can you show me your faith if you don't have good deeds?'" (2:18 NLT).

If you have faith, it's time to get to work. Live it out as the Lord leads and be grateful.

VERSES TO DEEPEN YOUR JOY

EPHESIANS 2:8–10; JAMES 2:14–17

Go share the joy today!

Supersized Faith

The apostles said to the Lord, "Increase our faith." So the Lord said, "If you have faith as a mustard seed, you can say to this mulberry tree, 'Be pulled up by the roots and be planted in the sea,' and it would obey you."

LUKE 17:5–6 NKJV

We often talk about faith that moves mountains. But what about faith that can cause a tree to uproot itself and relocate to the ocean? That was the picture Jesus painted when the disciples asked him to raise their level of faith. He was reminding them of the power of even a small amount of faith. In other words, they didn't need more faith; they just needed to *use* the faith that they had.

God has given each of us "a measure of faith" (Romans 12:3 NKJV). Your measure can be a big scoop if you'll only exercise your faith and let it grow. Pray regularly and rely on the Word for the content of your prayers. As you sow your seed of faith, you'll see it grow before your very eyes.

If you can move mountains and uproot trees with just a little seed of faith, imagine what will happen if the Holy Spirit supersizes your faith. Every test and trial you encounter becomes a chance for the hand of God to sprinkle some Miracle-Gro on your faith.

Doubt causes all kinds of things to die. But the good news is that God is in the business of resurrecting dead stuff—including our faith. Allow the Lord to resurrect and give life to those areas that Satan has tried to choke out with weeds of doubt.

VERSES TO DEEPEN YOUR JOY

MARK 9:23–25; JOHN 10:10

Go share the joy today!

Our Eternal Victor

Thanks be to God, who gives us the victory [as conquerors] through our Lord Jesus Christ.

1 Corinthians 15:57 AMP

For those whose hope is in the Lord, the race has been won; the war is over, and we're the victors. Why? Because we're on the Lord's side, and he always gets the victory. Christ is the ultimate overcomer, and he shares his winner's inheritance with all those who call him Savior and Lord.

When King Jehoshaphat was facing an onslaught from his enemies, the Moabites and the Ammonites, the Lord spoke to him through a prophet named Jahaziel, saying, "Do not be afraid or discouraged because of this vast army. For the battle is not yours, *but God's*...You will not have to fight this battle. Take up your positions; stand firm and see the deliverance the Lord will give you" (2 Chronicles 20:15, 17). God is ready and able to fight our every battle. We just need to stand back and let him work. Just as Moses encouraged the Israelites, let me encourage you now: "The Lord will fight for you; you need only to be still" (Exodus 14:14).

And when God wins, we should give him credit for the victory. In today's verse from 1 Corinthians, Paul was talking about victory over death. If death has been conquered, what else could possibly stand in our way? "Everyone born of God overcomes the world. This is the victory that has overcome the world, even our faith" (1 John 5:4). That's great news! When we acknowledge Jesus as the Son of God, we share in his conquering of this world—including death. That sounds like real winning to me.

VERSES TO DEEPEN YOUR JOY

Colossians 2:15; 1 John 5:5

Go share the joy today!

Leave a Legacy of Faith

[Jesus said,] "Very truly I tell you, whoever believes in me will do the works I have been doing, and they will do even greater things than these, because I am going to the Father."

JOHN 14:12

The book of Hebrews includes a section that many people call the Faith Hall of Fame (Hebrews 11:4–30)—a list of people whose stories are in the Old Testament and whose faith was commendable. The following is a summary of just a few of these faith-filled folks. I would recommend reading the whole section of Hebrews regularly. As we study the example of these faithful pioneers, we can strive to follow in their footsteps.

By faith,

- Noah obeyed God's instructions and built an ark (v. 7).
- Abraham and Sarah believed God's promise to give them a son, so they conceived (vv. 11–12).
- Abraham prepared to sacrifice his promised son, Isaac, in obedience to the Lord's command (vv. 17–19).
- The Israelites passed through the Red Sea when Moses, by the power of God, parted the waters (v. 29).

What an example these heroes of the faith have set for us! Let's endeavor to live by faith in such a way that we leave a legacy of faith for future generations. When our joy stems from the source of life, we can live in a way that gets our names written in the record book of heaven for the benefit of our children, our children's children, and beyond.

VERSES TO DEEPEN YOUR JOY

PSALM 145:4; ROMANS 1:17

Go share the joy today!

About the Author

Danette Joy Crawford is a powerful speaker, author, TV host, and international evangelist with a refreshing message of hope and encouragement. Danette has a master's degree in counseling from Regent University. She is the founder and president of Danette Crawford Ministries and its outreach arm, Joy Ministries Evangelistic Association. Danette Crawford Ministries organizes inner-city work with over twenty-three compassion programs dedicated to sustainable aid, and Joy Ministries offers educational and mentoring resources, assistance for at-risk youth and low-income families, and programs for single mothers. These programs include Cars for Moms, LIFE Group, the Mother's Day Celebration, and the Father's House.

Danette's television program, *Joy with Danette Crawford*, is broadcast weekly into millions of homes. You can watch her program on Daystar, CBS, TBN, NRB, ABC, Dove Network, and many more. Danette is also the author of several books: *Don't Quit in the Pit*; *Total Turnaround*; *God, You've Got Mail*; *The Standard Setters*; *Limitless Thinking, Limitless Living*; and her forty-five-day devotional, *Break Free*.

Danette's story of building an international television ministry and national outreach organization as a single mom raising her daughter has inspired millions. The heart of everything that she does is to change lives and to show others that they can overcome any difficulty that comes their way.